WOMEN WHO DARE

Merry Christmas
Allie
Happy Trails in
2015
Love
Cathy & Dave

Lisa Rands on a Looney
Binge (12c), Owens River
Gorge, California.

WOMEN WHO DARE

North America's Most Inspiring Women Climbers

CHRIS NOBLE

Forewords by Steph Davis and Sasha DiGiulian

FALCONGUIDES

GUILFORD, CONNECTICUT
HELENA, MONTANA

AN IMPRINT OF GLOBE PEQUOT PRESS

FALCONGUIDES®

FalconGuides is an imprint of Globe Pequot Press.
Falcon, FalconGuides, and Outfit Your Mind are registered trademarks of Morris Book Publishing, LLC.

All photos by Chris Noble
Text design: Sheryl Kober
Layout artist: Casey Shain
Project editor: Ellen Urban

Library of Congress Cataloging-in-Publication Data

Noble, Chris.
 Women who dare : North America's most inspiring
women climbers / Chris Noble.   pages cm

Summary: "A celebration of feminine beauty, athleticism, wisdom, and skill—*Women Who Dare* profiles twenty of America's most inspiring women climbers ranging from legends like Lynn Hill to the rising stars of today. The profiles are complemented by stunning color photographs by leading adventure photojournalist Chris Noble."

—Provided by publisher

ISBN 978-0-7627-8371-7 (pbk.)
1. Women mountaineers—North America—Biography. I. Title.
GV199.9.N626 2013
796.5220922—dc23
[B]

2013029033

Printed in the United States of America
10 9 8 7 6 5 4 3 2 1

Contents

Foreword by STEPH DAVIS

As a woman who climbs, I am often asked to reflect on women and climbing. This usually leaves me a little nonplussed. Having spent most of my life on the side of a wall or sleeping in a small space with one other person or a dog, I mostly identify myself as a climber, and if asked to supply another qualifier, I then go on down the list to a human, and if pressed further, I describe myself as a writer or a photographer or a BASE jumper or whatever I happen to be doing that day. Of course I acknowledge and value being female. It's on the list of things I am; it's just not at the top of the list.

In climbing it seems impossible to avoid qualifiers, such as difficulty, length, duration, speed, technicality, intensity, physicality, extremeness, maleness, and femaleness. One of the first things you learn as a climber is the Yosemite decimal system, so you know how to compare and grade routes. To an outsider, climbers must seem like a bunch of very athletic accountants. Quantification, I believe, is like a large clay pot that you plant a seedling in. At first it seems impossible that a little sprout could grow to fill the pot. Yet inevitably, the plant grows until its roots meet the pot's walls and become cramped and smashed. The plant withers, and dies, stifled by the same walls that once seemed impossible to reach.

I think I'm lucky to have lived this metaphor so intensely for the twenty-two years I've been a climber. It didn't take long for me to see quantification as a clay pot rather than a huge perimeter of infinite aspiration and to see that the world outside the pot is where that universe of infinite aspiration really lies. Living within labels and categories keeps us within the pot, where everything is great until our roots are crushed up against the walls. Then freedom comes only from smashing the pot to send off shoots in every direction and grow freely without restriction.

I've always been uneasy with putting myself into any category, taking up residence inside any pot. And I've been uncertain of how to think about the concept of women climbers. That label strikes me as a pot with very thick walls. Certainly climbers across the board seem to have the same dilemma. A female climber gains notice when she becomes the first female to climb a route, while at the same time, discussions are held as to whether first female ascents should even be discussed. There are women-only climbing groups, events, and expeditions with gender exclusiveness as the overriding goal, and though I've seen plenty climbing outings with only men in them, they never seem to be organized as such. For someone who aspires to see the world and living creatures in the most fundamental terms,

Steph Davis climbs Hidden Gem (5.13), Moab, Utah.

this type of separation is difficult to embrace. Personally, I've never chosen or rejected a climbing partner on the basis of gender. I've lived in a portaledge for weeks with men I considered excellent climbing partners and good friends and never thought more about it beyond wanting to reach the summit and get down again.

I grew up with one older brother. In 1991, when I started climbing in Maryland, rock gyms did not exist. There weren't many climbers in general and definitely fewer women in the sport, especially on mountain climbs and on expeditions. I climbed what I could and with anyone who wanted to climb, which meant that my partners included men and women who ranged in age from twenty to sixty. On expeditions, my partners were predominantly male, but I didn't think much about it, aside from learning quickly that women need to wear an extra layer of long underwear when climbing in cold places thanks to the different behavior of our circulatory system. When I think about my favorite climbing partners, they are categorized by the type of climbing they like and their attitude about life, rather than their gender.

Though I haven't spent much time reflecting on what it means to be a climber who is female, I've spent a great deal of time reflecting on what it means to be human. At this point in my life, I think one of the most significant qualities of humanness is the need to connect. Looking back, I can see that this desire is what made me become a climber. It's also what has kept me climbing for over half my life, and it will keep me climbing for the rest of it. Climbing is a conduit, a metaphorical plug that we can use to link ourselves into powerful, life-altering forces—forces like passion, discipline, purity, nature, and the universe itself. The desire for connection leads us down many avenues and ultimately leads us to be our best selves.

It makes sense that I never thought about the idea of male versus female for all these years, because when seeking connection, we focus on similarities. What makes climbers the same is our love of climbing and our desire to share that love with those who feel it as much as we do. As a climber who is also a woman, I think that shared experience is to be celebrated wherever we can find it.

From this perspective, I see women climbers differently. Finding common ground is one of the hallmarks of connection, and I think it's what inspires women who climb to seek one another out and what makes our experiences more meaningful to each other. Because connection has no perimeters, no walls, and no bounds, it is the ultimate aspiration, the deepest root of human desire. The quest for common ground makes climbers of us all and humans of us all. The details of our connection are the ties that pull us together.

—STEPH DAVIS
Moab, Utah, 2013

Foreword by SASHA DiGIULIAN

What is climbing culture? This is an ever-changing topic that has many definitions and contradictions. Climbing has long been defined as an outdoor sport peopled by independent, spirited men and women, challenging rugged rock faces. These climbers form a close-knit global community and are the core of the climbing culture. With the advent of competition climbing with events, such as the Rock Master Festival in Arco, Italy, came the growth of the indoor climbing gyms. These facilities first served as indoor training options for traditional outdoor climbers during the off-season, but they have quickly grown to a culture adjunct to and separate from traditional outdoor pursuits. Often the destination for birthday parties, Boy Scout trips, and corporate events, the gyms popularized and fueled the growth of the indoor climbing industry for both competition and for fitness. According to the gym directory on Mountain Project in 2013, there were 884 indoor climbing gyms in the United States and Canada. There are youth climbers who actively compete and are members of USA Climbing, the national governing body of competition in the United States. There are many more who utilize the gyms for fitness and social activities. Many of these climbers have never, and may never, climb a natural rock face in their lifetime. In the beginning the gym parking lots had muddy Jeeps and Subarus, and you now see fancy BMWs that would never make the approach to the "Motherload" in Kentucky's Red River Gorge.

Rock climbing is now more approachable and attainable than ever. It is fast becoming a commercialized sport, available to the mainstream. Magazines such as *Vogue, Seventeen,* and *Women's Health* are tuning in to the sport as a type of new workout. So, with this change in the interpretation of who climbers are and what composes the climber lifestyle, from seemingly outdoor "hippies" to more youthful vivaciousness that parallels the culture of snowboarding and surfing, can we say that climbing is evolving for the better or should we be preserving the past? There is no turning back the clock and to even attempt to do so would not be a good thing.

I have been climbing since 1999, and I have experienced this evolution of the sport during the short time I've been involved. My first exposure to climbing was at my brother's birthday party when I was seven years old. Something about the sport invigorated me. I was drawn to the excitement of advancing upward, defying gravity, and controlling my movements. I was enthralled by the experience. I had always dabbled in different sports: swimming, figure skating, soccer, ballet, and skiing; however, I was more than ready to give them all up once I joined the junior team at Sportrock, a local climbing center.

My drive to climb inspired me to climb both outdoors and in competition. I was lucky. My coach stressed to our team that climbing outside would make us better climbers. I learned how to lead belay with my teammate on a climb rated 5.12 in the New River Gorge in West Virginia.

Sasha DiGiulian focuses on True Love (13d) Red River Gorge, Kentucky.

I loved climbing outside, partially for the social aspects of the experience and partially for the cathartic exposure to nature. Spending time with friends, being able to laugh, and encouraging each other while pushing our own personal abilities highlighted my experiences in the sport. We bonded through this shared appreciation for being out in nature and attempting climbs together. No matter the age or background of the participants, climbing was a unifying undertone that created instant friendships. I looked forward to the Triple Crown bouldering comps, which were held outdoors. I climbed next to Lisa Rands, who completed boulder problems rated v9 and v6. Watching her motivated me.

For me, hearing about top climbers' achievements imbedded an awareness of pushing the standard, but more, I was intrigued to set goals in order to test my own boundaries. My friends were my role models, and climbing enthusiasts are exactly the motivating figures in climbing that are pushing the standards of climbing today. That being said, there are many climbers who love the sport, who are national and international champions, and who never climb real rock. Are they any less a climber than me? No, they just experience the sport differently. Is a swimmer any less a swimmer if he or she spends a lifetime training in a chlorinated, 50-meter pool and never dives into the ocean or swims to an island in a pristine lake? In my opinion they are all swimmers. Some compete in pools, some swim iron-man races in open waters, and some just swim to the island because they love to swim.

Inspiration will always be individual. Through climbing, I learned that true motivation will always be rooted in passion. As my passion for climbing increases, my interest in the history of the sport grows too. When I was a young girl, all that really mattered to me was the activity of climbing, but as I matured with the sport, I realized the importance of the roots of climbing, in particular, women in climbing, and I developed a deeper appreciation for the past. It is hard to directly relate to generations that I feel slightly removed from. I realize I am no longer the youngest generation of climbing. There are layers of history behind me for me to learn from and to progress from, as well as new layers of younger climbers to watch and to be inspired by. We can all give and take from our own distinct backgrounds. No matter how old or how young we are, personal progression is just that: personal. I will always have a new route or boulder problem that impassions me, a new grade, a competition, or a recreational climbing trip to a spectacular spot on the globe. The more entangled my life becomes with climbing, the more I realize that instead of melding together each generation's experiences of climbing and

climbing culture into one collective definition of climbing, we share our distinctive experiences and use these to annotate the greater picture. Climbing is freedom; it is a personal experience of realizing your goals through both mental and physical perseverance.

The standard for climbing will continue to rise to levels seemingly impossible. Inevitably the standard of the sport increases as the number of participants do. We saw Lynn Hill and Robyn Ebersfield-Raboutou set the standard; Josune Bereziartu realize 9a; and Angela Eiter stomp the competition scene for the past decade. Though now, an 11-year-old by the name of Ashima Shiraishi has bouldered v13 and sport climbed 5.14c and has a fearless tenacity to climb whatever that she envisions possible. I know, because I have trained with her, and I have witnessed her drive to excel and to define the next level.

I am endlessly moved and inspired by the past and present generations. I look to the past idols as role models in setting new levels of possibilities, but I look to the newer generation for motivation to conquer climbing frontiers yet to be discovered. In order to set the next standard and to be the next best thing, we must believe in ourselves and our capabilities. With mental perseverance, physical capability, and wisdom in the sport as a whole, the future of women in climbing will continue to progress at incalculable speeds. Brace yourselves, boys, women in climbing are progressing at full force and the next level is yet to be defined!

—SASHA DiGIULIAN
New York, New York, 2013

Introduction

Someone wise once said, "The greatest gift is the gift of good work." In that respect I've been fortunate, and this book in particular has been a gift in many ways. It's provided me the opportunity to meet and work with an exemplary group of individuals—twenty women who inspire through their vision, skill, commitment to climbing, and sheer love of life.

Even though I've been climbing for more than forty years, I learned something from each and every one of the women profiled in this book. In fact, the experience of collecting the wisdom of twenty of the world's best climbers has radically changed my own attitude toward climbing. Has it taught me to climb 5.14? Alas, no! I'm afraid I'm still going to have to wait to be reincarnated in Sasha DiGiulian's body in order to do that!

But the process taught me to think less about ratings and performance and to focus far more on the sheer joy of the sport in all its forms. It's made me realize how much of my climbing career has been spent attempting to shield my ego, rather than remaining open to new attitudes, techniques, and training methods. When I hear some of the most experienced climbers in the world talk about how they're always asking questions and continually learning, refining, and experimenting, it gives me permission to do the same.

And the *stoke* is infectious. Being around people who are passionate about the climbing lifestyle makes me appreciate and enjoy it all the more.

Perhaps the most important lesson this book offers is that each of us must find the courage to embrace who we really are. If, in your heart and in your soul, you know you're born to climb, then dedicate yourself fully to that passion. These athletes are a living testament to what can be achieved when you commit your life to what you love.

Books are journeys, too, and this one is no exception. Like many journeys this one started long ago, before I was even aware of it. I had been a photographer and writer for more than twenty years before I noticed that many of my best images featured women in relation with nature. This started me thinking about ways to organize those images into a collection, a winding circuitous path that brought me eventually to the book you're holding.

As a man, it's not my place to define how climbing, traditionally viewed as a masculine activity, has evolved through the influx and influence of women. Instead, my approach was to allow the women most responsible for that

Sasha DiGiulian samples the steepness of Kentucky's Red River Gorge.

transformation in North America to tell their own story, in their own words, and to let the power of their mastery speak clearly through photography.

In order to facilitate that process I provided each woman profiled in this book with a list of general questions about their lives and careers and then I conducted interviews with them based on those questions and recorded the conversations. Any errors are solely my own.

There's a quote by the Persian poet Rūmī that summarizes all I've tried to do with my life and work: "Let the beauty we love be what we do." I believe there are things in this world that are *intrinsically* beautiful. Horses for one. Running horses always awaken a brokenhearted sense of beauty—a longing for something that lies forever beyond words. Mountains are another. Driving along the Sierra Nevada, watching the ever-shifting play of cloud and brightness on John Muir's "Range of Light," I'm reminded of the profound beauty of mountains and why I've spent the better part of my life drawn to them, exploring their secrets, which as English writer Rudyard Kipling suggested, draw us ever farther, beyond the ranges, to dreamlike landscapes ever higher, more remote, and filled with mystery. And then, there is the remarkable grace of women who dare.

—CHRIS NOBLE
Salt Lake City, Utah, 2013

Kate Rutherford dances up the Free Nose (12c) Black Canyon of the Gunnison, Colorado.

DARING GRACE

There is a vitality, a life force, an energy, a quickening that is translated through you into action, and because there is only one of you in all of time, this expression is unique. And if you block it, it will never exist through any other medium and it will be lost. The world will not have it. It is not your business to determine how good it is nor how valuable nor how it compares with other expressions. It is your business to keep yours clearly and directly, to keep the channel open.

—MARTHA GRAHAM, AMERICAN DANCER AND CHOREOGRAPHER

One day, while riding in the car with her mother below Utah's Wasatch Range, my four-year-old granddaughter, Hannah, said, "Hey Mommy, look at those mountains!" And her mother said, "Yes Hannah, those are mountains."

To which Hannah replied, *"You know if you had a rope, you could climb those mountains."*

This book is dedicated to Hannah and all the children like her, girls and boys, who will one day discover their unique potential through the rapidly growing sport of climbing. At the ripe old age of four, Hannah is already a graduate of ABC for Kids, the climbing program created by former World Cup champion Robyn Erbesfield-Raboutou.

In the early seventies when I began climbing, there were only a handful of climbers in the entire United States. They were a ragtag band of misfits that Yosemite pioneer Yvon Chouinard accurately pegged as "a bunch of guys who couldn't get a date." Back in the day, we were slack jawed with surprise (and envy) when someone showed up at the crag with a girl in tow. It was rare indeed to see women climbing on their own or to see kids at the crag.

How times change! As of 2013, climbing is enjoying an explosion in popularity and participation impossible to imagine by us early adaptors. The advent of indoor climbing gyms took a fringe, counterculture activity and moved it swiftly into the mainstream. It's no longer necessary to live near mountains to be a climber. Sasha DiGiulian, one of the world's finest rock climbers, grew up in downtown Washington, D.C.; attends Columbia University in New York City; and travels, climbs, and competes at the highest level. By 2013 nearly every major city (and many small ones) in the United States had at least one gym, and in contrast to the past, the majority of people entering the sport today have their first experiences indoors on plastic, rather than outside on natural rock.

As Robyn suggests in her profile, climbing has the potential to rival gymnastics in popularity and possibly surpass it, since climbing has the added benefit of being an activity the entire family can enjoy together.

Kids naturally love to climb, whether it's on trees, jungle gyms, or climbing walls. That's good news in the United States, where if current trends continue, it's predicted that 50 percent of the population will be obese by 2030. Starting kids climbing at an early age provides an incentive for them to stay active and fit. In a society ever more concerned with the effects of passive entertainment, climbing offers a way for young people to *plug in* once more to a more primal, elemental world—one fashioned from sun, stone, wind, and sky.

Yes, climbing has its risks. Yet *sport climbing*, the most commonly practiced form, remains statistically safer than popular activities such as road biking and skiing. The women profiled in this book are living proof that climbing is a life-enhancing activity. As Lynn Hill points out, "climbing gives me life!"

While the women in this book agree that first and foremost climbing should be fun, for those who fall deeply under its spell, it can be more. Like yoga and meditation, climbing integrates body and mind. As big-wall climber Madaleine Sorkin points out, climbing raises the question, how can I take the calm, accepting state of mind I discover during meditation, and apply it to the emotional challenges found on the side of a cliff face thousands of feet above the ground? Ice climber Dawn Glanc states, "I feel like a Zen warrior out there fighting my warrior's battle with myself. Warriors don't go into battle thinking they're going to lose, and I don't attempt a climb thinking I'm going to fail."

For its initiates, climbing becomes a lifelong journey toward self-mastery. Climbing teaches competency, commitment, discipline, the ability to set goals and accomplish them, the perseverance to keep going when the going gets tough, and a discerning, yet pragmatic, quit-your-whining-and-get-after-it approach to the challenges life brings.

As a climbing friend of mine likes to say, "with the right attitude the *worst* day of your life can become the *best."* It's not uncommon to hear climbers say that when they were young, the sport served as a type of initiation that saved them from depression, drugs, delinquency, and worse.

While pop culture *loudly* promotes a cult of personality, climbing *quietly* promotes *character*—the strength and resilience of the human spirit that confronts the vicissitudes of life with confidence and good humor. Character was once a primary goal of higher education, but it seems all but forgotten in our modern age.

As French poet René Daumal writes in his book, *Mount Analogue,* those who remain in the valleys cannot even imagine the perspective of those who climb mountains. In the pages that follow, we are privileged to hear the personal stories of twenty amazing women who have dared the heights and returned. As they attest, the lessons learned in the gym; on boulders, cliffs, and frozen waterfalls; and in the world's great ranges can be brought home and applied to the more mundane challenges we all encounter in our daily lives.

Brought together by a common passion, climbers are a tribe. It's easy to recognize them by their broad shoulders, feline hips, droll humor, and love of travel. But perhaps most distinguishing is the faraway look in their eyes. Climbers are always gazing toward things unknown and unseen by the uninitiated—a spray of birds blown like sparks along a cliff's edge; the countless stars above a desert campsite; the crystal magic of a waterfall frozen to stillness by winter's cold.

Most of all, there's a bond of the soul between climbers that is impossible to describe to those who have not felt it; yet it is instantly recognizable by those who have—the distillation of days spent together experiencing the entire spectrum of human emotion, including fear, anxiety, exhaustion, doubt, and longing, as well as companionship, courage, exaltation, and joy.

Regardless of how long you have been climbing and regardless of your ability and experience, it is essential to *joyfully* embrace your own *inner climber.* The women profiled in this book did. Steph Davis, for example, describes how she horrified her parents by dropping out of law school in order to live out of her car and climb full time. Brittany Griffith describes learning about climbing and road-tripping from a boyfriend she would later marry. But in an interesting role reversal, when her husband decided he wanted to settle down, to his surprise, it was the marriage that ended, and Griffith has been on an endless road trip ever since.

Yosemite, Patagonia, Zion National Park, Hueco Tanks, Indian Creek, Rifle Mountain Park, the New, and the Red are the places that the women mention again and again. They think nothing of driving from Washington, D.C., to Kentucky's Red River Gorge for a weekend. At a moment's notice, they'll pack the truck and hit the road for weeks on end. Davis describes her early years of back-to-back expeditions, bouncing from winters in Patagonia to summers in Kyrgyzstan, the Karakoram and the Arctic, while waiting tables and living in her car between trips to make ends meet. Nomad extraordinaire Kate Rutherford has lived in one vehicle or another for a decade, mostly in Yosemite.

One could dismiss such devotion as one-dimensional, yet these women defy such stereotyping. Before dropping out of law school, Davis had already earned a master's degree in literature, and today, in addition to a remarkable array of climbing accomplishments she's the author of two books. Lisa Hathaway works as a wildlife biologist and plays music in several bands. Emily Harrington graduated magna cum laude with honors in international relations, and Alison Osius is not only an accomplished climber, but she's also a lifelong writer and editor, whose career focused on the climbing lifestyle.

Along with Alison, seven of the women are dedicated moms. Heading that list is JC Hunter, who magically finds time to climb 5.14 between working full time as a nurse and raising four children.

Yet while the climbers in this book (and their partners) certainly deserve respect, they'd be the first to point out they are not superhuman. They all share the same insecurities, worries, and self-doubt. Regardless of where climbers finds themselves outside on the ratings scale, inside they grapple with the same universal anxieties about finding balance, not living up to their own expectations, and managing intimate relationships. In addition to discussing their climbing accomplishments, the women profiled here talk candidly and courageously about the issues that confront and confound us all.

Most of all, this book is a celebration of the climbing lifestyle as experienced by women, and it acknowledges that women have quietly, yet surely, made a home for themselves within the climbing world. Each of the women profiled was asked whether she thought women approach climbing differently than men. Overwhelmingly, the answer was *yes,* but as Dawn points out, women climb differently than men, but those differences enrich the climbing experience and are something to be celebrated.

Alex Megos, a nineteen-year-old male climbing phenom from Germany who in 2013 became the first climber of either gender to on-sight 5.14d, points out, "You can learn something from every climber, especially from girls. Because on some of the routes you have a way, and it feels so hard, and you see a girl do it, and make it look so easy because she has different ways to do the moves, and different feet, different holds, and body positions. You think, 'why didn't I try that?'"

It's significant that *Women Who Dare* was published in 2013, the same year as the twentieth anniversary of Lynn Hill's free-climb of the Nose on Yosemite's El Capitan. The most elegant line on what is arguably the premier granite wall on Earth, climbing the Nose, by any means, is a lifetime achievement for most climbers. But Lynn did all the moves *free,* using only natural features and without resorting to *aid* or *artificial* climbing for purchase and upward progress, and her achievement was a watershed moment in the evolution of the sport. Some of the best male climbers in the world have tried to free the Nose and failed. When Lynn succeeded, it was a tremendous leap forward in what was considered possible for any climber regardless of gender.

Lynn's ascent was a *game changer*, a paradigm shift that occurs once or twice in a generation. It ushered in the era of modern rock climbing as it is known today, and it opened the floodgates for a whole new generation of women climbers. Free-climbing the Nose leveled the playing field in a way no amount of feminist campaigning ever could. Actions always speak louder than words, and Lynn's actions on the Great Roof and the Changing Corners state clearly and unambiguously that women can climb as hard as any man and that they are more than capable of making lasting contributions to the sport's evolution.

After all, the goal of any social movement is not superiority but equal opportunity. Evidence of Hill's enduring legacy can be seen today in the adventures and accomplishments of the women included here and in every climbing gym in the world, where tens of thousands of young girls, like my granddaughter Hannah, now learn to climb without any limit on what they can achieve.

ELAINA ARENZ

There are places you visit that immediately seem like home, and Fayetteville, West Virginia, perched on the edge of the New River Gorge (NRG), is one of them. This is Appalachia at its best—deep gorges, white-water rivers, and sixty-three thousand acres of protected forest, hill, and hollow. On crisp mornings mist flows above the New and Gauley Rivers, and by afternoon it's warm enough to swim. Perched above the gorges is some of America's best rock climbing. These elements alone make the region attractive, but it's the locals who make it feel like home. When I think of climbing in the NRG, memories of stellar rock are blended with the warm hospitality of the people who live there.

No one personifies the local openhearted friendliness better than Elaina Arenz. Growing up an army brat, Elaina understands how it feels to be a stranger, and she was once just one of the thousands of climbers who pass through Fayetteville each year. For five consecutive summers she and former husband, Kurt Smith, crisscrossed the United States with their *Kickin' Access Tour* on behalf of the Access Fund, a national advocacy group for climbing areas in the United States. Roving missionaries preaching the benefits of accepting climbing as one's personal salvation, Kurt and Elaina's efforts raised more than a hundred thousand dollars and signed up more than ten thousand new converts. Each summer she and Kurt passed through the NRG, and eventually when it came time to put down roots, they chose Fayetteville due to the strong friendships they had formed and the brilliant climbing the area offers.

Left, Elaina Arenz takes possession of Finders Keepers (12c) New River Gorge, West Virginia. Above, Arenz is lowered off a route at the Endless Wall in the NRG.

Elaina Arenz going for a Photo Finish (5.9) high above the New River.

Now the owner and operator of New River Mountain Guides (NRMG), Elaina introduces people to the wonders of climbing. With her office located in the same building as Water Stone Outdoors, the local climbing shop, Elaina and Water Stone's owners, Kenny Parker and Gene and Maura Kistler, form the diplomatic core of Fayetteville's outdoor community. Once you get to know these folks, it isn't long before you know everyone in town.

Through NRMG, Elaina offers a full spectrum of courses designed for the modern climber. For instance, you can learn not just *how to* climb but how to transition from the gym to outdoors. Each summer NRMG offers the successful Teen Rock Climbing Summer Camp, and it recently began offering retreats that combine climbing with yoga. Elaina is also a certified Warrior's Way trainer, the Arno Ilgner mental training for climbers interested in improving their ability to focus and work with climbing-based fears.

Elaina is a climber unafraid to give back. In addition to teaching and guiding, she serves on the board of directors of the New River Alliance of Climbers. She was one of the organizing members of the New River Rendezvous, an annual climbers festival considered one of the best in the nation.

Despite all her duties, Elaina still finds time to *crush it* out on the rock. Elaina has put up numerous first female ascents both in the NRG and across the United States. Along with Kurt, she was one of the original developers of El Potrero Chico, the sport-climbing destination in northern Mexico. Some of her first ascents there include Marklar (11b) and No Excuses (11a), as well as Flounder (11a) in the NRG.

An unrepentant tomboy who refused to play with dolls as a child, Elaina is sponsored by La Sportiva and Sterling Rope, and like natural-born *dirtbag* climbers everywhere across America, her favorite postclimbing beverage is PBR (Pabst Blue Ribbon beer).

ROOTS

My name's Elaina Arenz. I was born in Virginia in 1974. I grew up an army brat, so I've lived all over. After graduating from high school in Texas, I attended the University of Texas, and that's when I started climbing. A coworker introduced me to it. He was opening Austin's first climbing gym, so he took me along, and I was really psyched.

"Wait until I take you outside," he said. So the next weekend he took me to one of the local Austin crags, and I top-roped a route called Meet the Flintstones (5.9). My friend was impressed I didn't fall.

"You should lead that," he said. And I said, "What's leading?" He replied, "That's where you take the rope with you and clip it into the quick draws as you go." Then I asked, "If I fall, will I hit the ground?" "No," he answered, "not if you're high enough." So I decided to try it. He pulled the rope, and I led my first route.

Immediately, I realized the real fun was outside. However, for the first couple of years most of my climbing was at the gym, because I was in college, and the easiest place to climb was indoors. Soon I got a job working at the gym and that's when I started teaching. At the time, none of my friends were climbers, so I had to either make new friends or teach the old ones how to climb. So from the very beginning I was introducing people and showing them how to climb.

Today I identify myself primarily as a sport climber. That's the first discipline I learned, although I soon started bouldering as well. When I met Kurt, he taught me how to trad climb, place gear, jam, etc.

I love a lot of things about climbing. But first is the travel. I like the places it takes you, and the people you meet. You have meaningful interactions with different cultures as a climber that you wouldn't experience as a tourist.

ROAD TRIPS

After graduating from college, I took a year off to travel and climb. I had a friend living in Anchorage, Alaska. So in the middle of winter I

A squirrel's view of Elaina Arenz sending the trad classic Trojans (11c), Lower Meadow, NRG.

flew there to meet her, and we drove *all the way* to El Potrero Chico in Mexico! It was really fun, like Thelma and Louise on the Alcan Highway. On the way we spent a month in Hueco, Texas, and I got all my stuff stolen [laughs]. Somehow, I managed to scrape enough money together to make it through the winter. I know, living in

Texas, Alaska was a bit of a detour on the way to Mexico. But I *wanted* a climbing road trip. Since I'm an army brat, travel must be in my blood.

Fast-forward a couple of years, and Kurt and I are traveling on behalf of the Access Fund. We would book slide-show presentations where the climbing was best that season. Every June we passed through West Virginia, and we'd spend a couple weeks with Kenny Parker and Gene and Maura Kistler who own the local climbing shop in Fayetteville. We formed a close friendship with them and the NRG community. Every time we passed through, they'd ask, "When are you guys moving here?" They planted the seed then watered it with kindness. Eventually we got burned-out traveling. We knew we needed to park it and get some jobs [laughs]. So we moved to the New River Gorge, because there's so much great climbing, but it's the community that keeps you there.

GUIDING

I never set out to be a guide. As Kurt and I traveled, instructing was a way to make extra money. We'd offer clinics at climbing areas and gyms. Helping people work on movement and technique is something I've always enjoyed. When I moved to Fayetteville, I had a friend who owned a local guide service. He was ready to move on, so I took it over. It was perfect timing. I couldn't have planned it any better. Now, I've owned New River Mountain Guides since 2003, and the business has grown steadily.

For the past few years I've been working with Arno Ilgner, the creator of the Warrior's Way mental training method for climbers and author of the book, *The Rock Warrior's Way*. He approached me to see if I would be interested in offering clinics, and I said, "Of course!" I was interested in learning about his mental training techniques. So we started collaborating and offering clinics. Then he decided he wanted to certify Warrior's Way trainers, and I was one of the first to jump onboard. In 2009 I finished my training process and now I'm a certified Warrior's Way trainer.

Basically, the program teaches climbers how to focus their attention. Most people are distracted by the fear of falling or the fear of failure. The ego has a lot to do with this. So the training addresses those focus issues. I hold Warrior's Way seminars throughout the year in both private and group settings. It's great for people who have a fear of falling to learn how to focus and commit to climbing through their fears.

I've seen my own approach to climbing evolve through the Warrior's Way training. There are plenty of people who are *type A* personalities, who need everything broken down, and for those people I think it's *very* helpful. It gives people a systematic process they can follow to improve their focus and commitment.

Teaching these concepts has helped me apply them to my own climbing. I've been able to push through the grades better, keep my focus, and become more comfortable with bigger falls. Practicing how to fall is part of the training, and it prepares climbers on what to expect when they do fall on a real climb. Being aware of your surroundings and of the rate and depth of the breath is very important, because they can affect your ability to focus.

For example, I went climbing with a friend on a 12a that has a very long and precise sequence at the *crux*. I tried it fives or six times and couldn't do the move. I was distracted by the potential fall, so I took the pendulum fall several times. Then I lowered to the ground and wrestled with myself. "Okay," I thought, "I don't want to *have* to do this route again. I know I can do it if I just focus on climbing and don't worry about falling." So I sat there and planned exactly what I was going to do. I visualized every move. I set the intention that I wasn't going to *overgrip,* because fear was making me overgrip. I went back up, and the only thing in my head was this little mantra: *Breathe. Relax your grip.* I rested where I could and held on as lightly as possible, and it worked! I nailed the crux, and now I *never* have to go back and do that climb again [laughs].

The way I deal with fear is by focusing on my breath. I get scared. Everybody gets scared, and the natural reaction is to breathe shallow and fast. So I try slowing my breath as much as I can and being attentive to my surroundings. If I'm afraid to fall, I look down and ask, "Okay, why am I afraid? Am I going to hit anything? How big is the fall? Do I have experience with this type of fall?" My goal is to really objectify the components of the fall instead of being at the mercy of random imagining. And breathing is key in order to relax.

So first *evaluate the danger.* Then decide whether there's a *real* or *perceived* risk. That's a learned skill, one that you never stop learning, because there are so many different situations possible in climbing. It takes a lot of practice and a lot of time on the rock to know where it's safe to fall, where it's *not okay* to fall, when to trust your ability to climb,, and when it's time to listen to your doubts, pack your gear, and go home.

How do you psych yourself up for a hard route?

If I've been on the route before, I get psyched by rehearsing the moves in my head. If it's something I'm trying to redpoint, I visualize myself doing the moves flawlessly.

What's your favorite place to climb?

Whichever area I'm climbing at the time! But I do have favorite routes. Levitation 29 (5.11 Trad, nine pitches) in Nevada's Red Rock Canyon is absolutely amazing. In Joshua Tree in California I love O'Kelly's Crack (5.10c with a v4 bouldery start). For bouldering I love Hueco Tanks in Texas and, of course, everything at the New River Gorge.

If you could offer one essential tip to other climbers, what would it be?

First and foremost remember to breathe. Make sure you're having fun and don't get too caught up in the numbers. Numbers are a great way to measure your progress, but if you let them control you, they can become self-defeating.

If you could improve one thing about yourself as a climber, what would it be?

I would be eternally psyched, even on less than perfect days, and have the ability to go for it all the time.

CHROMOSOMES

As a female guide, I've definitely had to overcome some sexist behavior. As the owner of my own business, I do everything: book the clients and serve as guide. In the early years I had people show up and ask, "Where's the guide?" And I'd say, "I'm right here." Some were surprised at first to see a female guide, but once we were at the crag, they forgot all about it. That initial surprise happens less and less these days.

In 1993, when I started climbing, I could count all the female climbers in Austin on one hand, but now it's a whole new world. There are the Sterling Rope Women's Climbing Weekend, an annual event for female climbers, and Chicks with Picks, an organization founded to teach women about the sport. There are so many programs for women, and of course, the gyms have been incredible by introducing females of all ages to climbing.

EVOLUTION

Over time I've become a well-rounded climber. I started as a gym/sport/boulderer. It was several years before I learned about trad, which opened new possibilities for me. I like to dabble in it all and be as good at as many things as possible.

The NRG is a great place to mix things up, because you don't have to choose between sport and trad climbing. They're pretty well interspersed, and you'll have *splitter* cracks next to a sweet-face climb, bookended by another splitter. You take your rack of gear and your quick draws, and you can mix things up. It makes it easier to switch back and forth. If you continually practice placing your gear and clipping bolts, then the techniques stay fresh and more accessible to you.

Elaina Arenz considers the final moves on Mutiny (11d), Summersville Lake, NRG.

STRENGTHS AND WEAKNESSES

My greatest strength is my footwork, which I developed traveling for as many years as I did, experiencing many different climbing areas, different rock, and styles of movement.

My biggest weakness remains trad climbing. I wish I could climb as hard in trad as I do in sport. Physically I can, but it's the mental side that's another game: It's a different headspace falling on gear. Sounds like I need to take more practice falls on gear [laughs].

LESSONS

The most important lesson I've learned is to keep trying. Don't give up. If you fail at first, that doesn't mean you *can't* do it. It just means you can't do it *right now*. You've got to find a way to make it happen. You can apply that to everything in your life.

There's so much I still need to learn! I always tell my students that you're never done learning in climbing. Climbing teaches you so much about yourself, about the world, and about the way it all works. We need to be open to it all.

Elaina Arenz finds religion on Leave It to Jesus (11c), the Endless Wall, NRG.

COMMUNITY

I always like to say that in West Virginia things operate on their own time and by their own design. One of my friends called the NRG, the land of *misfit toys*. It's the place people go when they don't fit in anywhere else. Fayetteville works for them. The climbing community here is tight-knit. Everyone's open and welcoming. There are *no outsiders*. We go out of our way to make people feel welcome. West Virginia and all of Appalachia get a bad rap from movies like *Deliverance,* so we do our best to counterbalance that reputation. And where else can you live within five minutes of a national park and world-class climbing?

Plus it's affordable. It's a cheap place to live, if you can find a way to make a living [laughs]. Every year *Budget Travel* magazine creates a list of the coolest small towns in America, and several years ago Fayetteville made the list. So the town government put up a sign at the city limits publicizing Fayetteville as the "coolest small town in America." Of course when you call yourself the *coolest,* that's about the *uncoolest* thing you can do, so it makes us locals cringe!

But it is cool! You can get outdoors to recreate in a matter of minutes. In an hour after work you can top-rope some routes, go for a bike ride, or go kayaking.

THE FUTURE

I'm definitely a *lifer.* That's the thing about climbing: It's not just a sport. It's a way of life, and I embrace it. I don't see that changing. I'll climb as long as my body allows.

MOTIVATION

When I have a solid consistent partner, I'm much more motivated. For me a big part of the sport is the quality of the time you spend with the person you're climbing with.

I definitely have a tick list of routes I'd like to do. However, I'm really bad at *projecting*. It was not really an option during all those years that I traveled, so I'd try to *on-sight* a route or do it in a few tries. If I couldn't do it, I'd move on to the next one.

But it's hard to progress as a climber if you're not projecting, so I'd like to be better. Since there are so many routes in the NRG, I try to get on a new one every time I go out. But I do have projects, and I pick a project depending on where people want to go climbing that day. So I have projects everywhere [laughs].

KITTY CALHOUN

hen I first accompanied Kitty Calhoun into the mountains, I realized with a shock that this woman, who is half my size with an easy laugh and a warm Southern drawl, was the strongest person, man or woman, I'd ever climbed with. Not only could Kitty break trail through waist-deep snow longer and faster than any man I knew, but she was also mentally tougher. When we attempted the unclimbed north face of Thalay Sagar in the Himalayas in 1996, Kitty chastised us men mercilessly for taking too many showers. Since those early experiences, I've also accompanied Kitty and her husband, Jay Smith, on climbing trips large and small. We traveled along with the original North Face "dream team" to the Aksu Valley in Kyrgyzstan, where Kitty and Jay climbed the *north face* of the Bird (V, 5.11+), made the first free ascent of the *south face* of Peak 4810 (V, 5.10+), and put up a new route on Slesova called Fat City (VI, 5.12)—all while Kitty was pregnant with her son, Grady.

Kitty is America's premier woman alpine climber. To put that in perspective, it's important to understand that out of all the climbing disciplines, alpine climbing is also the most challenging for a woman. The reason is simple physiology. Overall, women are smaller than men,

which means that when alpine climbing, they have to carry a larger percentage of their body weight simply to be in the game. Just to carry the basic kit—sleeping bag, pad, shelter, stove, food, water, clothing, boots, crampons, ice axes, harness, rope, and protection—requires a woman to carry close to 50 percent of her body weight.

Left, Kitty Calhoun out for a winter stroll in the Ouray Ice Park, Colorado. Above, Calhoun tapes for the splitter cracks of Maverick Buttress, Southern Utah.

There are few men who can perform for long when burdened by as great a load.

Not only has she overcome such challenges, but Kitty also thrives in the mountains with enough good humor, energy, and enthusiasm to buoy up the rest of the team.

Kitty has made winter ascents of Colorado's Mount Sneffels, Wyoming's Grand Teton, and Washington's Mount Shuksan. She's climbed the southwest face of Alpamayo and the north face of Quitaraju in the Cordillera Blanca in Peru as well as Alaska's Cassin Ridge. In 1987 her team climbed the northeast ridge of Mount Dhaulagiri and in 1990 the West Pillar of Makalu, both in the Himalayas. After our experience on Thalay Sagar, she and Jay got right back on the horse, establishing Ride the Lightning (VI, 5.10, A4, WI3) on Middle Triple Peak in Alaska's Kichatna Spires. On El Capitan in Yosemite Kitty has climbed Lurking Fear, the Salathé Wall, Zodiac, and the Nose, all with female partners.

When Grady was born in 1996, Kitty brought the same fierce commitment she has for climbing to motherhood, and today one her favorite activities is lifting weights with her son, who now plays high school football.

Kitty has introduced hundreds of individuals to climbing through her years of guiding

Kitty Calhoun belays during an attempt on the North Face of Thelay Sagar, Garwal Himal, India 1996.

and teaching for organizations, such as Outward Bound, the American Alpine Institute, and Chicks with Picks. From 1990 to 1998 she served as the director and chair of the American Alpine Club Expeditions Committee. She has won both the Catherine Freer Memorial Award from the American Mountain Foundation (later renamed Rocky Mountain Field Institute) and the Robert and Miriam Underhill Award from the American Alpine Club.

ROOTS

My name's Kitty Calhoun. I was born in Greenville, South Carolina, in 1960, and I've always liked sports. Growing up, I did a lot of downhill skiing, and I liked tennis. I also played field hockey and liked running.

When I was eighteen, I took a course at the North Carolina Outward Bound. I signed up because I wanted to go hiking on the Appalachian Trail, and my mom said no, because I didn't know what I was doing. So I thought, "Okay I'll show her." I signed up for Outward Bound because I knew there was going to be rock climbing.

Climbing was something that scared me, because I'm afraid (or was) afraid of heights. So I decided that the best thing to do was to get really fit, so I'd be able to endure the experience better. So I started running. I was superfit when I went to Outward Bound. And, then, when I got to the climbing part, I decided not to look down and to stay focused on the next move. That worked pretty well.

What appealed to me most about climbing was the challenge. I'm the kind of person who likes to work on my weaknesses.

FEAR

I was hooked on climbing from the beginning, even though it took me a *long* time to get over this fear of heights. I'd still like to do that [laughs]. The fact is I'm not afraid of heights in terms of looking down. I can do that. I don't mind exposure. The thing I don't like is falling, but that's because I quickly became involved in alpine and ice climbing and it's not okay to fall in those two mediums.

There are two kinds of fear when it comes to falling. The first is imaginary. Yes, it would be scary to fall here, but I know I wouldn't get hurt. The second is realistic. If I fall here, there will be serious consequences. The second kind of fear takes the fun away.

I get butterflies the night before a big climb, but for me the best way to deal with anxiety is to get the first lead and focus on getting up the route. Focus on the next thing I have to do. That worked for me in my first class at Outward Bound, and it still works today.

ENJOYING THE SPORT

I think the thing I like most about climbing is the movement, figuring out how to stay in balance and work with different kinds of rock. I still enjoy working on cracks that aren't quite my size and figuring out how to do that efficiently. And I like sport climbing. It's fun trying to learn how to stay on an overhanging piece of rock long enough to climb it. Then there's *slopers*—how to work with those. And I like ice climbing, learning to work with the ice to climb efficiently. And, I like mixed climbing too. These are all things I enjoy.

CAREER

I feel fortunate to be sponsored by Patagonia, Scarpa, PMI, Black Diamond, and Julbo. And I feel fortunate that they still appreciate me even though I've been venturing away from alpine and into other aspects of climbing. A lot of what I do now is to give back through teaching. I lead ice- and rock-climbing clinics for women through Chicks with Picks, an organization founded to teach women about the sport.

I've always guided. When I fell in love with alpine climbing and started doing it a lot, I needed a job. I figured I wanted to go climbing in ranges all over the world, so either I needed to be sponsored, or I needed a job. At that stage it was easier to get a job, so I began guiding for the American Alpine Institute. They let me guide all over the world right away.

I got to guide in Peru, Bolivia, Alaska, Argentina, and Nepal. I spent years climbing and guiding big peaks and getting to experience different cultures. I was able to get familiar with the logistics of other countries, so I could set up my own expeditions. So guiding has worked out really well.

It's important to realize that guiding and teaching are different things. I enjoy both, and right now I'm enjoying teaching. When I have to verbalize, organize, and present things clearly, in a way people can easily grasp, I learn a lot as well.

CLOSE CALLS

I've had so many close calls. I'll tell you about one in the Himalayas. In 1987 Matt Culberson, John Culberson, Colin Grissom, and myself were on Mount Dhaulagiri (8,167 meters, the world's seventh highest mountain). I had a permit for the east face, because it had only been climbed once. It's a beautiful ice line. But when we got there, the east face wasn't frozen. So we had to come up with plan B, which was to try and get permission from a Japanese expedition to get acclimated by climbing as high as possible on their route, the Northeast Ridge, which is the standard way up the mountain. Then hopefully while we were acclimatizing, the east face would freeze. That's what we were hoping.

In the meantime the Japanese got caught in an avalanche. Luckily they were all okay, so when they got back to their tents, I went over and asked if we could share their route until we

Kitty Calhoun busts a move on Hoedown (rating unknown), Maverick Buttress.

got acclimatized. They said, "Sure, but to begin, you go tomorrow and break trail." So the next day we started postholing up their fixed lines. We got to the very top of their fixed line, which was anchored by eight *snow pickets*. Then we stepped on a wind slab. John and Colin were just above me. Matt had stayed below, because he wasn't feeling well.

John and Colin set off the slab. It wasn't a very big avalanche, but it pulled us over the north face, which is really steep. We were about three thousand feet up, and we started tumbling. I felt the rope come tight, so I went into self-arrest and tried to stop, but the rope pulled me

Following a successful ascent of a frozen waterfall in Iceland, Kitty Calhoun rappels in an arctic storm.

off my feet. I got back into self-arrest, but the rope yanked me even harder. Now I was just tumbling. I knew I couldn't arrest our fall, so I just curled into a ball, put my arms up, and tried to protect my head.

We were falling fast, and the first seven snow pickets all ripped out, one by one. But the last one held. We came to rest with Colin hanging on John, and John said, "Get off me Colin," but Colin couldn't. It turned out that Colin's locking *carabiner* had somehow come *unclipped* from the fixed line, then during the fall had *reclipped* to John's harness. If that hadn't happened, then Colin would have fallen to his death. So because of a single snow picket and one locking *carabiner*, we all survived. We went down and told the Japanese we were sorry we'd ripped out their fixed ropes. The next day the Japanese packed up and went home.

Despite the accident, we decided we wanted to give Dhaulagiri another shot. The east face still hadn't frozen, so we decided to try to summit via the Northeast Ridge, and we made it. But the real story was surviving that avalanche.

EVOLUTION

I think climbing has changed me as a person in a number of ways. I've developed more confidence. For instance, when I'm taking exams in school (I went back and got an MBA), I would think, "I can do this," because I've done certain challenging climbs. I've even brought a picture of me climbing into the exam room.

Climbing also helps me keep things in perspective. For instance when I was in school, there were times when I'd get upset if I didn't do as well as I'd hoped. Then I'd go climbing and

I'd realize, "Kitty, it's not the end of the world. I mean, you're still alive."

And finally, climbing helps me appreciate simple things, things as simple as bread and water, because sometimes on a climb you have to do without. In mountaineering it comes down to what matters for survival, and I think you can use those experiences to figure out what matters in life.

STRENGTHS AND WEAKNESSES

One of my greatest strengths as an alpinist is persistence. That's gotten me up big mountains and through hard situations. Another strength is being a woman, because women have a higher percentage of body fat. So when I'm climbing with these scrawny guys and we run out of food, I have more fuel to carry on [laughs]. My biggest weakness is still my fear of falling. That's held me back in sport climbing.

CHROMOSOMES

When it comes to differences between men and women, there are all the stereotypes. For instance, women tend to use balance more than men. However, there are always exceptions. I've seen men with really good footwork. So it's hard to say. I think that definitely in groups, women feel more comfortable asking questions. And that helps them learn better, because they're not afraid to ask questions, and they're more open-minded.

I've always climbed with men, because in the past there weren't as many women climbers. But now there're more, and I've been able to climb more with other women. It's definitely different than climbing with men, because in general, women are more supportive. They pay attention when they belay. If they feel I need encouragement, they give it. However, if I've been climbing with women, it can sometimes be difficult going back to climbing with men. Because sometimes when I'm climbing with a guy, I look down and he's reading the guidebook! That's taught me I can't rely on someone else to give me encouragement or confidence. It's nice if I can get it sometimes, but I can't rely on it. I have to rely on myself, and climbing with men has taught me that.

LESSONS

The most important lesson I've learned is to keep things in perspective. It doesn't even have to be a serious life-or-death situation. It could just be a day *cragging*. When I'm done climbing, everything seems to fall into place. Everything has to do with your frame of mind. When I go out and focus on something other than my personal problems, I come home with more creativity and an improved ability to figure out solutions. Things don't seem so overwhelming anymore.

What do I still have to learn? Well, one of the things I've been thinking about lately is that I'm getting older. So I'm trying to figure out how to grow old *gracefully*, which could be challenging. We'll see. I've been challenged before, and I've come out fine. But undoubtedly, there's going to come a day when my performance declines, and I'm going to have to learn to deal with that. It hasn't hit yet, but I'm beginning to wonder.

ACCOMPLISHMENTS

My most important climbing accomplishment was my expedition to the west face of Makalu in 1990. Considered one of the most difficult eight-thousand-meter peaks (also called "eight

Kitty Calhoun and husband Jay Smith embrace on the North Face of Thelay Sagar, India.

thousanders," there are just fourteen peaks on Earth higher than eight thousand meters), Makalu, at 8,481 meters, is the world's fifth-highest mountain. I believe we made the fourth ascent of the West Pillar.

The *beta* was that the West Pillar had ten thousand feet of sustained technical climbing. I called John Roskelley, who had done an earlier ascent, and I asked him how much fixed rope they'd taken, and he said ten thousand feet! *Whoa boy!* I didn't want to take ten thousand feet of rope, but I figured that maybe, *just in case,* we should, because at that time John was one of the world's most-respected alpinists.

So we got to base camp with these potato sacks, each containing a thousand feet of rope. And we really didn't know what to do with it, because none of us had ever fixed rope before.

There were six of us—myself, John Culberson, Colin Grissom, Mark Houston, Kathy Cosley, and John Schutt. We were all good friends, and eventually we figured out how to string that rope.

And it was wise that we brought it, because the technical difficulties really were ten thousand feet long. There's a knife-edged ridge nearly a mile long between camps one and two, and the entire time you're exposed to the wind. And of course, we had to make multiple trips. There weren't any possible *bivy* sites between the camps because the route is too steep.

So for safety's sake we fixed the entire ridge. We spent two weeks above twenty-one thousand feet, which was a *major* effort, but we all worked together flawlessly.

Altogether we spent sixty days on the route. At the end of that time, John Schutt and I summited. No one knew in advance who was going to summit, because we were all strong, and everyone gave themselves selflessly to the effort. In the end John and I were the only ones left standing, but we only made it because of the combined effort of the other members.

That was teamwork like I've never experienced before or since. It was definitely some sort of synergy, or pure magic, at work.

Today most big peaks are guided and team members don't really know or care about one another. On that expedition we were all friends. We didn't choose Makalu because it was a big peak; we chose it because the line is beautiful and offers high-quality climbing. I don't think there are many expeditions like that anymore.

The biggest gift climbing has given me is the bond I formed with my partners, those intense experiences climbers share with one another in situations that no longer occur in modern human life. In alpine climbing there are life-and-death experiences, when you have to work together to figure out what your best move might be. Those types of bonds are unique.

RELATIONSHIPS

The biggest challenges in my life and in climbing are my relationships. They are the most rewarding and, at the same time, the most challenging. In climbing it's difficult when your partner has his own goals and they don't coincide with yours. How do I be a supportive partner and work that out? It can be complicated.

Early in my career when I had difficulty with a partner, I'd tend not to climb with him or her anymore. Now I'm trying to learn how to work things out, even though it's painful. I'd say I'm more willing to make personal sacrifices, and sometimes that means I have to set aside my personal climbing goals. It's not easy, but I feel it's a better approach.

PHILOSOPHY

My personal philosophy about climbing is that style matters. What's important is not whether or not you get to the top, but how you do it. How you treat your partner and how you treat the environment are important. Climbing is the medium through which I've been able to develop as a person.

THE FUTURE

Climbing is definitely a lifelong activity. However, I questioned that assumption a few years ago, when I had both my hip joints resurfaced. I thought, "This is a window of opportunity! I can make a break and become whoever I want to be. I can do whatever I want to do. This would be the time."

Then I thought about it for a while and decided I wanted to keep climbing, because climbing's still fun. And I feel I've got a lot of experience to offer through teaching. My hopes and dreams for the future are to keep improving in all aspects of climbing: ice, mixed, sport, crag, big wall, and alpine. I think I can still improve and that I still have a lot to learn. That's what makes climbing fun.

MOTIVATION

I stay motivated by making goals. The goal may be a particular trip or a particular climb. It might be the number of days a week I want to climb or whichever weakness I want to work on.

How do you psych yourself up for a hard route?

What psychs me up for a route is the beauty of it. I'm attracted to a beautiful line on a peak in the same way I'm attracted to a handsome man. How can you put that into words? It's just a feeling you get.

If I'm preparing for a difficult route, I'll use visualization. Even just walking to the climb. Let's say it's an ice climb that I'm afraid of, because, you know, I can't fall. Right? So I'll think of something that gives me confidence. There have been times when I've thought back to leading one of the last pitches on the Salathé Wall on El Cap. I'm up there, and my belayer can't see me. It's early morning, freezing cold. I've been aiding, but there's this place where I have to bust a free move and run it out. So I keep saying to myself, "I've got God and sticky rubber on my side! God and sticky rubber!" Positive thinking got me through that section on El Cap, so I remember it and use that kind of visualization for other challenges as well.

What's your favorite place to climb?

I love Utah's Indian Creek and Colorado's Black Canyon of the Gunnison because it's so beautiful. I love Yosemite, because it's so unique. Iceland is awesome, because when I was there, nobody else was around, and there are tons of ice routes to do. For alpine climbing I really like India, because the rock is solid. There's really good mixed climbing in India.

As for specific routes, I like the classics. For desert sandstone there's Fine Jade (11a) on the Rectory in Castle Valley, Utah. For alpine I like the Cassin Ridge on Mount McKinley in Alaska and for ice the Aimes Ice Hose (WI5) near Telluride, Colorado. And I really like the Salathé Wall (5.9 C2 or 13b) on El Capitan in Yosemite.

If you could offer one essential tip to other climbers, what would it be?

My advice is to live each day like it's your last, because it could be. You never know. And it's so very important to follow your dreams. Life is wild and full of surprises, and that's why we were given passionate hearts and searching minds.

How do you train?

The best way to train is to go climbing. But if I'm not going climbing, my ideal training is a half hour of warm-up exercises, such as push-ups, pull-ups, and an eight-minute abdominal routine, followed by a thirty-minute cardio workout. I use a bike with a heart-rate monitor. I get my heart rate up to a target level and keep it there for the full thirty minutes. Then I lift for a half hour and stretch for a half hour. I also practice yoga when I can fit in a class. That's how I train.

STEPH DAVIS

When I think of Steph Davis, I see brown eyes and a wide smile, and I think of the desert with its towers, cliffs, and canyons, stretching away into the blue distance. It is a landscape both beautiful and perilous. The Wingate sandstone of the Colorado Plateau offers some of the most challenging climbing in the world. The moment you insert a fist, fingers, or toes into those smooth splitter cracks, you immediately begin learning about levels of strength, technique, and endurance previously unimaginable.

Yet Steph makes it look easy. In 2003 she became the second woman (after Lynn Hill) to free-climb Yosemite's El Capitan in a day (via Free Rider, VI, 12d/13a) followed by a return to El Cap two years later for the first female ascent of the Salathé Wall (VI, 13b). In 2008 Steph climbed Concepcion (13b/c) near Moab, considered to be one of the hardest pure-crack climbs in the world.

And that's just the stuff she does with a rope. Steph is one of the few women in the world who free solos (climbing without rope or belay) on a regular basis, and she is perhaps the only woman who has free soloed at the 5.11 grade and above. She's free soloed the Diamond on Longs Peak in Colorado *four times,* along with test pieces, such as the Coyne Crack (11+), at Indian Creek in Utah, and in 2008 she free soloed the north face of Castleton Tower (5.11) outside Moab, Texas, then BASE jumped from the summit. (BASE is an acronym for skydiving from buildings, antennas, spans [bridges], and earth [cliffs].)

Which brings us to the other thing that puts Steph in a category all her own: She not only likes to *climb up* vertical terrain, she also likes to *jump off.* When she and her husband, Mario Richard, one of the pioneering developers of modern BASE jumping, got married, they held the ceremony atop Parriott Mesa, a vertically walled desert plateau near Moab, Utah, so they could celebrate their vows by jumping. Not to be outdone, half the wedding party followed Steph and Mario into the air that day.

Left, Steph Davis considers her next move on Glad To Be A Trad (5.13) Southern Utah. Above, Davis at home in Moab, Utah, with beloved companions Mao the cat and Cajun the blue heeler.

Steph is the author of two books: *High Infatuation: A Climber's Guide to Love and Gravity,* published in 2007, and *Learning to*

Steph Davis begins the long journey up Glad To Be A Trad, Southern Utah.

Fly, published in 2013. In *Learning to Fly* she describes the remarkable mental aikido required by a climber who free solos then purposefully learns to fall. She writes, "Falling into dead air felt nothing like I thought it would. I'd spent much of my life trying not to think about it. It was my worst nightmare. . . . Because you can't think about falling when you're climbing, or you won't go climbing anymore. . . . I figured if the big fall ever came, it would be over, *wham,* just like that. I'd slip off. I'd start falling. A stab of panic. Then somehow I would just disappear or everything would go black or something. . . . As it turns out, nothing could be further from the truth."

When she isn't traveling the world to climb or BASE jump, Steph lives in Moab, Utah, with Mario and her beloved animal companions, a dog named Cajun and a cat named Mao. In her spare time she gardens and blogs about the climbing lifestyle, veganism, and animal rights. (Postscript: On August 19, 2013, Steph's husband, Mario Richard, was killed while BASE jumping in Italy. He was 47.)

ROOTS

I'm Steph Davis. I was born in Illinois in 1972. I first started climbing as a college freshman. When I started, I didn't know anything about outdoor sports. I was a serious student and a musician, but one day I skipped a calculus class to try climbing, and that was it for me. After that, I was all about climbing.

I think what appealed to me most was that climbing was a dramatic difference from what I'd been doing. I started playing piano when I was three, and up to that point my whole life was

Steph Davis boulders near Moab.

oriented toward music. So here I was at eighteen, and I wasn't at all familiar with the outdoors. I played outside as a kid, but my family wasn't into hiking, camping, or anything. I didn't know there was mountain climbing. I had never heard of Mount Everest, the highest mountain in the world. So climbing opened up a whole new reality. For me the most exciting thing in life is to always be learning. And I saw immediately that climbing offered infinite learning.

When I learned how to climb, the sport was still relatively unknown. It was the East Coast in 1991, and climbing was not what it is now. There wasn't the whole gym scene or any kids climbing. In fact it was still a bit countercultural, which I think for me was part of the attraction. But for my parents it was really rough. I did stay in school, earning a master's degree in literature, but then after only one week in law school, I left to go live in my car and climb full time. So my parents thought that I was not only dropping out of school to pursue a dangerous activity they couldn't relate to but that I was also ruining my life.

For probably the next fifteen years, life was really hard for *everybody* [laughs]. It was hard on me, because I felt sad that I didn't have the support of my parents. I felt alone and scared about what I was doing. And it was hard on my parents, because they felt the same. So I guess everyone was scared and sad [laughs]. But now we're all happy! So the moral of the story is to hang in there! After twenty years, your parents will accept what you're doing [laughs].

Now I've been climbing half my life, and climbing defines who I am. It shaped my life, the places I've visited, the people I've known, and the things I've done. For me climbing remains a very individualistic pursuit. By that I mean I like to do things on my own. I like the fact that climbing can be something that's community oriented—that's important. But at the same time, climbing can also be very personal. Just going out there by myself, doing my thing at my own pace in my own way, is what really suits me.

STYLE

I've always been really curious. So right from the start I became attracted to climbing with gear (*trad* climbing), because it offered more things to learn and understand.

Don't get me wrong. I enjoy sport climbing, but for me the process of mastering the gear, the rope work, big-wall climbing, aid climbing, ice climbing, and expeditions is really compelling and always has been.

When I first started climbing, sport climbing existed, but it hadn't become the sport that it is today. Climbing with gear was typical. So if I wanted to be a climber, I needed to learn how to place gear.

You know, sometimes when you're doing it, you're like, "Oh, there's all this stuff! What a pain!" But to me it's really engaging. Learning how to climb is not just understanding and training for the moves, but it is also learning how to use the gear, all of which adds a whole new dimension to the experience. And then say you want to do a multipitch route. You've got to figure out which ropes to take, how to be efficient, how much water you'll need, and how much food to take. It's a whole new level of knowledge, and I like that.

So I love *cragging* with gear. I love the purity of it and the technical nature of it. But it's more than that. For me, the daily life in Moab, Utah, where I live, is as important as the climbing. Climbing is something I do, and it's important, but climbing by itself is not enough.

For example, for a long time I lived in Yosemite. That was important too, and I'm glad I did it. But the lifestyle there was not healthy. There was too much driving and too many regulations. To me that was not a healthy lifestyle.

In Moab life is very free. Very simple. I ride my bike. I do what I want. I can BASE jump. I can climb. I go places with my dog. To me it's more balanced than living in a place where climbing is the only thing to do.

LEARNING TO FLY

I've noticed that I *really* like being in high places [laughs]. And I think that's one reason I like the desert, because when you climb there, you always end up on top of a mesa or tower. I like that. I like being in high places, and climbing gives you that. BASE jumping gives you that. So in some ways, the reason I do all these things might be as simple as that.

You know, BASE jumping's interesting to me because it's a lot like climbing. People have different approaches. With BASE it's possible to go with the *dude bra* ski approach, where you're like, "Hey dude, watch this!" You know? You're psyched, and you *hope* it all works out.

That's definitely one style, but there's another that is very precise. I would say more intellectual. The emphasis is on the beauty of the experience, when you put yourself in danger. You have the right tools. You have the right gear. You have the right skills. Then instead of being a death-defying experience, it becomes this amazing feeling of being able to take that extra step and go to a place you wouldn't normally go. It's not just *surviving*: It's doing it well and having the experience of doing everything right and feeling the way you do when you're in that zone, where everything's happening the way you want it to and you know you can control things. So in that respect BASE jumping is a *really* amazing way to experience the cliff, just like climbing.

"3, 2, 1, Go!" Steph Davis BASE jumps from a cliff above Utah's Green River.

In fact I wrote a book about this. It's called *Learning to Fly.* It's about the time in my life when I *truly* learned how to fly. Everything I did for a long time was focused on climbing and *free soloing.* During the period I learned to sky dive, I was in a phase where I was extremely focused on free soloing. That's the only kind of climbing I wanted to do. Then I literally *jumped* into this new world of skydiving, learning how to fly a wing suit, learning to BASE jump. That was a very transformative period because obviously

Steph Davis finds the treasure on Hidden Gem (5.13), near Moab.

when you solo, you spend all of your time wanting *very much not to fall!* Then to suddenly become someone who is actively seeking to fall and fly—that's a world-altering shift.

CLOSE CALLS

The first time I went to Patagonia, a region in South America, mostly in Argentina, was in 1996 with Charlie Fowler and that was my first trip to real mountains. And we definitely had some, you know, *interesting* adventures [laughs], trying to climb Fitz Roy and getting stormed off. At one point, Charlie rappelled, and while he was rappelling, the ropes blew right off the bollard we'd chopped in the ice! So I was up there with no ropes, and he was somewhere down

"Nice neighborhood!" Steph Davis climbs near her home in Moab.

below. It was windy and sleeting, and we had zero communication. I thought he was dead and that I would have to down-climb all of Fitz Roy. So I started down-climbing, while Charlie was climbing back up with the ropes. We met partway, relieved we were both still alive. I had some of my closest calls on that trip, probably because I had little experience at the time, and I just went for it. But since then, I don't feel I've had a lot of close calls.

I went to Patagonia seven seasons in a row, seven consecutive winters. And during that time, I was going on summer trips as well. I went to Kyrgyzstan. I went to the Karakoram Range and the Kondus Valley in Pakistan. I went to Baffin Island in Canada. So yeah, during that phase of my life, I was going on a lot of expeditions.

I'm still interested in expeditions, but I'm also equally passionate about BASE jumping and wing-suit flight now, so it's hard for me to dedicate two to three months to a single trip. What I prefer now is to go to Europe, where I can do big wing-suit jumps and also be climbing at the same time.

THE CLIMBING LIFESTYLE

It hasn't been easy making a life from climbing. It's different today. There's more money in the sport; companies sponsor more established climbers. I suppose I'm trying to say that it's a little more of a solid path these days. When I started, the path wasn't as easy.

When I started, there was so much uncertainty. I left school, to the disapproval of my family. I lived in my car and waited tables and guided. I liked what I was doing, but I didn't know where it was going. And I certainly didn't

have any kind of stability. No home base, no financial stability, nothing.

Now I have a home. I'm more established as a climber. So that's really nice. It makes me feel grateful. But as far as my feelings about climbing, they're just the same. I still want to climb. It's still important, and everything revolves around it.

LESS IS MORE

The nice thing about climbing is that it affirms the desire to live a simple life. Climbing affirms that a simple life is the right way to go, because when you climb, less is more. You don't want to carry too much. You've got to have as little as possible and still get by. You want to eat as little as you can, drink as little as you can, and carry as little as you can. Do the easiest possible moves to make it through a difficult section. You know, you want the minimum of everything. That feels best.

In society that's not always clear. But it gives climbers a lot of inner strength to know that simplicity is right. That's really shaped me. Don't be wasteful. Follow the natural path. That sort of minimalism shapes everything I do.

I don't like anything excessive. I'm always trying to figure out what's the smallest thing I can do. So you want a car that's the most economical and gets the best mileage. And I'm vegan, because that's healthier and simpler. It's an easier way to live, a better way to eat. I live in a simple house that doesn't tax my resources. Every little choice adds up to a simpler lifestyle. That's what gives me freedom and happiness.

What I've learned is that it's really important to have the basics, but beyond that, what I value most is my time and my freedom. My belief is that once you have those things, you have everything.

STRENGTHS AND WEAKNESSES

I think my greatest strength is focus. I see things very directly. That's probably my biggest weakness as well. You know your strength is also your weakness! Because sometimes I feel too focused. When I was younger, I was so focused that sometimes my projects were all I cared about.

These days I try not to be so single-minded. It's hard when you want to do something, and there are all these other demands. It can be a struggle. So I've been trying to be a little more balanced in my approach.

But I've learned that in order to get something done, you have to have focus. But as life goes on, it's never that simple. As you get older, your world gets bigger. There are more relationships and more responsibilities.

So I think the important thing is to learn how to work with that. Learn how to say, "Okay, it's really important I do this thing I want to do." But it's also important to acknowledge, "Okay, I'm not doing exactly what I want to do right now, but I'm still going to enjoy it, embrace it, be here fully."

People have different tendencies. Some people don't have the ability to put their own goals first. So that's something they can give themselves. And other people *only* want to put themselves first, so they might want to look at the other side.

RELATIONSHIPS

It's really nice when a couple shares the same interests. But, as important as climbing is in my life, I've learned that everything else is equally or even more important. It's important to realize that there are plenty of people who are fun to climb with. But there are *not* a lot of people who would make the perfect life partner for you. That's an important distinction.

ACCOMPLISHMENTS

If I had to choose my most important climb, I'm not sure what it would be. I feel all my adventures have influenced me. Freeing El Cap in a day was a huge breakthrough. Freeing the Salathé Wall was huge. Soloing the Diamond was huge. But my favorite thing I think was free soloing the north face of Castleton Tower then BASE jumping off—because that really combined the things I find most special. It felt very pure.

Castleton was an adventure completely on my own, and that's what I like, the aesthetics, you know? *No rope. Climb up. Jump down.* To me, that's beautiful.

It certainly wasn't the most harrowing. The Salathé Wall really took a lot out of me, and the Diamond was pretty intense, but Castleton went exactly as I'd planned, so I think it will always be my favorite.

Typically when I'm soloing and going to jump, I'll pull the BASE rig up on a little cord. I'll take a piece of five-millimeter cord, and I'll hang the rig from a *fifi* hook on an anchor, then I'll solo the route, get to a belay and pull the chute up after me. However, when I soloed the north face of Castleton, I had already climbed the route a few days before with Mario to make sure I was ready for the free solo. When Mario and I do that, we always bring the jumping gear so we can jump from the top. But on that day it

How do you psych yourself up for a hard route?

Usually I just train on the route. The advantage of this approach is that I learn the route really well. If it's hard and it's going to take some time, I don't like to bother other people to get a belay, which is why I like to self-belay. But rigging a self-belay takes longer. You can't easily lower back down to work one section, so it takes a lot longer to actually get ready to do the redpoint. The flip side is that all the time invested makes me better prepared.

And I do visualization. I rehearse the moves in my mind. If I'm getting close and I think I'm actually ready to send, then I get serious about visualizing. I lie in bed and imagine myself doing each sequence, remembering every detail. For example, where you place each piece, how to rack so you grab the right piece. All those little things matter. If it's not working for you, it's working against you.

What's your favorite place to climb?

Obviously Moab. But I really like the Diamond on Longs Peak in Colorado as well. I think all of the routes there are great, but one of my favorites is Ariana (six pitches 12a), very classic. And I love Rifle Mountain Park, also in Colorado. Rifle's not the place I climb my best, but I like it very much. As far as favorite routes, I like everything on Castleton Tower. I like almost everything at Indian Creek [laughs]. And what else? All the Yosemite classics, such as the Rostrum, Astroman, and the Regular Route on Half Dome free. Every classic route in the valley is classic for a reason.

If you could offer one essential tip to other climbers, what would it be?

Don't be a number chaser. Don't get bogged down in ratings. I meet a lot of younger climbers, and in every case they stop having fun when their focus starts being about the rating. They start calling the route a number instead of its name. They start saying, "Oh, I should have been able to do that 12," or "I'm upset because I couldn't do that 13." Let go of all that! Just enjoy the fact you're climbing.

How do you train?

I climb a lot on rock, and I also have a training wall in my backyard. I do yoga every morning for a half hour. And with BASE jumping there's a lot of hiking with weight on your back. That helps keep me fit. In winter I used to lift weights, but now I'm doing a more climbing-specific regimen using a hang board, a campus board, and a system board—all things Mario built for me.

was too windy, so I stashed my rig. I buried it in a little cave on the summit. So when I went back and soloed the route, it was really nice, because I didn't even have to deal with the parachute. I just climbed, and the chute was there waiting.

I did Free Rider in 2003, and there wasn't a lot of free-climbing action on El Cap at that time. In fact, pretty much none. So there weren't many people on the wall, and to me that was attractive. I would go up there and get out of the valley and all of the craziness—the cars, the commerce . I would go up there and be by myself. That's why I did it.

I wanted to get into nature and not have other stuff going on. To me that's the way to feel happy in Yosemite. In a place like Moab, I don't need to escape, because it's so nice [laughs]. But again, I like doing things by myself. Sometimes that requires extra motivation, but it's a lot simpler. There are no distractions. Nobody's talking to you. You're just on your own program. You can listen to music. Go whatever time you want. If you feel good, you stay. If you feel bad, you bail. When I work a route in this way, I use a solo system, which involves a fixed line and two minitraxions attached to the rope that allows me to work out the moves alone. It's not as efficient as having a belayer, because it takes longer, but I really enjoy the freedom and process of being on my own.

SASHA DiGIULIAN

first met Sasha DiGiulian in 2010. She was a senior in high school and had just driven from her home in Washington, D.C., to Kentucky's Red River Gorge, a six-hour commute that she shrugged off as a normal part of being an East Coast climber.

At the time, Sasha was on the cusp of fame. She'd been dominating US climbing competitions for several years but had yet to make a name for herself outdoors. As we reached the trailhead to the crag, I was amused to see she was about to hike Kentucky's muddy trails in neon-pink *moon boots*. I remember thinking, "Wow, she really is a city girl."

While she may have skidded a bit on the approach, Sasha showed her true colors once we reached the crag. Jumping on an unknown 5.12 in the still cold morning air, Sasha "warmed up," trailing my static line in order to hang it for the subsequent photos. Then she proceeded to climb two 13s without seeming to draw a deep breath. I was impressed. The photos were wonderful, but as the world and I were about to find out, commuting long distances, and climbing 5.12 and 5.13 on-sight is not really a big deal for Sasha.

The next time we met was a year and a half later in Saint George, Utah. The moon boots were gone, replaced by Five Ten approach shoes and a wardrobe by Addidas Outdoors. Sasha

stepped off the plane less than twenty-four hours after winning her third US National Sport Climbing Championship *in a row*. She was fresh off her send of Pure Imagination, a Jonathan Siegrist 14d in the Red River Gorge. At the time, Sasha was the youngest woman in the world to climb 14d, and Pure Imagination was the most

Left, Sasha DiGiulian finds a rest on Golden (14b) at The Cathedral near St. George, Utah. Above, DiGiulian stays warm between routes at The Cathedral.

difficult route yet climbed by an American woman (although there has been subsequent discussion about whether Pure Imagination should be down rated, Sasha went on to substantiate her claim to the grade by redpointing Era Vella 14d in Spain). Sasha is now the top-ranked female outdoor sport climber in the world. She was profiled in an article in *Rock and Ice* magazine and won the 2012 Golden Piton Award from *Climbing* magazine. Six-hour commutes to the Red had been replaced by round-the-world air travel to Spain, China, Scandinavia, and South America to climb and to attend public presentations with legends of the climbing world, such as Reinhold Messner. Sasha still found time to graduate from high school and be accepted at Columbia University in New York City.

Her mission before starting at Columbia in the fall of 2012 was to climb as many 14s, in as many locations, as she could. Initially tired from the challenges of a multiday competition, Sasha was stoked to jump on Golden, a beautiful 14b line bisecting the center of the Cathedral, a limestone cave that lives up to it's name outside Saint George, Utah.

Sasha represents the latest generation of climbers who are remaking the sport in their own image and bringing it into the new millennium. She started at an early age and is a shining example of the precedent-shattering talent the indoor gym system can produce. Unlike many climbers who had to defy their parents to start climbing, Sasha has always had the full support of her parents, family, and friends. She also cares as much (or more) about the level of her grades in the classroom as she does on rock. And even though Sasha is young, she's already

sophisticated beyond her years, a consummate professional who is kind, courteous, humble, and responsive.

While bad weather prevented a successful redpoint of Golden, Sasha easily redpointed Atonement 14b, another Siegrist route in the Virgin River Gorge, then went on to win the US Lead Climbing Championships as well as three gold medals in the Continental Championships in Venezuela.

ROOTS

My name's Sasha DiGiulian. I was born in 1993, and I started climbing at a local gym when I was seven years old. Climbing and I clicked right away. I liked the sensation of going higher and higher. I started frequenting the gym, and I advanced quickly due to my passion and dedication.

I consider myself primarily a sport climber. I compete at the World Cup level in both sport climbing and bouldering. I try to be diverse. I like sport. I like bouldering. I like to climb outside, and in the future I'd like to do more trad. I think it's important to explore the diversity of climbing, because the sport offers such a wide array of experiences. I think that competing and climbing outside can be challenging. Obviously, since the holds indoors are *plastic* rather than natural rock, there are major differences between climbing indoors and out. I do most of my training indoors, so I try as best I can to convert that experience into outdoor performance.

I think that climbing from such a young age has helped me translate skills learned in the gym and in competitions to climbing difficult routes outside. However, the more I climb outside, the

Sasha DiGiulian on her way to winning the 2010 Sport Climbing Series National Championship at Momentum Climbing Gym, Sandy, Utah.

less intrigued I am to climb in a gym! And at the same time, there's something about the energy of competition that I thrive on. When I'm not competing, I start longing for that vibrant energy that pushes you up a wall in a competition. I think the practice of indoor and outdoor disciplines provides skills that enable you to succeed in both.

My experience in competition climbing has definitely aided me *on-sighting* harder routes outside. I've learned to keep pushing, even when I'm tired. I just concentrate on the next move and the next, instead of thinking about reaching the anchors. I think of a route as a journey rather than a final destination.

If you can keep pushing throughout that journey and make personal high points each time you attempt a route, your success comes faster. Same goes for *on-sight* climbing. Keep an open mind, know your pace, and really push yourself through the moves. I've learned about pacing largely through competitions. Competition climbing has also aided my ability to read sequences and figure out ways to move efficiently through difficult sections.

ENJOYING THE SPORT

I think what I love most about climbing are long sport routes, where everything else fades away and all you're thinking about is the movement. All you feel is the rock and the natural surroundings. This beautiful aspect of climbing outside, in particular on long routes, is what really ignites my passion.

The aspects of climbing that I like least are *thrutchy* sequences, where I have to abandon my technique and rely on pure power. Bouldering can sometimes be difficult for me due to my physique. I'm not a very big person, and I don't have a masculine build, so sometimes dynamic powerful sequences can be more challenging than technical sequences. But when I succeed in overcoming my weaknesses, there's a great sense of satisfaction.

INJURIES

When I'm bouldering a lot, I find I get injured more, and that's created a new challenge for me: overcoming fear of injury. I injured one ankle three years in a row. It became quite vulnerable,

to the point where I was on crutches and could only do one-footed climbing for a long time. I've also had a serious back injury. I cracked the L4 vertebra in my lower back in a bouldering fall. I've also had finger injuries, but primarily when I was younger. From about age nine to age eleven, when my body was still developing, I trained hard on campus boards. The tendons in my hands developed before my bones, so now my middle fingers are crooked because I'm missing bone fragments from the middle of the joint. But now that my bones are settled and I'm not growing any more, I don't have pain in my fingers.

Overall (knock on wood), I've been pretty lucky. I think as long as you trust your belayer and your gear, do things properly, and have patience, then climbing is quite safe, especially sport climbing.

I find the most important thing to prevent injury is to listen to your body. There's no point in pushing your muscles to the point of failure. Obviously, you don't want to have a mildly sore shoulder and say, "Oh well I can't train today," but if your fingers feel really painful, I'd say stop climbing and rest. The worst thing you can do is drive yourself to the point of injury. And if you do, you'll decrease your motivation as well. I try to climb when I'm motivated and take time off when I'm not. Fortunately, I'm motivated more often than not, so you'll usually find me climbing. But if I go through a period when I'm not motivated or really sore and tired, I'll take a break.

STRENGTHS AND WEAKNESSES

Over the years I've gained a lot more knowledge, an overall sense of body awareness, technique, and experience. Going on thirteen years of

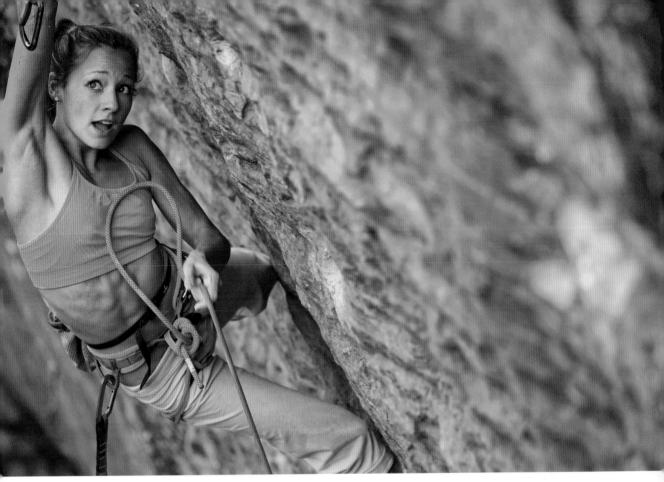

Sasha DiGiulian eyes the clip on Golden Boy (13b), Kentucky's Red River Gorge.

climbing, I feel like every year I learn something new, such as new techniques I can use with my hands, feet, or body. The more you climb the more you become aware of your physical and mental capabilities. Climbing is a mental sport. So I've developed a strong belief in myself. I've learned to become *less* concerned with pushing the number (rating) scale and *more* focused on pushing my own personal limitations, working on my weaknesses, and exercising my strengths.

As I said, my weakness is *thrutchy*, powerful, dynamic movements. Generally this is a mental issue for me. I'll see a big move and think "Well, I can't reach it. But if I open my mind to the fact that I can jump and I work on that jump, working my way through the entire sequence, then eventually I'll be able to do it. The most important lesson I've learned, one that I keep on learning, is not to shy away from my weaknesses. And for a long time I was shying away from *dynos* in particular. The more hard routes I attempt, the more difficult the crux sections become, and the more I need to *boulder* out the moves.

My strengths are mental perseverance and the ability to see different technical possibilities. Through competition, I've improved my ability to read sequences, so when I'm on-sighting, I can keep a calm mind, see what needs to be done, and then move through the sequence efficiently. I think I can improve in all areas of my climbing, but I think where I've improved most is with crimpers and resistance (endurance) climbing.

LESSONS

The most important lesson I've learned from climbing, one that translates to every other aspect of my life, is goal setting. More and more, I'm realizing that the greater your dream, the greater the success that you can achieve. And here, I define *success* as personal satisfaction. I think that once you can see that success is not a material thing but a mental state, you begin to realize all the benefits and passion that climbing brings to your life.

I still have a lot to learn, and that's why I'm going to Columbia [laughs]. I think I still have a lot to learn in climbing as well. I have plenty of technique that can be improved! Even a climber like Adam Ondra, who's currently leading the world, has a lot to learn. I think that's what's so great about climbing; we all learn from one another.

CHROMOSOMES

Overall I think women tend to be more *fearful,* and less *fearless* than men, but it's been inspiring recently to see women climbers worldwide challenging their own personal limits, not being daunted by hard grades, and just going for it. I believe that's the key to women's progress in climbing. For a long time men were progressing faster than women, and I think that was due in large part to the mental limitations women place upon themselves. The ability to see a route as a whole—as an aesthetic, inspiring line—rather than a difficult grade is the key to improving.

Women can climb just as hard as men on certain routes. In Spain there's a route called Mind Control, which is 8C+ (5.14C). More women have done it than men. I think this is a good example of women climbers' progress in their mastery of the sport. Mind Control is an example of a resistance-oriented climb. It's fifty-five meters of pure resistance, without too many powerful or dynamic moves. I think when technique and resistance are the key factors, you'll logically see more female ascents.

CHALLENGES

I tend to be relatively fearless when it comes to pushing my own limits. I don't like being told I *can't* do something. Sometimes when I hear that, it inspires me to want to try it even more. I like to challenge myself, and I try not to be daunted by hard tasks. I believe everyone should have the attitude that challenge is good. Once you see that challenges are not impossible obstacles, you can really begin pushing your own limits and confronting challenges head-on.

I've always been self-motivated, but I'm also motivated by my peers, each of whom inspires me in a different way. I think *everyone* can teach you something. No one has all the answers. Time management is key. I learned this in high school, trying to balance good grades with good climbing results. I think the secret is clearly seeing the task, then attacking without procrastination.

ACADEMICS

In the fall of 2012, I began attending Columbia University, which is another challenge but not an obstacle to my climbing. I'll just do both. I like to have multiple things going on. If I'm only

Sasha DiGiulian sends Atonement (14b) in Arizona's Virgin River Gorge.

climbing, I start putting too much pressure on myself about performing well. It's important for me to have other passions to look forward to in addition to climbing.

Even though I keep really busy, I don't ever feel left out socially, because I have a strong network of friends. I can connect with many of them on a deep level, and I'm really grateful for that.

My parents have always stressed that academics are of equal importance—*make that more important*—than athletics. They definitely raised

Sasha DiGiulian demonstrates her flexibility on Golden (14b).

me to value education. Columbia is located in New York City, my favorite city in the world. New York is this incredible energy center, where you constantly feel a part of something vast and powerful. I'm really excited to attend Columbia and pursue the academic part of my life. After high school, I took a year off to travel and climb, and it was amazing. I visited really beautiful places, and I increased my frequent-flyer miles a lot [laughs]. It was great, but I also feel that if I'm only climbing, something's missing. Climbing will always be my number-one passion, but I don't feel there's a reason to limit myself, so going to school and exploring what I'm capable of through studying and learning about other ways of life is important to me.

While attending Columbia, I'll be training, competing, and going on climbing trips. It will be challenging, much more challenging than if I was pursuing climbing alone, but it's another way for me to express myself as a human being rather than just as an athlete.

I think it's important to have other things going on in your life. If I get injured, I'll have studying to do. I also know I can't be at the top of my climbing game forever, and I'm open to the fact that next year I might not be as successful. What I most hope to accomplish through climbing is to inspire others to find what's best in themselves, and I think that going to school and having a good education will help me do that.

How do you psych yourself up for a hard route?

Generally when I'm working a route, I'll go up and figure out the moves, whether it's bolt to bolt with rests or every other bolt. I work from the bottom up. The goal is to find the best sequence. Then during my next try, I rehash those sequences and try to make bigger links. With every subsequent attempt my intention is to master the sequences, learn to move ever more efficiently, and climb longer without resting. Sometimes I break the route down into sections. It can be as many as eight sections to start, then I whittle it down to six, five, four, and so on. The goal is to climb the route in total.

How do you train?

In my opinion training needs to be self-motivated. If I'm not motivated, I rarely push myself. I think that listening to your body and following your heart are the two main components of succeeding. I've always been inspired by my peers and my family. I've been inspired to push myself, and I think that's the most important point. You need to have your own goals and to want to succeed for personal reasons. When I train in the gym, it normally consists of about two hours, five days a week. I approach training as something I do frequently for short periods rather than long hours taken to the point of exhaustion.

The percentage of roped climbing versus bouldering depends on what I'm training for.

There's really no one-size-fits-all approach to use. If I feel like bouldering one day, that's what I do. If I feel like sport climbing, then I'll grab the rope. Often I do circuits when I'm training. Circuits can range from thirty-five to seventy boulder moves at a consistent angle. The goal is quick, challenging movement that leads either to exhaustion or to a fall. I'll count seventy moves in my head, and I'll do three minutes on, then three minutes off resting. Because that's a more concentrated training session, I may only do circuits for an hour before I'm tired and call it a day. Or I may be bouldering with friends and climb for three hours.

What's your favorite place to climb?

My favorite place to climb is the Catalonia region of Spain. There's so much limestone, so much potential, and so many beautiful lines there. The options are endless when you're in Spain. It's hard not to spread yourself too thin during a short trip, because you want to experience every area, and every area has world-class routes waiting to be climbed. I understand why Chris Sharma moved to Spain. Right now, Spain is the mecca for hard sport climbing.

How do you choose your climbs?

I want to climb anything that looks aesthetically inspiring. I try not to worry about the grade, whether it's easy 5.12 or hard 5.14. There's really no reason not to try something.

Continued on next page

Continued from previous page

The worst you're going to do is fail, and failure isn't really failure. It's simply not climbing the route. Overall I believe the more you climb, the more you're benefiting, garnering new skills and knowledge. I think what's most important in climbing is to be open to all different levels and not to limit yourself by what I would call grade fixation.

Do you ever feel unmotivated to climb?
Definitely, and during those times, I don't push myself, because if I do, then that period might last even longer! But if I do take a break, then before long I'm eager to climb again. Every December I take a break from climbing and spend time skiing with my family. That's one of my rituals to rest my body. I think it's very important to physically give yourself a break, even if you don't feel like you need one. And it's also important to always exercise the muscles that are oppositional to the ones that are used in climbing.

ENJOYING THE SPORT

When I'm climbing, the thing that excites me most is when I just relax with friends and really *feel* the rock and have all my senses in tune with nature. When you're climbing a hard route, you don't really have room for negativity, and your thoughts can't wander because your focus has to be on the movement. I think that's the most enriching experience. When I've achieved long-term goals, it's a truly satisfying feeling. When I completed Pure Imagination, I was ecstatic. It was something I'd dreamed about. Reaching the anchors was one of the best feelings of my life.

When I started climbing, I thought, "Wow, if someday I could just climb 14a, I'll be content, my dreams will be accomplished!" But as you progress, your goals become greater, so when I climbed my first 14a, I *was* satisfied but certainly not *finished.* So I started setting higher goals and seeing what else I could do. The following year I climbed 14b, then I set my sights

on 14c, and I accomplished that. Pure Imagination is a 14d (9a on the French scale), and that's the hardest grade ever attained by a woman, so it was a big challenge. I didn't pursue it for the grade; I wanted to do it to find out if I was capable of pushing my limits that far. I saw a video of Jonathan Siegrist climbing it, and as soon as I saw that, I knew I wanted to climb that beautiful route. It's a long, steep, sustained climb up a honeycombed wall of sandstone. It's a daunting route. Climbing it required pushing through the hardest sequences I've ever attempted. When I got to the top, I was surprised, emotional, and *very happy!* It was one of those moments when you have to pinch yourself to make sure you're not dreaming!

RELATIONSHIPS

I've always found myself connecting with people who are passionate about something, whether it's climbing or something else. I really enjoy the friends who remain friends even if we go long periods without seeing each other. When we do see each other again, it's as if time had stood still. Those are the strongest bonds. The most important thing in a relationship is that you respect one another's passions and the demands accompanying those passions.

THE FUTURE

I see myself climbing for the rest of my life—certainly. Competing on the World Cup circuit—certainly *not*. Climbing with friends outside and in the gym is both a hobby and a lifetime pursuit for me.

Sasha DiGiulian celebrates on Golden Boy (13b), the Red River Gorge.

ROBYN ERBESFIELD-RABOUTOU

Climbing's undergoing a radical revolution. As of 2013, indoor gyms are proliferating. Each day in gyms around the globe, more young people are introduced to the sport. And when millions of individuals are introduced to climbing at an early age and their natural talents are fostered by expert training and coaching, standards soar. Climbs of a technical difficulty, which only a few years ago were deemed impossible for all but the world's best climbers, are now being climbed on a regular basis—*by children.*

Given the potential impact these new participants will have on climbing's future, it's not too bold a statement to say that Robyn Erbesfield-Raboutou may be the most influential American climber of her generation. She was the first to see the incredible potential in teaching young children how to climb.

One of the world's top female sports climbers since 1989, Robyn has won five US Sport Climbing championships and four World Cup titles. At the age of forty-five, she was the third woman in the world to climb 5.14, and she still climbs regularly at that standard, sending five 5.14s in 2012 alone.

But it's Robyn's work as a teacher, coach, and businesswoman that places her in a class all her

own. In 2005 she founded ABC Kids Climbing to offer climbing classes and clubs for children at the local Boulder Rock Club. Her own son, Shawn, and daughter, Brooke, became ABC participants at five years old and two and a half years old, respectively. Shawn went on to climb

Left, Robyn Raboutou and daughter Brooke (age 11) boulder in Utah's Little Cottonwood Canyon. Above, Former world champion and elite climbing coach Robyn Erbesfield Raboutou.

14b when he was thirteen, and in 2012 Brooke, at the age of ten, became the youngest female in history to climb 14b. Also in 2012 Robyn and her husband, legendary French climber Didier Raboutou, completed construction of ABC's own climbing facility, ABC Kid's Climbing Gym, in Boulder, Colorado, the first climbing gym in the world built specifically for youth.

Robyn brings the same tireless energy and fierce determination to coaching and business that she brought to World Cup competition. She's served as the head coach for the USA Climbing team and has been coaching junior elite athletes for fifteen years. Not content to limit her influence to Boulder, she's creating a network of ABC programs in other gyms around the United States, and during the summer, she and Didier go international, offering a summer camp for children in France called Planete Grimpe.

ROOTS

My name's Robyn Erbesfield-Raboutou. I was born in 1963 in Atlanta, Georgia, and I've been climbing since I was eighteen. I started competing in the United States and in Europe when I was twenty-seven.

I fell in love with climbing the very first day I tried it. A high school boyfriend took me climbing for the first time, and I loved the sport, was enthusiastic about getting better, and wanted to be a great female rock climber right from the get-go. So I started to train and develop my skills, and then eventually was asked to compete at the World Cup level. In 1989 I went to my first World Cup in Leeds, England, and I won. That was a *wow* moment for me. That win motivated me even more to become the best I could be.

Robyn Raboutou and daughter Brooke coach children during the dedication of the ABC for Kids program at Momentum Climbing Gym, Sandy, Utah.

ABC KIDS CLIMBING

If I had to narrow down what I love most about climbing, then I would say it's the mental and physical challenges.

My passion for the sport led me to start my own business, ABC Kids Climbing. *ABC* stands for agility, balance, and coordination. When I started ABC, my children were young and showing a lot of passion for climbing. At that time there weren't a lot of other kids climbing. So I started looking at my career. I'd been coaching mostly adults and young juniors. I started thinking that if I created a team, or at least a group of young kids, who were passionate about climbing, it would allow my kids to have companions to share the sport with. So in 2004 my husband and I started ABC, and now I have a national champion team of which both my children are members. We have forty kids, climbing 5.13 or harder, who range in age from seven to seventeen. I'm pretty proud of where my idea has led. In my mind I was starting a business plan in which agility, balance, and coordination would serve as a foundation for an athletic program for the very young child, with rock climbing as an accent. I knew it was something that wasn't already out there, which is why I was creating it. Then every year my team got bigger, my business became better known, and I realized I had a good thing going. With rock climbing becoming so popular now, it's certainly great timing. There are gymnastics facilities in every city, right? And there are a lot of climbing gyms. Yet there are no climbing gyms dedicated specifically for kids. So that's my thing. My latest and greatest accomplishment is creating a gym in Boulder, Colorado, that's specifically for youth and a whole new generation of climbers. I look at what I do a little bit like what Coach

Robyn and Brooke wrestle during a bouldering session in Utah.

Béla Károlyi did for gymnastics. To me, he's a role model. I think about what he's done in the world of gymnastics, and I'd like to do something similar in the world of climbing.

Gymnastics facilities are full of kids. But there are few times when parents actually do gymnastics *with their kids.* That's the biggest difference. Adults like to climb, just like kids like to climb. So I wanted to make sure that parents have a place to climb with their children.

Most of ABC's programs focus on teaching kids climbing through a lot of obstacle and adventure-course type activities. Agility, balance, and coordination is basically everything that moves and wobbles. So in class the kids are always in an unstable position. Yet at the same time they're gaining confidence that if they trust the system and themselves, they'll be safe.

Once the kids go through our program, they'll be great at anything, because we do a lot of core conditioning and speed training. It's so complete that they can go and play baseball, football, gymnastics, or whatever they choose, and they're going to be ahead of the game.

KIDS AND CLIMBING

If you're a climber and you want your child to like climbing, then keep it really fun. Take them outside, take them inside, but remind yourself regularly that it's gotta be fun. It's like teaching your child to use the potty or ride a bike: Keep it constant, keep it simple, and keep it light.

So many times I've heard parents say, "Oh my gosh, my child is almost three and still won't potty train, or my kid is almost four and is still depending on the training wheels!" Hey, it's okay! They won't go to college in diapers. They'll

be great bikers. And if they love climbing, then they're going to love climbing, but not because their parents pushed them. So I say, just kick back and make sure it stays fun.

In ABC's programs we don't take three, five, or seven year olds and say, "we're going climbing," which is perhaps too specific for them. We make it an adventure. We hang ropes and let them swing. Wherever you take them, just get your kids in a program. Make sure they're learning all the basics and that someone competent is teaching them. Invite friends along. If you take your family climbing, try to take along another kid to keep your kid company. That can make all the difference in the world.

PROUD PARENTS

The kids in our ABC programs have all types of parents, and I really admire all of them. The *soccer-mom* and *soccer-dad* types of parents are some of the most motivated, and at the level I teach, particularly for my elite team, we have to have parents like that. If the parents are not really motivated to take their kids to the top level, to bring them to practice four to five days a week, and to pay for the program, then the kids don't have a chance. So I really get it. I get that their investment is huge, and they care deeply. I'm okay with that. I have a great relationship with all the parents.

Shawn just had his fourteenth birthday. He's been climbing since he was tiny, and he's very gifted. He climbed 5.13 at nine or ten years old. He climbed his first 5.14 at twelve, and he climbed his first 14b at thirteen. That's pretty *wow* because I haven't climbed 14b yet! So that just blows me away.

Shawn's the kind of kid who doesn't do a lot of training. He shows up to practice honorably, and he climbs *really* well. But he's not the guy who's going to stay late. He's not the kid who climbs six days a week when practice is only for three. He's satisfied giving everything he's got three or four days a week. It works really well for him. I understand that for Shawn that's the best plan. So a lot of times after school, he'll ask, "Mom, should I climb or skate?" And I'll say, "Well you climbed yesterday, so maybe you should skate today." It surprises him that I don't say, "Oh you really need to climb if you want to do well at Nationals." Then there's Brooke, who just had her eleventh birthday. She's been climbing since she was in diapers, old enough to walk. But she's different from her brother. She's a lot more like I am. She likes to train really hard. She has no problem dedicating five or six days a week to practice. She'll call a friend and go climbing. She'll ask me to go climbing outside of practice times. She's a go-getter. She'll do a boulder problem even if it takes her ten tries. She won't go home without it.

So different strokes for different folks. Brooke's approach works well for her. She's bouldered v11, and she just did her first 5.14. In fact, she's the youngest female to ever climb that grade—by many years I believe. But they're also humble, both of them. They're good kids.

Often it's difficult to coach your own kids, but I'd say I'm pretty lucky. Both my kids are very coachable and very open to *my* coaching. Both kids listen to me more than the other coaches, but they also need a break sometimes. Occasionally they bark at me and tell me it's hard to be coached by their mom all the time. But at the end of the day, they whisper in my ear and say,

"Thank you so much!" In our family we pass a lot of notes between us saying, "Sorry I was a bit short with you today, or a little frustrated, but you're awesome." At the same time, I'm good at picking other coaches. So we're all one big team.

I recognize that there are *many* kids out there who don't want to do *anything* their parents want them to do. And I'm always thinking to myself, *really?* I am *so lucky* that my children love what I do. When Shawn and Brooke are not with me, just out there climbing with their buddies, they are *passionate.* They're not climbing because I climb. They're climbing because it's their thing.

A GYM FOR KIDS

We're very excited to have a facility that's both recreational and professional. Half of the gym is set up for elite climbers, and the other half is for beginners, because we recognize that our youth program is where we cultivate our elite climbers. We start children off with all the ABC activities, and we can see right away which kids are hooked. They come back. They want to come twice a week. Eventually they want to come three days a week, so we move them onto the team and watch how they develop. We help nurture these kids to be the best athletes they can be.

Kids can begin competing at any age. There isn't an age limit for the junior divisions, but there are age groups. *Eleven and under* is the youngest age group. Brooke went to Nationals as a seven-year-old, and she placed.

So kids can go at any age. They might get a little slammed because the smaller you are, the harder climbing is, which is another thing that makes these young kids so impressive [laughs].

Robyn Raboutou introduces a young boy to climbing at the Momentum Climbing Gym.

FEAR

I've never had any really close calls climbing. Back in the day when I was doing a little more *trad* climbing, I had to down climb a very long sequence of moves one day in order to avoid a bad fall. But to be honest with you, I'm lucky, because I've had few scary moments like that.

But I'm like anyone. If I haven't climbed for a while and we go outside, I need a little time to get comfortable. I have to manage the same fear that anyone else would have, whether it's finding out a move is trickier than you thought or a clip isn't right where you want it, and you've got to do some hard moves above the last protection.

In sport climbing there's typically a lot less danger than in traditional climbing, so generally we're safe. But I'm human and sometimes it takes me a couple of days to get used to the cliff and be back on the sharp end of the rope.

In a similar way, if I'm working with a child who is experiencing fear, I will start by saying that *fear is completely normal.* We do what we call *flight school,* where we let the kids take falls on purpose. We'll have them go up, clip into the draw, do one move, and then fall on purpose. Then they do two moves and fall and then three moves and so on.

We never ask them to fall farther than is realistic for the climb. But it's amazing how they will say, "Oh my gosh, I'm having so much fun!" And the most important lesson I teach kids is that I'm the best belayer anyone could ask for. I'm a *world champion belayer,* and I want *you* to be the best climber you can be! So they're focused on climbing, and I'm focused on belaying. And when they leave the ground, they can completely focus, because I've told them that it's my job to keep them safe. You can't skip clips, but aside from that, it's my job. So just get up there, and be the best climber you can be.

CLIMBING MOM

As far as my personal climbing, I have less, make that *a lot less,* time for training. So it's a little bit more social than it's ever been. I like to climb with Lynn Hill and a lot of my other Boulder friends. I'm also fortunate to be training other elite athletes. So if time permits, I can put on my shoes and rally with some of the best climbers in the world, whether it's Daniel Woods, Paul

Robyn and Brooke boulder in Little Cottonwood Canyon.

Robinson, Garrett Gregor, or Alex Johnson. They all live in Boulder.

So I'm surrounded by incredible athletes, and I like to be strong, so I never give up trying to be the best I can. But the main difference is I have less time, so I have to be stronger mentally. When I see my kid do a 5.14 before me, it's like, okay, I've got two days to pull this off or I'm getting slammed by my own kid! I wouldn't have that expectation of myself if I didn't still want to keep up.

EVOLUTION

I think there could potentially be some sort of limit regarding how difficult a grade people can climb. But first, I believe we will see more climbers like Adam Ondra and Sasha DiGiulian, because the pool of newcomers is growing rapidly. So I think there will be three or four instead of just one amazing male and one amazing female. I suppose you will see people stacking the most difficult routes on top of one another to make the grade harder. That's one way climbing will evolve, but

5.16 would already be so hard I imagine that if we get there, the question will then become can anyone do two pitches of 5.16? I see that happening before reaching the grade of 5.17, because at some level the rock just becomes blank. But you can definitely stack hard on top of hard; that's where I think the numbers will go up based on intensity and duration. Another factor is actually discovering routes at those grades. I've heard Chris Sharma say it's actually quite difficult to find a 5.15 route, so that may be a limiting factor as well.

STRENGTHS AND WEAKNESSES

At this point in my life, I gravitate to other climbers who are climbing hard and who climb with heart. I never go easy. I don't climb 5.12. I climb 5.14. I don't boulder v6 if I can boulder v10. I like to climb hard. Even if I can't do it right away, I try and I'm always progressing.

I don't know what sets me apart. I guess I would say a huge strength of mine is my mental attitude and perseverance. Whether it was during comps or redpointing a route, I'm just like, "Grrrr! I can do this."

In the climbing competitions, one of the reasons I think I won so many World Cups was because a lot of the athletes would arrive at the competition and they were beat just by seeing my name on the list. In their minds it was like, "Oh, Robyn's here. She's already won." That made it kind of easy for me. But I was just doing my thing. One more comp, yeah! The more the better. I've always been really hungry and determined.

My greatest weakness as a climber? Hmm. . . . I never thought of it like that. I don't think I have a weakness as a climber. I don't think I have a weakness as a person. I don't look at life that way. I think I'm full of strengths. Sure, there are sometimes difficult moments where I need to find *a solution,* but I don't look at it as being weak.

CHROMOSOMES

How do women approach climbing differently than men? We always say that women are more technical. Men are more physical. So I think women have a more technical approach. I mean guys have big muscles, and we have itty-bitty muscles. But you could say that having small muscles is an advantage, because we're hauling less weight.

I love climbing with guys. Before I met Lynn, it had been a long time since I met a girl to climb with and I thought, "Wow, she's really fun to be around." I've had other women in my life who I climbed with and really enjoyed, but most of the time I climb with guys. I love climbing with guys and with my kids [laughs].

ACCOMPLISHMENTS

Looking back over my career, I'm most proud of my climbing right now. I'm a bit older, with a lot less preparation and a lot less training, but that allows my biggest strength—my mental approach—to come through. During a recent trip to Kentucky's Red River Gorge, I was trying a climb that was hard for me, and I was already tired from trying to get the new ABC facility in Boulder going. It was interesting, because even when I tried the route two or three times and fell, I was hanging on the end of the rope, proud of my climbing! I thought, "*Wow that was a really good effort,*" even though I didn't get to the chains. And sure enough, after a rest day, that same positive attitude got me to the top. So

Brooke Raboutou spots her mom while bouldering in Utah's Little Cottonwood Canyon.

that's amazing to me. I'm no longer twenty-five and not able to train as much as I'd like, but with a positive attitude I can still do amazing things.

PHILOSOPHY

My personal philosophy is *respect*. Respect other people; respect nature. I make sure I'm educated, and I educate others in a way that ensures we're all going to be able to enjoy this sport and live our lives well for a very long time to come.

RELATIONSHIPS

When it comes to finding balance in our relationship, Didier and I have done tons of climbing together. Then he switched to cycling. So he's doing a lot less climbing. In fact, I would say he does almost *no* climbing, while I'm still passionate about it. My whole business revolves around climbing, and both of my children climb! But what's cool about my husband is that he's an open-arms guy. For example, he might go for a bike ride, but afterward he has no problem coming to the gym and hanging out with us. Or he'll go on a two-week climbing trip with us and climb 5.12 right off the couch, because he loves to be outside. He's passionate about the rock and seeing the kids climb. So he likes to be a part of our lives even if his focus has changed. He's

---

How do you psych yourself up for a hard route?

The advice I give to myself and to students is that if you get on a route that's a project, then you want to learn and understand the climb down to the smallest nuance. Sometimes we can get a route really fast if we spend a lot of time the first time we go up. So if you take your climbing seriously from the moment you leave the ground until the moment you get the rope to the top, you've learned a lot of information. Then you log that information in your mind, and when you're home at night about to sleep, rehearse it in your mind. This is visualization. *Nobody needs lessons to know how to do it. Just think about it. See yourself climbing. I think the greatest tip I could give anyone is to get as much information you can from the climb.*

Then when you go for the redpoint, *try to not switch things around too much. For example, you're not sure if you want to do it like you practiced or the way Johnny did it. Do it like you practiced it. If you fall, no big deal. Then try Johnny's way, and choose the right sequence for you.*

Try to understand your position. Okay, my left foot's here, and my right foot's there. Where are you going to clip? Or not clip? Learn the ins and outs of the route, then when you're home relaxing, use that time to see yourself making the moves, getting to the top, and experiencing the satisfaction of clipping the chains.

What's your favorite place to climb?

I love to climb at Hueco Tanks in Texas. We have some beautiful moments there when we take the team kids, and we're together for a two-week period. Life is so good. I think, "This is a job?" It's so much fun! We rally on hard

also building our ABC climbing gym right now. So he's a huge part of our lives, and he wouldn't expect us to stop climbing, anymore than we would expect him to stop exploring new things.

In contrast, Didier could constantly be saying, "Oh my god, climbing is all you do! Are you kidding? You're going climbing *again?* You guys are going on a trip *again?*" Well, yeah, because we're passionate about climbing. But he gets it. He doesn't hold that against us. He honors what we want to do. And it's a great lesson for me as well, because when he wants to go on a three-hour bike ride, I just have to say, "Have fun honey!" It teaches me to be open as well.

GIFTS

Climbing has given me so many gifts. It's pretty much who I am. But on a day-to-day basis, I'm continually aware and satisfied with the mind I've developed through climbing. I'm grateful for the person I've become and how it's shaped my family. Literally, my kids are my best friends! I adore spending time with my children, and I feel incredibly lucky they love doing what I do. I have a lot of confidence because of climbing. I really know who I am. When I talk to other people, whether it's about their children, their grandfather, or their broken car, I feel I have something to give. Truly, it's all come from my career in climbing.

climbs. We cook together. The ambience of going to Hueco with the team is just fabulous for me.

And I love to climb at the Red River Gorge. I think it's a beautiful place. I also love to climb near our home in France. In addition to Boulder, we have a home in St Antonin Noble, which is in the southwest of France. Didier developed a lot of the climbs in that region, so there's big heart in climbing there.

And I would say that one of my top places to climb is Spain, especially Rodellar, where we spend a lot of time as a family over the summer.

If you could offer one essential tip to other climbers, what would it be?

What I say to the really inspired climber, someone who's already completely hooked but wondering how to get better, is mileage! The more you climb, the better you get. Any kind of climbing. Climb with your friends. Climb with a team. Outside. Inside. Go with your family. Whatever. It's mileage that makes the best climbers. I see kids all over the world, whether they're French, Spanish, or American, and they're either in the gym or at the cliffs all the time. Those are the kids who are really progressing. So the more you climb, the better you get.

How do you train?

I think it's best to go really hard every session, followed by a rest. Rest days are important, but if you're going to rest, go into it completely wiped out. The body needs to heal. And the mind needs to heal, so that you retain your motivation. That said, I rarely take months off from climbing, but two or three days can be really healthy.

NANCY FEAGIN

Nancy Feagin's one of the finest, all-round climbers of her generation, and due to her low-key, unassuming personality, she's also probably one of the least known. As Nancy says, "I climb for myself, not to impress others." I've known Nancy for nearly twenty years, and she's always seemed like an old soul to me, someone lucky enough to bring the wisdom and calm perspective of all her former lives along with her into this one. She's also one of the most natural climbers I know, born with an uncanny ability to make it all look easy. Whether she's working sport routes in Utah's Maple Canyon, speed climbing in Yosemite in California, climbing Mount Everest in the Himalayas, or weathering the challenges of parenting, Nancy does it all with humor and grace.

Nancy's climbing career began at age thirteen with an ascent of Wyoming's Grand Teton. Only three years later, she became one of the youngest people to climb the Grand's north face, a serious undertaking for mountaineers of any age. As an adult, she went on to guide in the Tetons for Exum Mountain Guides. She's redpointed 13b sports routes and climbed Le Chant du Cygne (V, 5.12a), a route on the north face of the Eiger in Switzerland. She's climbed both Yosemite's El Capitan and Half Dome in a day and climbed twenty of America's most classic climbs in twenty days, a feat that includes an epic ascent of the Diamond on Colorado's Longs Peak during a snow and lightning storm. Teaming up with Lynn Hill and Beth Rodden in 1999, she established a new grade V, 13a, AO route in Madagascar, and in 2001 she summited Mount Everest via the south ridge. Nancy has also competed in speed climbing competitions, taking third in the 1992 World Cup in Nürnberg, Germany.

Left, Nancy Feagin nears the top of the Frendo Spur in Chamonix, France. Above, Feagin in her Salt Lake City home.

Nancy is currently treasurer of the board for the Access Fund, a national advocacy group for climbing areas in the United States, and has served two terms as a board member for the American Alpine Club. In her spare time she likes to run canyons—as in the Grand Canyon—from rim to rim.

ROOTS

My name's Nancy Feagin. I'm an April Fools' Day baby—born April 1, 1966. I live in Salt Lake City, Utah, with my husband, Jonathan Carpenter, and our son, Connor. I'm a rock climber, an ice climber, and a snow climber, basically an *everything* climber! Earlier in my career I was also a mountain guide and sponsored climber. Now I work as an accountant.

I've been climbing since 1979. I started when I was thirteen, when my family moved from New York to Jackson Hole, Wyoming. My father was an orthopedic surgeon. He traded a climbing guide the cost of his knee surgery for climbing lessons for our family. After the guide recovered, he took us up the Grand Teton, and that was my first climbing experience. I was instantly hooked. I loved being in the mountains and feeling the thrill of exposure climbing steep cliffs. I was also a gymnast, and I loved the feel of the movement while climbing.

It's a long way up and down the Grand Teton, especially for a thirteen-year-old, but I thought it was great. It was exhilarating. I don't remember thinking it was hard or tiring. I was a pretty serious gymnast, so I was in good shape from all the training.

I love all forms of climbing. I've never been able to stick with just one discipline. I joke that

I have ADD (attention deficit disorder) and that when I start to get good at something, I get bored and want to do something else. But the truth is I like variety. If I stuck with just one aspect of climbing, I think I would lose interest.

ENJOYING THE SPORT

What I love most about climbing is the fact that when I'm doing it, I'm *in the moment.* When I'm focused on climbing, I'm not thinking about my to-do list or any problems in my life. I'm completely absorbed in the task at hand.

What I like *least* is that to stay at a high level of performance in climbing requires an incredible amount of time. I love the feeling I get when I'm fit and climbing well, but it's hard to keep that performance level with all the other responsibilities in life.

CLOSE CALLS

I've had a few close calls. Several times when I was climbing near the top of mountains, I was almost hit by lightning. Once was near the top of the Grand Teton, when I was in my early twenties. We were only about two hundred feet from the summit, and a snowstorm hit. There was no visibility. It was full white-out conditions. At the time, none of us knew the mountain well, and we didn't know any escape routes. The only way we knew to descend (besides doing a slow, rappel descent; setting our own gear; and leaving it behind) was by going to the summit and then going down the Owen Spalding route. The four of us were huddled together, trying to figure out where the route to the summit was when the electrical part of the storm hit. My brother, Randle (who is usually incredibly calm in dangerous situations), started screaming that we needed to get going. Over the sound of the howling wind, I started yelling at him to calm down. Seconds later lightning struck just a few hundred feet away. It turns out that Randle, who was the tallest of the group and had all the carabiners on a sling around his neck, was feeling the building charge of the impending lightning strike!

We quickly figured out which way to go and started moving FAST. It was a huge relief when, thirty minutes later, the storm passed!

I had another close call with lightning on Longs Peak in Colorado. I was with three friends, climbing the D1 route on the Diamond. We were ten days into an epic adventure, trying to climb twenty classic climbs in twenty days (the list of climbs comes from a book by Steve Roper and Allen Steck called *Fifty Classic Climbs of North America*). The route wasn't in good condition, and the weather was marginal. But Longs Peak was on our list, and we had nine more climbs to do in the next nine days, so we decided to climb anyway. By early afternoon we were two pitches from the top, when our progress slowed to a crawl. The route ahead (which was normally dry rock) was filled with ice from the previous winter. We had no ice tools or protection. It was terrifying climbing. Then the storm hit. It was hailing, and thunder echoed all around us. We had two choices—do a slow, tedious, rappel descent or keep going to the summit. We chose to summit. It took forty-five minutes, but we got to the top. By this time the lightning was striking at almost the same instant the thunder was clapping. The full fury of the storm was upon us. I knew many people had been killed by lightning on top of Longs Peak, and I was pretty sure

we were going to become another statistic. We ran to a small shelter and waited for about an hour for the electrical storm to pass. Afterward we savored a long, quiet hike out that evening.

I've had two incidents rappelling when I almost died, because I was distracted. One was in Colorado's Ouray Ice Park. I was at the top of the cliff talking to a friend I hadn't seen in a long time. I put the rappel device on the rope while talking. I was a hundred feet up, and I started rappelling. I just happened to look down and notice that I hadn't properly doubled the rope. I almost rappelled off the end! The second incident was in Utah's Big Cottonwood Canyon. I threaded the rope though my rappel device incorrectly, again while I was talking to my partner. It was the same kind of thing. Momentary distractions almost led to catastrophic consequences.

Many of the risks we hear about in climbing these days have more to do with socializing and not paying attention than with objective hazards. Many of the things people consider dangerous about climbing have not been as risky for me, because I've been focused on what I'm doing. It's when I'm relaxed and not paying close attention that climbing becomes dangerous.

Another close call was when my partner, Doug Heinrich, and I were hiking up to climb in Little Cottonwood Canyon in Utah, and some people knocked off an enormous boulder. It bounced off a few other rocks, and Doug and I each jumped different ways. A small piece of rock hit Doug in the head. He was bleeding heavily, so we went to the nearest emergency room, where he got stitches. I wasn't injured. But the boulder could easily have killed us both.

LOSS

I've lost some friends. When I was in my mid-twenties, I lost my best friend, Pattie Saurman, in Alaska. Pattie was leading a snow gully on the southwest ridge of Mount Hunter when she fell. She was roped in with three partners. Her fall pulled everyone off, and they all fell seventeen hundred feet down a couloir. Pattie and one partner died, but the other two survived. Losing Pattie was *very* hard.

I was also close friends with Alex Lowe, who was killed October 5, 1999, in an avalanche on Shishapangma in Tibet. I guided with Alex in the Tetons, and we were both sponsored by The North Face. Seth Shaw, another good friend, died in a serac collapse on Alaska's Ruth Glacier on May 25, 2000.

All of them were so passionate about being in the mountains. They loved it, and I felt the same way at that time. I don't feel exactly the same way now. But I understand. That's where they wanted to be, and that's what they wanted to be doing. They died doing what they loved. I don't think you can go through life being scared. You have to live life as who you are and how you want to be. It's important to follow your dreams!

FEAR

After climbing for so many years, I am still *ridiculously* afraid to fall. Which is silly [laughs].

In general, whether it's a mountain experience or big-wall experience, I try to look at my fears rationally and figure out which part of the fear I can control and which part I can't. For instance if it's the weather I'm worried about, I can move faster and more efficiently.

If I'm truly terrified, I'll try to breathe deeply and talk myself through the situation. I try to stay focused on what I need to do in order to get out of the dangerous situation. Maybe being an accountant, having a logical mind and thinking through problems step-by-step, helps in situations like that!

EVOLUTION

Climbing has changed me by giving me more self-confidence. Over the years in the mountains, as I've succeeded or failed, I've tried to learn from my failures. I've learned what it takes to accomplish things, how to set goals, and how to work toward those goals. That knowledge has really helped me throughout my life, in all sorts of different areas.

At the same time, since becoming a mother, I don't take nearly as many risks as I used to. Even breaking an ankle would upset my life drastically. So even a short, ground fall is a concern. Things like that didn't faze me in the past. I felt invincible. But now I want to make sure that at the end of the day, I come down in one piece.

STRENGTHS AND WEAKNESSES

I think my biggest strength is my brain. I'm strategic. I'm good at planning, and I'm very tenacious. I'm relatively strong, but regardless of the type of climbing you're involved in, whether in the mountains or sport climbing, it's your brain that takes advantage of your strength and makes it work, such as knowing how to read a route, how to *redpoint,* and how to train efficiently. As sport climber Wolfgang Güllich once said, "your brain is your most important climbing muscle."

Nancy Feagin climbs Resurrection (13b), the Wailing Wall near St. George, Utah.

My biggest weakness is the fact that I still don't like to fall, despite all the sport climbing I've done. That's one aspect of my climbing I could improve. If I could go up on any route and not care if I fell, I would probably *on-sight* higher ratings. However, I don't think it would make much of a difference in my *redpoint* level.

Obviously all climbers have to be discerning about when it's safe to fall and when it's not. This goes back to identifying rational fears. But that said, I'm probably *too* conservative about where to draw that line when I'm sport climbing. I'd like to have the ability to climb to failure on a sport route and not stop due to fear of falling. I think it's important to keep going, paddling up those last few moves, even when you don't know if you can hang on. I don't do that enough.

Some of my fear is a result of growing up as a traditional climber in the big mountains. When I learned to climb, I was told I always needed three points of contact with the rock, I needed to be in control at all times, and that the leader is never supposed to fall. I've done my best to forget all that advice when I'm sport climbing, but it still creeps back into my brain! I usually find that the more I take falls (safe ones), the less I'm held back by the fear of falling.

CHROMOSOMES

I don't like to generalize about men versus women. But I do think that overall, women are less aggressive than men, and that tends to make them approach climbing differently. Often women need to be more focused about being aggressive and going for it, which is something men find easier to do. But to offset that, women tend to be more technical and agile. The fluidity of climbing tends to come more naturally to women.

LESSONS

The most important lesson I've learned from climbing is that it's all about the journey. It's not so much about *getting* to the top or *being* on top. I've learned through expeditions that I have a tendency to be focused on summiting. Then I realized that along the way there are so many incredible things to learn, see, and appreciate.

It seems our society wants us to check things off, then add more to the list, and that's part of my nature, too. I have a type A personality, so I tend to want to check the box and move on. Climbing has taught me to try to appreciate all those little moments along the way.

And what do I still have to learn? I *still* have to learn to slow down and appreciate the little moments on the journey [laughs]. It's a daily lesson for me to be in the moment and appreciate what I have. I think that will be a lifelong challenge for me.

ACCOMPLISHMENTS

I'm most proud of climbing the Nose on El Capitan and Half Dome in a day. Mostly because I dreamed about doing it but didn't know if I could pull it off. It seemed like an enormous goal, and at the time we did it, it hadn't been done many times. I had a lot of doubts. It was incredible to get to the top of the Nose, look over at Half Dome, and know we were going there next! I remember being really tired but just pushing on. My partner was Hans Florine. He's a brilliant, big-wall speed climber. We were dating at the time, and we'd been climbing together a lot, so we were

Nancy Feagin negotiates a snow and ice couloir in the French Alps.

completely in synch. I'd done both the Nose and Half Dome separately several times before. Hans and I had this system, where one of us would lead in blocks of four to five pitches. If the difficulty was below 5.10, then we would *simul-climb* (moving simultaneously on the rope without setting up belays), putting in about five pieces of protection per pitch. If it got harder than 5.10, we set belays. The second climber would stop at a belay, clip in, and start belaying the leader. If it got *much* harder than 5.10, then the second jumared the pitch. We were very fast at making transitions, at jumaring, and at cleaning gear. We were also good at all the tricks that big-wall speed climbing requires. It didn't really require free-climbing at a super high level. I don't think I ever did a move as hard as 5.12 on either the Nose or Half Dome. If the climbing got hard, then we just put in a piece and pulled on it. It's great fun being up that high, going superfast.

Getting down off El Capitan and then hiking up the slabs to the base of Half Dome is sort of an epic journey. I got to the base of Half Dome first, but it was Hans's turn to lead. He led the first three pitches on Half Dome, and I jumared those pitches. I remember my biceps cramping up so badly from dehydration and fatigue I could barely let go of the ascenders. My arms wouldn't straighten out! Luckily we brought a fair amount of water, so I drank, and the cramping subsided. All told it was just under twenty-four hours from the time we left our car to the time when we returned to it.

Another favorite climb is on the north face of the Eiger. It's called Le Chant du Cygne, a twenty-one pitch, 5.12 climb that's amazing. Getting to the base of the technical difficulties required a lot of scrambling up loose talus with plenty of exposure. To be safe, we had to do it fast, which meant moving unroped. If you fall there, then you go a long way. You would definitely die. It was wonderful being on that big face, looking over at the ultraclassic routes up the Eiger north face. I was psyched to be able to do a climb like that. The Eiger had always been on my to-do list of alpine climbing.

I am also proud of climbing Mount Everest. The first time I went up to Camp II (on the South Col route), I had giardia. Then I got pulmonary edema. It would have been *really* easy to give up. Everyone wanted me to quit. But I recovered for a week in Namche Bazaar, a village near Everest base camp in Nepal, then I went back and made it to the summit. I'm proud of my perseverance.

Then last year I did something unrelated to climbing but still a big accomplishment. I joined a couple girlfriends to run from the South Rim of the Grand Canyon to the North Rim then back again in a day. That's forty-six miles round-trip with over eleven thousand feet of elevation change, and by far the longest I'd ever run at a stretch. It was a huge goal, and to accomplish it, I had to use a lot of the lessons I learned from climbing about goal setting and training. For example, I used lessons learned from climbing for twenty-four hours at a time, about hitting the wall, and about not quitting. The next day I could barely walk, because my calves were so sore.

EMBARRASSING MOMENTS

A big part of being a professional climber is getting your picture taken. In the early nineties I was sponsored by Reebok, and there had been a series of photo essays of female athletes in *Vanity Fair* magazine taken by Mark Seliger, a famous New York photographer. Reebok asked me if I wanted to be the subject of one of Seliger's essays, a photo-driven piece on climbing, so I said sure.

We drove to the City of Rocks National Reserve in Idaho. I didn't realize Seliger had done lots of covers for *Rolling Stone* magazine and photographed lots of famous singers, musicians, and other artists. As it turned out, he had very little interest in my athletic ability or rock-climbing talent. The first thing he wanted me to do—well maybe not the *first* thing, but very soon after arriving—was to wear as little clothing as possible.

He tried to pose me upside down, so my breasts were hanging out of my sport top. Then he wanted me to drape myself over a rock in a very seductive way. Then he decided it would be much more artistic if I wasn't wearing *any* clothes at all. He begged me to pose nude, insisting it would all be very tastefully done and that no one would really see that I was naked. But I didn't give in.

Eventually he talked me into putting on fake eyelashes and wearing a bikini. We were done climbing, but he wanted a few more *artistic* shots, with me draped on the boulders of the beautiful City of Rocks. So I put on the fake eyelashes. It felt like I had windshield wipers on my eyes. I put on the bikini and wrapped myself around a rock. And just as I did, one of my coworkers, another Exum Mountain Guide from the Tetons, walked around the corner. At first he didn't recognize me. Then someone asked me a question, and when I answered, my friend recognized my voice. "Nancy?" he said. "Is that you!"

I'm sure my face turned five shades of red. I was so mortified I almost died. My friend started laughing so hard he couldn't stop. He was delighted he had discovered Nancy Feagin, *the climber and mountain guide,* wearing next to nothing. Luckily for me, the series was canceled, and the photographs were never published.

CHALLENGES

For me the biggest challenge is to stay present in the moment, because I tend to set a goal and just focus on that. I've realized throughout my life that when I achieve a goal, there has sometimes been a sadness or emptiness afterward, because I didn't take time to appreciate what I'd done. If you don't appreciate the whole journey, then reaching the summit is not nearly as meaningful, and you are left with a sense of *unfulfillment.*

PHILOSOPHY

I try to make a difference in the world. A lot of the time, that's as small as letting the people I work with know that they've done a good job or trying to make someone's day better in some small way. I try to do my part to be green and preserve the environment. I try to give back. I've been involved with Access Fund since 2007. It's a great organization, and I am committed to helping it be successful! I want our climbing areas to be kept open for future generations!

My climbing philosophy is to remember that I make my own rules. I try not to compare myself with other people. I try to get out of it what I need. Sometimes my goal for the day is simply to spend time with a friend in nature. Sometimes my goal is to send a hard route. I climb for myself, not to impress or please others. Climbing is my own creative expression, nothing more.

RELATIONSHIPS

I've always struggled to achieve balance in my life. I tend to overbook myself. I commit to too many different things. I feel lucky that my husband is very supportive of my climbing. Even though he doesn't climb as much as he used to, he still understands the passion. He's helpful by giving me time to climb. And simultaneously, he knows our family is my first priority. My work is important, too. I love to climb, so balancing all that is a constant juggle.

OTHER PASSIONS

Right now my son is seven. I feel like I'm still important in his daily life, so motherhood is a big focus right now. Spending time with Connor, my son, and Jonathan, my husband, is certainly a passion. And athletically, in addition to climbing I love trail running, and skate skiing. Those are my other favorite things to do.

THE FUTURE

My climbing goals are now all related to sport climbing because that's what works best with my available time. Recently I came really close to climbing a 5.13c sport route in American Fork Canyon near Salt Lake City. So one of my goals is try that route again. If I can do it, it will be my hardest redpoint to date. I've done a bunch of 5.13b's, but never a 5.13c. (Author's note: Nancy subsequently sent her 5.13c project.)

I'm hoping to be able to climb for the rest of my life. I've always told myself that if my fingers go, then my next thing will be climbing *via ferratas.* Italian for "iron roads," *via ferratas* are climbing routes in the Alps and elsewhere, equipped with steel cables, iron rungs, pegs, ladders, and bridges that allow safe climbing without the need for roped belays.

I'm sure as I age, I won't be able to climb like I do now, but I'm certain I'll always enjoy being outside. Maybe when I'm ninety, I'll just be sitting in a wheelchair, on the porch. I feel grounded when I'm in nature. It will always be part of my life.

Nancy Feagin climbs at the Hellgate Crag, Little Cottonwood Canyon, Utah.

How do you psych yourself up for a hard route?

I try to imagine what it will feel like when I get to the top, those last few moves, followed by clipping the chains. There's a feeling of exhilaration and a special kind of adrenaline buzz when that happens. I find that listening to good music is helpful when I'm visualizing the moves, but really being able to see myself at the top or making the last hard moves on the route is the most motivating and inspiring.

What's your favorite place to climb?

Yosemite. I don't get there often anymore, but I just love the fact that the rock is solid, you can get fifteen pitches up on relatively easy terrain, and the weather is usually great. There are not many places in the world like that. I've been pretty much all over, and in most areas the rock is not nearly as safe and solid on multipitch routes.

My favorite route, hands down, is Astroman in Yosemite (10 pitches, 5.11.c trad, Washington's Column).

If you could offer one essential tip to other climbers, what would it be?

My best tip is to climb for yourself. Don't climb for anyone else or to impress someone.

How do you train?

I do lots of different kinds of climbing, but as far as specific training goes, I think the most important thing is to set goals then follow a timeline with some periodization. The fundamentals of training for climbing are building up a solid fitness base, being realistic about what your strengths and weaknesses are, working on your weaknesses, and building toward your goals.

I try to climb three days a week. I boulder once a week, because I tend to be an endurance climber and my power declines if I don't boulder. The rest of the time I climb routes. If I have a trip coming up, I might do back-to-back days to make the training more like the trip will be. If I have a project that's got lots of crimpers, then I'll try to do some hang-board training or focus on routes with crimps. I've done things like four by fours and campus-board workouts from time to time, depending on whether or not I was trying to train power endurance. At the moment I'm just having fun doing routes at the gym. I try to on-sight as much as possible, and if not, do the route on my second or third try.

DAWN GLANC

L ike many climbers, I have a love/hate relationship with ice climbing. On one hand I love the beauty, the outrageous situations, and the surreal terrain ice climbers explore. On the other hand, I'm concerned by the risk inherent in climbing such a fragile, dynamic medium and the potential for long, potentially catastrophic, falls.

Outside climbing, most people consider *all* climbers to be a bit touched in the head but ice climbers even more. Then there's mixed climbing, using ice axes and crampons to climb rock where there's no ice at all! That's a level of crazy that makes even most climbers shake their heads.

And I was one of them, until I had the opportunity to watch Dawn Glanc in action. Prior to seeing Dawn mixed climb, I didn't get it. I was one of those people who couldn't stand the sound (reminiscent of fingernails on a chalkboard) of crampon points grating over bare rock.

And I love my ice tools! I wince every time I swing too hard on thin ice, and the pick rebounds in a shower of sparks. Why subject my lovely axes and crampons to naked rock where there's no ice at all?

But after watching Dawn perform her vertical ballet, gracefully linking sections of ice and rock, I began to understand the aesthetics and admire the incredible precision required to *gently*

position crampon points and the picks of the two axes on tiny, nearly imperceptible placements, as well as the stillness of body and mind required to move with exquisite delicacy between sequences. After witnessing Dawn's mastery, I began to see mixed climbing, which I'd previously considered to be perhaps *the most masculine* form of climbing, to be instead a particularly *feminine*

Left, Dawn Glanc gets her ab workout on Pull the Trigger Tigger (d11, Dry Tool 11), Colorado's San Juan Mountains. Above, Mountain guide and mixed ice climbing champion Glanc, Ouray, Colorado.

pursuit, where precision, delicacy, and grace are tantamount to success. And I got an inkling of how, if you were to learn such skills in a relatively benign environment like Colorado's Ouray Ice Park, you could carry those skills to the high ranges of the world and use them to unlock swift passage up ephemeral threads of ice, rock, and snow, in previously unimaginable ways.

Dawn's irrepressible humor and enthusiasm don't hurt either. Whether discussing her "booty-quake" method for getting psyched for challenging climbs or the satisfaction she finds in helping other women discover their own inner climber, you can't help but want to be more like Dawn, living a life confronting your limitations in spectacularly beautiful places.

Dawn grew up in the Midwest, far from the mountains, and she came to climbing relatively late by modern standards. Dawn is a certified mountain guide, who guides for Chicks with Picks, Chicks Rock, and other companies. She's also a dedicated student of Warrior's Way, a mental training method created by Arno Ilgner, author of the book, *The Rock Warrior's Way*.

As she discusses below, Dawn is a fierce competitor, who won the women's division of the Ouray Ice Festival Competition in 2009 and 2011, took second place in 2007 and 2012, and third place in 2010. In 2012 she won first place in mixed climbing at the Teva Winter Games (later renamed Winter Mountain Games) held in Vail, Colorado.

Outside the competitive arena, Dawn has completed first ascents in Cody, Wyoming, ranging from WI3-4+, and six first ascents in Iceland, ranging from WI5-5+. She's redpointed Gold Line (M10) at Poser's Lounge in Ouray, and in 2008 she was a member of the Big Expedition for Cancer Research, an expedition sponsored by the Fred Hutchinson Cancer Research Center of Seattle, Washington, to scale an unclimbed, unnamed peak in Alaska's Glacier Bay National Park and Preserve. Outside the United States and Iceland, Dawn has climbed in Canada, France, Norway, Greece, Montenegro, and Croatia. She's sponsored by Mountain Hardwear, La Sportiva, Black Diamond, BlueWater Ropes, and Julbo. And she's so naturally funny, that if the climbing gig doesn't work out, she may have a second career as a stand-up comedian.

ROOTS

My name's Dawn Glanc. I was born in 1975 in Brunswick, Ohio. Growing up, I was a Dr. Jekyll and Mr. Hyde kid. In school I was a genius. I got straight As. I got my homework done early. Teachers loved me.

But as soon as I left school, I was the worst kid in the world. My sister (three years younger) was my partner in crime. I'd get these crazy ideas like, "Hey, let's go to the mall and shoplift!" and "Let's go to this party and do this just awful thing." I won't even admit the things we did. I think we were really seeking a sense of adventure, that sense of pushing it, but in a negative way. In climbing you have a similar excitement. Are we going to get away with this? And when you do, it feels good.

But I grew up in a suburb of Cleveland. I had no outdoor outlet. What was I to do? The only sport I had was softball. *Give me a break!* Softball is *not* an outlet! So I'm superhappy that I found climbing. Honestly, I don't know what would have happened to me otherwise.

After high school, I attended Kent State University for three years, and that's when I began climbing. When I was twenty-one, I moved to the Black Hills of South Dakota to attend Black Hills State University. In 2004 I moved again, this time to Bellingham, Washington, in order to pursue a career as a professional mountain guide. Now I live in Ouray, Colorado, when I'm not traveling the world to climb.

At Kent State I was dating a guy, and believe it or not, he invited *my roommate* to go climbing with him. I was livid! I couldn't believe this guy would do such a thing, because I *really* wanted to try climbing. So to calm me down, he took me to this tiny place called Whipp's Ledges in Hinckley, Ohio. For the first year my entire climbing experience was top-roping thirty-foot cliffs. It wasn't until I moved to the Black Hills that I really learned to rock climb.

The first time I went sport climbing in South Dakota I said to my partner, "How do we get around to the top?" And he said, "We don't. We have to lead it." And I didn't have any idea what that meant. Then that winter the same friend called me and asked if I wanted to go ice climbing and I said, "Yeah, I think so" [laughs].

Honest to God, I had no idea what he was asking me to do. But I thought, "Hey, it's climbing," so I figured I would love it. And sure enough I did. I loved it from the very first moment.

I like all kinds of climbing. I really love rock climbing, but I think my true passion is ice and mixed. There's something that comes over me when I get those tools in my hands. I feel like I can climb anything!

I believe that I excel most in ice and mixed, because I have complete confidence that I can hang on to the tools, no matter what. With rock climbing I'm not so sure. I'm never sure I can hang on to that *crimper,* and I'm more scared rock climbing because of that uncertainty.

But when I have ice axes in my hands, I know I can hang on to those tools for as long as it takes. If I can get them set in the ice or rock, I'm good to go. That gives me confidence to push through routes and grades I never imagined I could.

MIXED CLIMBING

When it comes to accessibility and the sheer number of routes at different grades, Ouray is the greatest place in the United States to live for ice and mixed climbing. And the beauty of the Ouray Ice Park is that you can top-rope all sorts of routes when you're first learning. I definitely did my fair share of that, but, as I like to do with lots of things, I also threw myself into the fire. You only get better at your weaknesses if you work on them. And mixed climbing was my weakness. I knew that if I moved to Ouray, then I would compete in the annual Ice Festival competition and that would require mixed climbing.

But I didn't know how! It was humbling, because I felt like I could climb any kind of ice, but when it came to mixed, I was starting all over again. But confidence in the tools came quickly to me. I was able to push all my mental fears aside as soon as I grabbed hold of the ice tools.

So I'm superpsyched that I can hang on to these awesome handles, but sometimes the pick of the ax wobbles and teeters on the rock. When that happens you have to move with complete stillness in mixed climbing, and that's why it is so intriguing to me.

*Dawn Glanc picks
her way up Flying
Circus (M8+,
i.e. mixed 8+),
Colorado's Ouray
Ice Park.*

It's crazy, but when you put your tool on a placement, you cannot make any unnecessary movements, because if you do that, then the tool's going to pop. Most of the time the tools are only sitting on the very tip of the pick. I always joke that if you blink—you're outta there. Suddenly it's just *poof,* and you're falling.

That's a big difference from rock climbing. On rock I can feel my hands slipping. I feel my toes slipping. I don't feel that when I have metal connecting my hands and feet to the rock. I don't have the same sensory connection. But at the same time, I can stand on things that are completely different. I can pivot and do things with my body that I can't do when my rock shoe is smearing. So when I'm mixed climbing, I feel perhaps a different freedom of movement and a little more gymnastic quality to what I'm doing.

Many people think that lack of connection is much scarier. Wobbling tools and the sound of crampon points screeching over rock scare most people. The sounds of mixed climbing freak people out. But to me, that's just part of the chaos of the sport. The fun is to accept the chaos and the craziness and still be able to focus and make it all happen.

ENJOYING THE SPORT

I love anything that has to do with climbing. I have a very addictive personality; I'm very compulsive. I do the same things over and over. Climbing provides this 100 percent laser focus where nothing else matters. I can't get that from anything else, and I need it. My personality is the type that if I don't climb on a regular basis—either daily or a few days a week—I go crazy. Literally. I can't go without it. I've gotten so used to having climbing be a major part of my life I can't give it up; there's nothing else that would fill the void. Sure, I could try skiing. I could try all these other things, but my brain would be all over the place.

Then there's the social bonds. There's no way I would give up the time I spend with my climbing partners. You know how modern life is. You go out to dinner with your friends and everyone's on their stupid phones, they're texting, everyone's busy and distracted.

But when you go climbing together, that's your time, and you're 100 percent there for your partner. I'm beginning to realize that kind of connection is rare in today's world. So I value it more.

The thing I like *least* about climbing is hiking uphill with a heavy pack. I love to work hard. I love to push myself, but humping heavy loads is grunt work. So when I'm approaching a peak in order to climb it, having a heavy pack is not my favorite thing.

COMPETITION

I've been doing the Ouray ice climbing competition since 2007. I've competed at Ouray six times, and I've been in eight comps overall. I hold the Ouray comp in high regard. The best climbers in the world come here to compete, and I wanted to see if I was as good. Could I beat them? Could I even compete or was I just going to be laughed off the stage? I was lucky each year I competed. I did well. I made the podium not just first, but second and third as well. In 2012 I gave a slide show about my journey as an ice climber during the festival, and during the show, I mentioned I felt even more honored to be giving a slide show than to be competing, because presenting means you have made it, you're recognized by your peers.

Then in 2011 mixed climbing was added to the Teva Winter Games in Vail, and I was invited to compete. And Bozeman, Montana, held an Ice Fest in 2013 in which I competed. I'm hoping that all the time and energy I've put into competitive climbing will help me make the Olympic team in 2014. The International Olympic Committee will hold a World Cup–style, mixed-climbing event as an exhibition. It's just an exhibition, but I don't care. I'd be honored to represent America.

GUIDING

I feel lucky I get to work as a climbing guide. Taking people into the mountains to rock climb, ice climb, travel on glaciers, and so forth is really fun. I enjoy sharing with the students the crazy learning curve they experience, which, *luckily,* is something I don't remember very well from my own early years [laughs].

It's cool, because if you can get students when they're still fresh, before they develop bad habits, and before they say something like, "Oh my friend told me to do it this way," you can help them avoid having to relearn the skills

So that's the cool part. Watching people excel. And later I'll be in the ice park, or out in the mountains, and I'll run into a former student and realize, "Hey, I had you in a course." And they're out there on their own, and I'm proud I was an important part of that process.

When it comes to ice climbing, everyone is scared of the same things. It doesn't matter whether you're a man or a woman. We're all scared of freezing to death. We're all scared of

heights and falling, of a tool popping and hitting you in the face, or of ice falling on your head.

Working with other women is cool, because we naturally have a better bond. Female students feel freer to ask female guides lots of questions. They usually say, "I've got a hundred stupid questions for you." But they're *not* stupid questions. They are just the same questions everybody wonders about.

If you can empower women, it has amazing results. Let's face it: Most of the time women are the head of their household. They make everything run. Sorry men! You may not want to admit this, but it's usually the case. And if you give a woman the sense that she can do anything, it's amazing what she will take home and do with that knowledge.

Women who complete ice-climbing courses achieve a newfound sense of accomplishment. They think, "Hey, I didn't freeze to death! I didn't die when I fell. I was able to tie knots and belay my partner safely." Newly trained female climbers walk tall. Their attitude becomes, "Bring it on! I can do better. I can manage every aspect of my life better."

Many of the women we teach through Chicks with Picks were not athletic growing up. We've had women in their fifties and early sixties as students. We have even had seventy-year-olds. These people had no sports opportunities as kids. Climbing class is their first athletic experience, and they realize that they have the ability to dig deep and the mental toughness to push through fear. Most of them didn't know they had that in them. You show them that they can push beyond their comfort zone, and it's absolutely amazing the change that occurs.

CHROMOSOMES

I think women definitely approach climbing differently than men. Our body types are different. Our shapes are different. The size of our hands are different, and all these things affect the way we climb. And the mental aspect is different as well. Most women I know (I'm not going to say all women) have a different level of risk that they're willing to take. It's not that they hold themselves back but that they are more calculated. Women think things through. And they have a different sense of caring when it comes right down to it. You know, when I'm out climbing with Kitty Calhoun, she's tough as nails, but if I'm having a bad day, then she's going to give me a little *more love* than if I'm out with some dude. So there's compassion and a sense of sisterhood that women climbers celebrate together and that brings a whole new element to our climbing experience.

STRENGTHS AND WEAKNESSES

My biggest strength is my ability to remain calm. I had a climbing accident in France, where I got

Dawn Glanc searches for a way out of Confinement (M8) Ouray Ice Park.

smashed in the face with some ice and the friend who was with me says she's never seen anyone remain so calm through such a traumatic experience. My face was split open. Blood was everywhere. My friend was freaking out, because she can't deal with blood or guts or stuff like that [laughs]. She's seeing my skull right through the wound in my cheek, so she knows things are bad. But I didn't lose my cool.

I've had plenty of partners who are all over the place emotionally. Freaking out, getting pissed off, kicking the rock, and dropping *F bombs*. But I don't. I think my ability to remain calm has helped me through a lot of scary scenarios.

My biggest weakness is the fact that I suffer from migraines. I suffer from headaches a lot, so I feel that if I don't have one at the moment, I better take advantage of the time. When I'm on an expedition, I can do well as long as I take care of myself. But if a headache comes on all of a sudden, *you're* taking care of me. So I try to give my best and my all when I can, because I know my healthy time is limited. I've had headaches my whole life. My entire family has them. It's something you learn to deal with.

LESSONS

The most important lesson I've learned from climbing is goal setting. I know that if I have a goal, I can reach it if I work *really* hard. Another lesson I've learned is how to work with my fear. This was huge, because now I can face things in other parts of my life and realize, "Hey this isn't so bad. It's not life or death. We're good!"

Huge lessons guiding taught me are to look at the simple things in life and to look at what really matters. This makes you calmer. It gives you a more relaxed way of looking at things, because whatever I'm going through right now is not as bad as some of the spots I've gotten myself into climbing.

The way I deal with the stress is to stay physically healthy. I'm a huge advocate of weight training. If I have a goal I'm working toward, then you're going to find me in the gym putting in overtime. I'm an advocate of going to the weight room three times a week. That helps me, because when I'm there, I can visualize. It's like meditation in action. Yes, I'm trying to push my body and become physically stronger, but at the same time I'm thinking about my goal. If I'm training for a comp, then I'm working out while envisioning myself finishing first. The same goes for working a route. I'm certainly not going to visualize *not* making it to the top. So that's something I get from the weight room. It's been a huge help for me, because in my mind I've already seen that I can do what I need to do.

And when I'm out there climbing a project or competing and things don't go as well as I'd like, I try to learn from the experience. That's the only way to move forward. When I'm performing, I do my best. If I fail, I come home and say, "Well I didn't make it because my heart rate was going through the roof. I let myself freak out. Okay, why did you freak out?" I'm constantly picking this stuff apart, trying to learn and improve.

I used to beat myself up like crazy. I would think, "Why can't I climb this?" I realized I needed to take a hard look at why. Complaining wasn't going to make a difference. Being pissed off wasn't going to make the situation go away!

That's how I've managed everything in my life. "Okay, that didn't work. Why didn't it work? Let's figure this out, then come back and do it better."

CLOSE CALLS

I've been really lucky. I haven't had too many close calls. The accident in France, when I got smashed in the face, was a freak occurrence. There's nothing we could have done differently; nature just knocked a massive chunk of ice down on me. Lots of people laugh at me and say I'm going to win the climbing safety award each year, because I really go out of my way to take those extra steps to make sure we don't have problems.

For example, I don't like to solo without a rope. I almost fell off an ice climb soloing. I almost killed myself. It was one of those *holy shit* moments. So now, if you take my rope away from me, I'm paralyzed. If you give me my rope back, I'm fine.

Another close call was in Ouray Ice Park, where I was climbing a hanging dagger of ice. It was a route that started on ice, continued on rock, then finished on this massive hanging pillar. The pillar was probably fifteen feet around and thirty feet long, dangling in space.

It was a warm day. I shouldn't have been there. I did the rock moves then climbed out onto the pillar and traversed around to the front. I was climbing toward the top, when I looked up at the bridge across the canyon and my husband and one of our friends was there. So I shouted up to them, "Hey how's it going? The ice is soooo good right now!"

Then I swung my tool and *pop!* The entire icicle broke off. I didn't realize what was

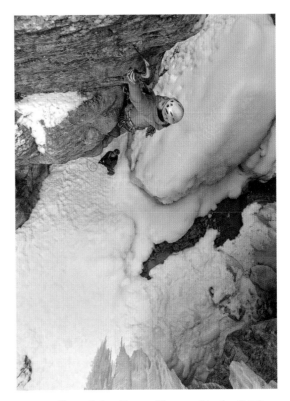

Kitty Calhoun belays Dawn Glanc on Bipolar (M9) the Ouray Ice Park.

happening. I heard the pop. I'm still hanging on, but I was falling with it, wondering, "What the hell?" I'm on a giant icicle, and it's falling!

Luckily I had not put any screws in the ice, so when my rope came tight, it sucked me back to the last bolt I'd clipped on the rock, and because I fell so far, the rope sucked my belayer up into the wall as well, way off the ground. If he had still been standing below the climb, he would have been smashed by the falling ice. But nothing happened to either of us. There have been many times I foolishly thought I could climb anything, do anything. I'm glad I got away with that, but since then, I've definitely looked at ice differently.

FEAR

I try to work consciously with fear. I try to think clearly about what is *real* fear and what is *irrational fear,* because irrational fear can be a total showstopper.

I know when the irrational fear is coming, because my heart rate soars. So now I focus on recognizing the physical changes that occur in my body when I get scared. Because things can be going great. I'm not pumped. I'm not tired. But the moment I feel my heart rate begin to increase I feel the whole thing falling apart. Your heart rate is naturally elevated when you're doing something physical. But if it increases past a certain level, then your vision narrows. The world closes in. You can't see the next move, and that's when you blow it.

So I try *really* hard to watch that, whether I'm on rock, ice, or mixed. It doesn't matter. I try to be aware of the tendency and manage it. Luckily for me I can hang on all day! That's been a big help in keeping calm, taking some deep breaths, and remembering, "Okay, I chose to be here."

I feel like a Zen warrior out there, fighting my warrior's battle with myself. Thinking I'm not going to let this fear get the best of me! Warriors don't go into battle thinking they're going to lose, and I don't attempt a climb thinking I'm going to fail. I learned this mental aspect of climbing from Arno Ilgner, the creator of Warrior's Way, a mental training method for climbers. When I'm working with my clients, I see that what I'm really teaching them is confidence, the idea that they are engaged in a battle within themselves that they are choosing to fight.

I'm *choosing* to go up that climb. I'm the one who picks this crazy project, and in order

Dawn Glanc bridges the gap on Bipolar.

to succeed I've got to have a strategy. *Not hope.* Hope is not a strategy. But it's not about conquering the rock, the mountain, or your competitors. What you conquered is the part of yourself that said you couldn't do it. You pushed through your weakness. You grew within yourself. That's what's important.

ACCOMPLISHMENTS

My most important climbing accomplishments are those climbs that I completed even though I had doubts. When I chose them, I thought no way. But I planned and trained for each goal, and I succeeded! They are not necessarily climbs that mean anything to anyone else. They include my first 5.9 trad lead and my first M9 (mixed climbing 9), climbs that are important to me. I would never give those experiences up.

But the most meaningful experiences I've had in the mountains are those I've shared with a great partner. If you have someone on the other end of the rope pushing confidence up to you, *keep him or her.* Do not let that partner go! Say, "Okay fine. You need to have Peet's Coffee in the morning before you go climbing. Great! No worries. We will always have Peet's." The beauty of a great partnership is to discover the quirks in each other, to realize we're all weird, and to understand that we all have things that scare us and that make us goofy. I would never trade for anything the experiences I shared and the bonds I formed through climbing.

CHALLENGES

The biggest challenge I've had to overcome has been being female. *Honestly!* Now that I'm married dudes don't just call and say, "Hey, we're all going to the gym today. Hey, we're all going to the crag. Come along." It just doesn't work that way. So it's been hard to find partners. It's hard to have a sunny day free and not have a climbing partner. I suppose I feel it more since there are so few women ice and mixed climbing. So that's why being a woman has been a challenge for me.

THE FUTURE

I want to climb until I'm *very* old. I don't want to give up my friends or my climbing experiences. I don't want to give up the amazing places I get to see.

I'm reminded of the time I attended my ten-year high school reunion and ran into a former classmate who asked what I was doing for a living. At the time I was running the outdoor program at an air force base. So I said, "I take military personnel outside—bike riding, climbing, hiking, skiing, all these awesome things." Then I said, "What do you do?" And she crinkled up her nose and said, "Well, I hope I'm past the stage of riding my bike."

And I just thought, "Please God, don't let me ever become like her! Don't let me ever grow out of this stage! Let me be outdoors, climbing and biking and enjoying life as long as I can."

RELATIONSHIPS

I have a fantastic husband, Patrick Ormond. We've been married since 2011.

Pat and I met on Alaska's Mount McKinley. I was guiding, and he was on a personal trip. My group got stuck in a snowstorm at eleven thousand feet. I got out of my tent to start shoveling one morning, and there he was, right on the other side of the snow wall. I thought, "Whoa, that guy is kinda cute." Then we kept running into each other, but we were either dating other people or living in different states. This went on for five years. Then a mutual friend came to Ouray and took some photos of me climbing. He went back to Salt Lake City and showed Pat the photos. And Pat said, "Hey, I know that girl." And Jeremiah said, "Well, you should *know* that girl. She's *single.* You should *call* that girl." So Pat called, and after six months, we finally reconnected, and it's been magic ever since.

I was single a long time. I didn't date anyone, because it was impossible. I didn't live anywhere.

How do you psych yourself up for a hard route?

In the morning before going climbing, I'll put on what I call booty-quake music—really loud, hip-hop, dance music, much to the chagrin of my landlord, who lives upstairs. That gets me motivated. And when my partner picks me up and we've got a drive ahead of us, I'll try to keep the booty quake pumping! I climb with Kitty a lot, and if you can believe it, she's not into booty quake, so she's had to learn to deal [laughs]. And so has Pat and everybody else around me, because no one else I know listens to that kind of music.

What's your favorite place to climb?

I love desert crack climbing, and when I went to Yosemite for the first time, I discovered I love granite crack climbing as well. And for ice climbing, you can't beat Ouray. But if I had to choose a place other than Ouray, then I would choose Iceland because it has the craziest ice I've ever seen. The wind is insane there. It's strong all the time, and as the water freezes, the wind bends it in all these amazing ways. There are horizontal icicles and wind-sculpted caves. So climbing in Iceland is challenging and beautiful at the same time.

If you could offer one essential tip to other climbers, what would it be?

The advice I give to all climbers, regardless of whether they're young or old, is when learning how to climb, spend some time with a certified mountain guide. When you learn from a professional, you learn the correct information the first time, and you learn the

I would rather go climbing than spend my time with a boy. I'm selfish. I'm happy to miss a social event and go climbing instead. Climbing's my thing. So relationships are hard.

But Pat's been a climber his entire life. He started climbing when he was two. He's also a mountain guide. So I feel very lucky, because we both understand that there are going to be times we're apart to pursue our passion. We've created a committed relationship in which we accept that we're going to spend five to six months apart every year. But entering into a relationship knowing that has been beneficial, because we look at the times we are together in terms of quality, not quantity. We have limited time together, so we make the most of it.

safest, most efficient way to deal with the risks you encounter.

And secondly, there are so many girls and young women out there who don't think it's cool to exercise, because it makes their hair messy or their nails dirty. And I say, "Sisters, if you really think it's cool to just be a bump on a log and never do anything with your life, fine." But the things that set you apart in life are the passions you have. Follow those passions. If you want something out of life, go for it. You're not going to accomplish much sitting on the couch.

How do you train?

I've been lifting weights since I was thirteen. I started because some girls in school were bullying me. After I took care of that problem, I wanted to be thin, but I knew I wasn't going to starve myself, so I kept lifting. And as I grew older, I wanted to stay young, and I believe exercise is the fountain of youth. I know that if I want to still be climbing when I'm ninety, then I have to keep up with my training. As a climber, I think it's superimportant to weight train in order to balance your body. My program aims to balance my muscles, keep me strong, prevent injuries, and help me with my life in general.

I do train specifically for mixed climbing, but when the comp is over, I don't stop going to the gym. I'm right back in there the following Monday. That consistency is important. It makes me feel amazing. I like feeling that my body is strong. It gives me confidence in all areas of my life, not just climbing.

BRITTANY GRIFFITH

Brittany Griffith's a funny, irreverent, midwesterner with more energy than a truck full of Red Bull. She's also an ambassador for outdoor clothing company Patagonia and a full-time climbing evangelist who, along with her husband, Jonathan Thesenga, a global sports marketing manager for Black Diamond Equipment, travels the world searching for obscure cliffs to practice their unique brand of adventure rock climbing. When Brittany and Jonathan are home in Salt Lake City, Utah, they never miss an opportunity to load up their Mercedes Sprinter van and head for Indian Creek, Zion National Park, St. George, or Maple Canyon.

Some of Brittany's most notable accomplishments include a free ascent of Zion's Moonlight Buttress (V, 5.12+), the first ascent of Cracker Pterodactyl 5000 (V, 5.10+) in Oman, the first ascent of Ten Pounds of Tequila (VI, 5.12+) on the Acopan Tepui in Venezuela, and the first ascent of Battling Begonias (V, 5.12) in Yemen, which is known more for Predator drone strikes than tourism. Brittany has climbed 5.13 sport routes, holds a black belt in tae kwon do, and was ranked twelfth in the US when she raced downhill mountain bikes on the NORBA (National Off-Road Bicycle Association) circuit. Before becoming a professional climber she

worked at McDonald's, where she estimates she served more than twelve thousand Happy Meals.

But some of her more harrowing stories have nothing to do with climbing. They are hair-raising and hilarious accounts of visits back home to Iowa, where marathon tailgating parties can rage for more than twenty-four hours and a famous bike race has mandatory stops for a drink at every bar along its a two-hundred-mile course.

Left, "Now that's a splitter!" Brittany Griffith samples the spicy Six Star Crack (13a) Indian Creek Canyon, Utah. Above, Griffith appears on the Gong Show (12c) Utah's Maple Canyon.

ROOTS

My name's Brittany Griffith. I was born in 1969, and I grew up in Missouri and Iowa. I didn't grow up climbing. I grew up doing all the normal Midwest sports—detasseling corn, track and field, basketball, and volleyball. In college I got involved in tae kwon do. I was really into the mind control, the focus, and the fitness aspect of martial arts.

When I was twenty-three, I was dating a guy who asked me if I wanted to go on a road trip. "Huhh?" I didn't even know what a road trip was. He explained that's when you travel around climbing and mountain biking. At the time I wasn't very outdoorsy. But A, I was really into this guy, and B, I had always wanted to get out of the Midwest to explore the rest of the country. So to me this road-tripping business sounded like the perfect opportunity.

It wasn't the climbing that attracted me to the trip. It was the travel. And to be honest, that's still true today. I love the physical activity of climbing, but it's the traveling lifestyle that I became addicted to. My love affair with travel has been going strong ever since that first experience in 1994.

From the very start I was never interested in competition climbing, which is strange because I've always been a competitive person. But now I think, "Ooooh!" That's because most climbing competitions are held *indoors,* and indoor climbing has never particularly interested me. I like climbing at the gym when I can't go outside, but that's not where I want to focus.

Honestly, the focus for me is *not having* a focus. I enjoy being *very* focused on *all* parts of climbing, rather than on just one. The emphasis

right now is free-climbing on rock. I really like rock climbing. The problem with other aspects of climbing is that I don't like downtime. I don't do well with nothing to do, so waiting out weeks of bad weather in order to go alpine climbing or spending hours on a ledge belaying while aid climbing, has never been attractive. Mostly I like adventure rock climbing. I like going to different countries, exploring, and doing first ascents. My claim to fame is I've climbed 5.12 on every continent except one. That's good enough for me.

CAREER

People ask me, "Oh gosh, how do you get sponsored and how do you become a professional climber?" Starting with that first road trip in 1994, I knew I loved the climbing lifestyle. It was the first thing in my life that really made sense. So I knew that climbing is what I want to do. I didn't have any other career aspirations. I never wanted to be *something.* I just knew *how* I wanted to live. What I did to attain that didn't matter. I mowed lawns. I painted houses. I babysat. I cleaned houses. Whatever. It didn't matter that I had, you know, five hundred bucks. I could earn five hundred bucks a month, put gas in the car, travel, and go climbing.

So the first thing I did was commit to the lifestyle, and the rest is what you might call serendipitous. I don't know if I would call it luck. Lots of times people say, "Oh you're so lucky." But to me, luck is winning the lottery. Believe me, I did *not* win the lottery. I wish!

Instead I made scary decisions. They didn't seem scary to me at the time, but I think that many people would consider it scary to leave everything they know and figure out how to survive later. There were times (many) when I had no more than fifty bucks in my bank account.

But through it all, I had this crazy belief that it would all work out. I wasn't scared about not having money, because now I had this whole new passion that was climbing. I believed I would be able to figure things out and support the life I wanted.

So I traveled and climbed, and as I did, I began meeting people who worked for companies in the outdoor industry. The community is pretty small, so eventually you meet people who work for Patagonia or Black Diamond, and I guess I made an impression on them. For example, one day I was at the crag, and I met some guys who worked for Five Ten, and they were getting ready to go to a trade show. I'd worked trade shows in college for a T-shirt business I helped start. So I knew my way around, and I said, "Hey if you need some help, I'll work the show for you." And from then on things fell into place. I would see something I could do for a company, and I'd offer to do it.

To figure out what service you can *provide* that a company *needs* is key. Most people have it backward. "What can you do for me? What can you give me?" But I'm always saying, "No. Figure something out you can do for them." People outside the industry think it's like, "Hey, here's some money. Why don't you go on a climbing trip!" But that's not how it works [laughs].

I was at Smith Rock State Park in Oregon, and there was a photographer who took a picture of me. He sold the photo to Patagonia. The company used it, and then it sent me all these clothes. Then another shot ran, and Patagonia

kept sending me all these clothes. Finally I called the company and said, "I can't just keep taking all these clothes! I've got to do *something* in return. This is too generous, what can I do?"

So Patagonia had me talk to the head of marketing. He had many different responsibilities, and dealing with this chick named Brittany was probably the last thing he wanted to think about. But he told me that Patagonia was starting a new clothing line called Rhythm, which would be a nontechnical part of their brand, more oriented toward rock climbing. So I was excited, because that was exactly what I was into.

So he said, "I'll send you a contract," and I went back to Bend, Oregon, where I was living. Months go by, and there's nothing in the mailbox. So I think, all right, I've got to do something.

So I jumped in my van, and I drove all the way to Patagonia HQ in Ventura, California. I walked in, and he was sitting at his desk—barefoot of course. And he says, "Brittany? Okay. Right now. Let's get this going."

So we went to the beach to talk, and I said, "Here's what I do. Here's what I'm good at. I'm *not* ever going to do competitions. I'm *not* ever going to be a 5.14 climbing superhero. This is who I am, and this is what I can do for you. Does this interest you or not?" And based on that I got a contract.

In the beginning my job was to give feedback on Patagonia's products and work for them at the Phoenix Bouldering Contest and other grassroots events. Then it evolved. I became interested in writing. I've been to a lot of places. I've got a lot of funny stories, so I said I could write stories for Patagonia. So now I write for the

Desert climbing at its best.
Brittany Griffith cruises
Sicilian Crack (5.11)
Indian Creek Canyon,
Utah.

company's blog. I also write copy, and occasionally I'll write for the catalog.

There are times when I'm busy with climbing events that take a lot of energy. I work the booth. I take people climbing and teach them how to climb. I represent the brand, and I have to be *on* day and night. It's not just a nine-to-five thing, where I can clock out, go home, and sit on the couch. Because then there are the parties [laughs]. So poor me!

I'll be honest. There are times when I feel like I can't keep doing it weekend after weekend. But then I get to the next event, and I meet all these great people. They're *so* psyched and enthusiastic, and I feel like this is my *one* chance to really make a difference in these people's lives and to inspire them to experience the thing that has transformed my life. So that's what keeps me stoked.

ENJOYING THE SPORT

It's difficult to put my finger on what I love most about climbing, because it's all encompassing. First it's my health—physically and mentally. People don't realize the amount of mental strength and fitness that climbing gives you. You have to focus—a lot. You have to solve problems. You're scared a lot, and I think that's all stuff you need to have going on in your brain in order to keep it sharp and alive.

Then there's the community. Climbing is everything I'm involved in. It sounds pathetic, but I probably only have two friends who are *not* climbers. The partnerships and friendships I've made through climbing are like no other.

Climbing provides what I call *the essentials.* If I get bogged down with accounting, house issues,

or my job, basically the stuff in life that can bog you down, I know that ultimately I don't need any of it because of climbing. I can go to Indian Creek, and the view of the Six Shooter Peaks will provide more peace and contentment than material possessions will ever give me. So that's what I love most, the peace of knowing that climbing is all I really need, the simplicity of it all.

What I like least about climbing is the fear of losing people close to me. I have irrational fears about my husband getting hurt. Friends getting hurt. It's funny; I'm never scared for myself. When shit happens, I'm always afraid it's going to happen to the other person *way* more than to me. That part frustrates me. You do everything right, and shit still happens. God, it's irritating you know [laughs]. I *know* it's part of the game! Like I said, it's *irrational,* so what can I do?

TRAVEL

In the past twelve months I've been to six countries and ten states. In 2011 I was away from *my domain* for two hundred days. And even when I'm *home,* I might be away from home, for short periods of time, such as five days. I have platinum frequent-flyer status on Delta, which means I fly a minimum of seventy-five thousand miles a year.

But like anything, traveling all the time is a mixed bag. For instance, occasionally I'll have to fly an airline that I don't have any status with, and man, that really sucks [laughs]. But seriously, people think it's glamorous and I'm like, "Really?" Because I have friends who are moms with full-time jobs, and they get to climb more than I do. Seriously! They have a more regular, regimented schedule.

I don't have that. But I'm not complaining, because God knows, I'll be home for a week, and I'll start thinking, "I've *got* to go somewhere!"

Finding the balance in all the chaos is the challenge. It's a choice. I *don't have* to travel like this. I'm an adult, white female living in the United States. I can choose to settle down. So it's all about finding a balance.

RELATIONSHIPS

I don't think I could be in a relationship with someone who's not a climber. And it's not because I can't communicate on a different level; it's because climbing is all consuming for me. I climb four or five days a week. It's everything. My job. My community. So I think being with a nonclimber would be too hard; it would require far more balancing and juggling.

"Home sweet home." Brittany Griffith and husband Jonathan Thesenga in their Sprinter van in Indian Creek.

The fact that Jonathan is probably as crazy as (if not crazier than) I am about climbing is what makes our relationship work. It's still hard, because I leave a lot, but the time we're together and climbing is so powerful and enriching.

It's hard to find balance, but to me an even harder part of life is finding something you're truly passionate about. Once you find that, everything else becomes easier. Because you start to think in terms of values related to your passion. For instance, one *day* of work equals a tank of gas, and one *week* of work equals a plane ticket to Europe. That's how I think. It isn't money. It's a system of exchange that equals freedom.

LOSING FRIENDS

In 2006 I lost one of my favorite climbing partners ever—Sue Nott. She and Karen McNeil died climbing Mount Foraker's Infinite Spur in Alaska. She was the first girlfriend I climbed with in Indian Creek. Sue was one of those friends who didn't compete with you. You always felt Sue was 100 percent on your side. She wanted you to succeed more than she did herself. She was also one of the easiest people to make laugh, which I think is a great trait in people.

When you lose someone in a tragedy like that, it's surreal. To me, it's similar to a climbing trip, where you spend two weeks with other people, and you do everything together. You eat, sleep, laugh, drink, and climb. They're involved in every second of your world, yet when the trip's over, you go to your gate at the airport and they go to theirs, and you may never see that person again. Every time a trip ends, I feel this small tinge of panic. It's not necessarily a fear that my friends might die, but it's the realization that I

have no idea when I'll spend that kind of time with them again just because everyone's so busy.

That same realization hits me when people die too. In 2009 Jonny Copp, Micah Dash, and Wade Johnson died on China's Mount Edgar, and I don't feel like they're dead. It's just that I'm not going to see them again. We're not going to hang out and go climbing in Indian Creek. They've gone on a different trip. That's the way I deal with it anyway.

RISK

I don't deal with risk very well. There were times when I absolutely lost my mind and had a major breakdown during a climb, because I didn't trust that Jonathan was making the right decision or that he was going to remember to retie his knot after threading the anchors. I don't think it's a control issue, as much as it is an inability to believe that other people who I care about can take care of themselves. It's the caregiver gene run amuck. I want to take care of people. And I want to be the one doing it, so I can be in control and know it's being done right. So yes, there are times when I have to let that go and realize, "It's okay, Brittany. This person can take care of himself."

EVOLUTION

As far as basic skills, I've evolved very little. I climbed 5.12c fifteen months after I began climbing, and now I've been climbing 12c for fifteen years, since 1997. Sure, I could climb a whole number grade harder if I really tried, but that kind of focus and commitment to one aspect of the sport doesn't motivate me. Unless you're supergifted, you pretty much plateau at a certain level, and you will stay there, unless you try *very* hard to change. The honest truth is I can pretty easily climb 5.12 with a hangover, so I don't really care. I'm not going to give up all the other stuff in order to climb harder. Besides my life isn't set up that way: How can I *project* a route when I'm never in one place more than six days in a row?

INJURIES

I used to race mountain bikes, and I've crashed my bike going forty miles per hour. Riding my snowboard, I've hit trees head-on. But the most traumatic injury was a broken foot. It broke in five places when I was bouldering in a climbing gym.

And, of course, I'm really impatient. I *don't* want to stretch. I *don't* want to do yoga. I *don't* want to take rest days. I *don't* want to warm up, but *hellooo,* I'm forty-three. I'm going to have to learn to do all those things now. I can't not.

So I have a lot of massage and body work done, and I'm starting to do a bit of rehab, including strengthening exercises. One day recently I tried to pick up a glass out of the dishwasher, and my elbow was so sore I dropped it. And I thought, how's this possible? I'm climbing 5.12, but I can't pick up a glass? The point is I've always thought of myself as stronger than most people I know, but suddenly I realized I was weaker in a lot of areas than the average person. So I started doing some counterbalance stuff with my neck and shoulders. I'm still not very good at it, but every little bit helps.

STRENGTHS AND WEAKNESSES

I suppose my greatest strength in climbing is my focus. In fact, climbing is the one part of my life where I *can* focus. I've got ADD (attention deficit disorder) so bad. But when I'm climbing, there's peace knowing that's all that's going on in that instant of time. I'm able to deal with that.

My biggest weakness is taking on too much. Like I said, I travel two hundred days a year, but I also have a garden with *fifteen* varieties of tomatoes! I get bogged down not being able to prioritize. Overcommitting. It cripples me. I'll just sit at my desk, wondering how I'm going to get it all done.

LESSONS

The most important lesson I've learned is not to be afraid to follow my instincts. I don't give in to conventional wisdom. For example, when I first made the decision to climb full time, I felt so alone. Now I know hundreds of people like me, but at the time I was living in Iowa and I didn't know anyone facing the same dilemma.

The only other person I knew who was a climber was my boyfriend, who I ended up marrying. But it didn't work out, because I still wanted to live in my car. I still wanted to travel, and suddenly he didn't. So I was like, "Whoa! What just happened to the road trip?"

I figured there must be something wrong with me. Why don't I want a house and a job, with the security most people want? But I'm glad I found the courage to be different, because now I can't imagine life being any other way.

CHROMOSOMES

I think women approach climbing in a more emotional way than men, but that just parallels life in general. Women aren't as afraid to show their emotions, and that crosses into climbing.

Brittany Griffith basks in reflected light on Gong Show (12c) Maple Canyon.

I believe women try to deal with their emotions in a more open, honest way and don't try to hide them. But that isn't all positive; it can also hold them back. Because women aren't afraid to say, "Take!" or "I'm scared this bolt won't hold me."

I'm probably going to get a bunch of shit for this, but men don't want to show anyone that they're weak, so they'll put themselves out there more.

Most fears are irrational anyway. You shouldn't be afraid to fall on a bolt. That's irrational. So I try to practice a form of tough love on my girlfriends. I recognize that sometimes everyone needs support, because sometimes I want it too. But there are limits, and at some point I'm going to call you on it. I've friends I climb with who get scared, and believe me, if I didn't *care* about them, I wouldn't say anything, but I see how strong they are. I see their potential, and if the only thing holding them back is that they're being a chicken shit I'm going to let them know—*because I want them to be better!*

Of course the trick is not pushing it. Does that person really want to be better? If he or she does, then I want to help and that help might be TOH.—you know, tough on the heart! And I might have to use HTFU! Harden the f—— up! I've used that one before.

INSPIRATION

I've always admired what Lynn Hill did. She was doing climbs back in the day because she wanted to be the first *climber* to do it, not the first female climber. She was competing against the guys, and like it or not, that's the game. I admire her, because she was doing it for the purity of the sport and for the adventure. She wasn't doing it

to get a free pair of shoes from a sponsor. And it was harder for her, because she was breaking ground on all levels. Girls may climb harder grades now, but Lynn made that possible.

ACCOMPLISHMENTS

I've never been goal oriented. Yes, I've had objectives. For instance I wanted to free-climb Moonlight Buttress in a day, and I've wanted to do first ascents. But one climb that really stands out for me is a route we did in Oman with Zoe Hart. She and I were partners, and Jonathan and John Dickey were partners. We just walked up to this big chunk of limestone that was as big as El Cap, with a double set of cams and two ropes. And we climbed it to the top without any information. Well, let me say, we had only the limited information that we could glean with binoculars.

And that was really scary, because if you get in trouble, how do you get down? It's not like you yell to your friends in El Cap meadows that you need a rescue. It's supercommitting. The first day we climbed two-thirds of the wall. We slept on our ropes. We made a little fire on a ledge we found. The next day, we summited, and we didn't leave a single piece of gear behind.

I do a lot of the things I do, not because I really want to, but because I'm afraid of them. But once they're over, I'm so grateful. What I'm trying to say is that to follow through despite my fears and have these incredible experiences is enriching. I'm afraid of a lot of stuff. It's scary going to a foreign country where four days before we arrived a tourist was beheaded. It's scary not being able to call the police when a Chinese mob attacks you. But I'm so grateful to have had those experiences.

THE FUTURE

While floating down a river on a climbing/river-rafting trip, a friend and I talked about people we know who don't climb anymore. And we kept asking ourselves, how can people just walk away from climbing?

And Jonathan, who should know *everything* about me, said, "Well, you almost did! You were five seconds from quitting to become a professional mountain bike racer." And I said, "No I wasn't! Never! Never for a second have I ever felt that I wouldn't be a climber the rest of my life. Mountain biking was just a momentary thing to see if I could do it. I was never a mountain biker. I was a climber who mountain biked."

My hope is I can continue to find balance in it all. For instance, maybe sometime in the future, I'll only want to climb once a week. Maybe I'll want to take four months off. I think people continue to participate in this crazy sport

---

How do you psych yourself up for a hard route?

For me the most important thing is to choose an objective you really want to do. That's what Moonlight Buttress (V, 5.12+, trad,) in Zion National Park was for me. I wanted to be up there. Don't choose it because of the grade or because you need to get the first ascent; choose it because you can't live without climbing it.

What's your favorite place to climb?

If I had to pick one area (even though I haven't been back there in five years), it would be Squamish in British Columbia, Canada. Because Squamish has it all: bouldering, sport climbing, and multipitch. As for routes, I really like Northern Lights (linking two Squamish classics—Alaska Highway 5.11c/d and the Calling 5.12-). It is amazing climbing.

If you could offer one essential tip to other climbers, what would it be?

Stay enthusiastic. Attitude is everything. One thing about climbing that's different than any other sport I've been involved in is that it's so obvious when you're failing. In climbing either you can do 5.10d or you can't. It's very cut-and-dried, and it's maddening. You have to learn to keep your frustration and your other emotions under control. This is something I learned from tae kwon do: "Control your emotions, before they control you."

How do you train?

I hate training. I've never been a disciplined person. Well no, that's not completely true, because I did train when I was four years old. I remember doing push-ups and sit-ups for a fitness test. So I guess I have it in me, but I don't like doing things I don't want to do. I love climbing, and I climb four or five days a week, so I don't have to train.

even if they're no longer happy doing it. It's like an obsession they can't walk away from.

How old am I? I'm forty-three, so in twenty years I'll be sixty-three. I hope I'm still going on road trips and will be able to deal with the rigors of travel and climbing, because a lot of times the hardest part of climbing trips isn't the climbing. It's lugging your bags to the airport. It's getting them loaded on mules. Going through security. Dealing with the police. It's traveling for thirty hours, then staying up another night to go to a rave in Hong Kong. I'm not sure I'll be able to do that in twenty years, but hey, you never know.

EMILY HARRINGTON

I first met Emily Harrington in the summer of 2012, six weeks after she'd summited Mount Everest in the Himalayas. She was still struggling, literally and figuratively, to return to Earth, and to understand for herself and to explain to others how she, a competition climber who didn't begin to climb outdoors seriously until she was eighteen, had somehow come to stand on the highest point on Earth.

Writing in the American Alpine Club blog about the surreal nature of her experience, Emily zeroes in on the paradoxes that swirl around modern expeditions to Everest:

> Mount Everest isn't supposed to be a difficult mountain to climb. *Climbing* is (a word) often not even used to describe the world's tallest peak. "*It's just walking. It's not hard,*" was something I'd often heard. . . . Growing up in the climbing community gave me a unique and opinionated perspective toward a place I'd never even visited or bothered to learn about. When non-climbers asked me if I ever dreamed of climbing Everest, I would snidely reply, "Umm, no. That's *not* the kind of climbing I do."

> Well, I'm now eating my own arrogant words. . . . Everest is a controversial place full of both real-life danger and ego-crushing criticism. It's the most personal struggle I've ever had to undergo. . . . I've never been as sick as I was when I first

arrived at base camp with a respiratory infection. I've never fought so much physically to keep pushing . . . enduring the exhaustion, extreme heat, and bitter cold. I walked by dead bodies, human souls who'd . . . left this world in pursuit of the same goal I was trying to achieve. I was afraid a lot of the time. Never before have I faced such a reality; that

Left, Emily Harrington gets her "Grrr" on Hellion (13c) Ten Sleep Canyon, Wyoming. Above, Harrington rests between climbs in Ten Sleep Canyon.

my own life could be taken away from me by circumstances out of my control, and the unsettling knowledge that it was my choice to be there, but for what? I fought intensely . . . to justify this mission to myself, despite the danger, death and . . . harsh criticism I was receiving for even setting foot on the mountain in the first place, with no previous high altitude mountain experience.

In many ways Emily represents the best and brightest of the brave new world of modern climbers. She started climbing in a gym at age ten and began competing only two years later under the tutelage of former World Cup champion Robyn Erbesfield–Raboutou. Emily went on to win six Sport Climbing National Championships and place second in the 2005 World Championships.

Nor did it take her long to translate the technique and stamina she'd developed on plastic to sport climbing outdoors. At the ripe old age of twenty-five, Emily had already climbed *eleven* 5.14s and more than *sixty* 5.13s! She made the first female ascents of Waka Flocka (14b) in Rifle Mountain Park in Colorado and of Burning Down the House (14b) in Sonora, California. She was also the first female to ascend Living the Dream, Roadside Prophet, 7pm Show, and Zulu (all 14a), all in Rifle Mountain Park.

Emily's remarkable accomplishments earned her a place on The North Face Climbing team, which led to an invitation to Mount Everest. Climbing in the Himalayas opened Emily's eyes to the incredible depth and richness of experience that climbing in all its forms has to offer. As she explains below, her current focus is to evolve from a competitive sport climber to being

just a climber, one proficient in all aspects of the craft—trad, sport, alpine, and mixed. To further that end Emily has learned to ice and mixed climb, taking first place in the women's division of the Ouray Ice Climbing Festival in 2012 and placing third in 2013. When she isn't traveling the world to climb, Emily lives near Lake Tahoe, in California, and serves as a national ambassador for the Access Fund, a national advocacy group for climbing areas in the United States.

ROOTS

My name's Emily Harrington. I'm from Boulder, Colorado. I was born in 1987 and started climbing at the age of ten. Two years later, I started doing competitions, and I competed all through my teenage years.

I became interested in climbing over a summer break. My family was at a lake swimming, and one of those portable climbing walls was there. My cousins and I tried it, and afterward I told my dad I wanted to climb. He started taking me to a climbing gym. Fortunately, my dad loves climbing. He's really passionate about it, but he doesn't get to do it as often as he'd like. When I was younger, he was my primary partner, and I owe him a lot [laughs]. Now we go climbing occasionally, usually in the gym. I know he'd love to travel and climb, but he usually doesn't have the time.

I graduated magna cum laude from the University of Colorado, where I studied international affairs. I climbed the entire time I was in school. In fact, I did my first 5.14b while I was in college. I rearranged my schedule, so I could climb and train all the time. I competed a lot. I didn't really do anything but climb and go to

Emily Harrington investigates Number One Enemy (11a), Ten Sleep.

school. I didn't have any friends! I didn't have the full college experience, which is fine. But I did miss out a bit.

I'd like to be known first as *just* a climber—an *all-around* climber. But I'm primarily a sport climber. I used to be mostly a competition climber, but I've phased out of that. I've outgrown competition climbing. I want to continue to push myself in sport, but I want to explore all other aspects of climbing as well. I ice and mixed climb, and I want to get into traditional climbing more. I'd love to do big walls. I've summited Mount Everest, and I'd really like to continue to explore the mountains, perhaps doing more technical peaks.

What I want is to be a climber. Climbing is who I am. I started so young that I don't really remember who I was *as a person* before climbing. It defines who I am. It's taught me almost everything. It's not just a sport; it's the way I live. It's my community and my relationships. It's my family, and all the places I've visited.

ENJOYING THE SPORT

What I love most about climbing is the overall experience I have when I'm traveling. I love seeing different places and cultures, meeting new people, and forming relationships around the world. Without climbing I wouldn't have that. So in a way, it's not really about the act of climbing anymore. It's evolved into a lifestyle I appreciate, and it teaches me a lot about myself.

The thing I like *least* about climbing is that it can sometimes seem one-dimensional. With my lifestyle, sometimes I feel I don't use my brain enough, because I'm always traveling and focusing on climbing. There are times when I lose motivation because I'm not feeling engaged. Maybe it's just balance that I need? It's hard when your job, your passion, and your hobby are all rolled into one. This lifestyle is *amazing,* but at times it can be overwhelming. I start to set expectations for myself and put pressure on myself, when maybe I should just step back and let go.

LESSONS

I learned a lot about dealing with stress from competition climbing, because it's definitely the most intense form of the sport. It's the most intense, because you're not *supposed* to be competing against other people, but you *are.* You can't really escape the feeling of being competitive with your friends.

In a way I had to distance myself from what I learned in comps, because I was so intense and focused. Occasionally I start to slide back into that, and I have to remind myself that intensity is not really what climbing is for me anymore.

So I took some lessons away from competition climbing, but I also had to let go of other things I learned in order to appreciate the sport in a whole new way. For instance, I used to put a lot of pressure on myself to train all the time, to always be at a certain level, and to always have a certain amount of fitness. But I realized that if I want climbing to be my life, I can't be that way. If I do, my life's going to be a roller-coaster ride. There's naturally going to be peaks and valleys, and I have to learn to accept them because otherwise I'll just burn out. Professional athletes who compete at a really high level don't do it their entire lives. They move on. But with climbing you don't have to retire. You can move on to other types of climbing.

Emily Harrington in the Super Final, on her way to winning the 2008 Sport Climbing Series National Championship at Momentum Climbing Gym, Sandy, Utah.

So I'm starting to realize it's okay not to be at the top. It's okay to do other things. It's okay to go on a climbing trip with friends and just go *tribe climbing* for a weekend and top-rope 5.9! I've learned that climbing can be the most enjoyable thing ever.

MOUNT EVEREST

I've evolved from being a serious climbing competitor to a serious outdoor sport climber focused on climbing 5.14. Then I got a little bored with sport climbing, so I thought I should try mixed climbing and ice climbing. Then I was asked to go to Mount Everest and I thought, "That sounds cool, I should do that too." There was a point when I never would have considered Everest, because you can't go to Everest and come back and still climb 5.14! It just doesn't work that way. And that's a *big lesson* that I'm still trying to accept [laughs].

In 2008 I joined The North Face team and became good friends with Conrad Anker, our team captain. Maybe he saw some sort of interest or potential in me. I'm not sure. But he asked if I'd be interested in climbing Everest in 2012. At the time I was going through a lot of changes, personally and with my climbing, and I saw it as a good opportunity. So I said yes. In some ways, I suppose I didn't really think it would happen. It was one of those things where it was still two years away! "Whatever! We'll see what happens. But yes, I'm on board."

Then Conrad called again and confirmed the trip was happening. "Are you in?" So I had to make a decision. I was planning to go sport climbing in Spain, but instead I went and lived in a tent on a glacier for three months. It was really an amazing experience in both positive and negative ways.

We were sponsored by The North Face, a well-known retailer of outdoor equipment and apparel, but the trip was also a partnership with National Geographic, the Mayo Clinic, and Montana State University. So part of the expedition was to participate in medical research. Actually, that was a big part of it.

Doctors did a bunch of tests on us before, during, and after the expedition. They were trying to make a connection between the effects of altitude and cardiovascular disease, because a lot of the symptoms that people experience at altitude are similar to the symptoms of heart disease. My understanding is that they were looking for connections so the research could be used to find treatments and cures. To me that was cool, because it was one of the first times I felt like my climbing had the potential to help other people.

We also did some geological research on the mountain that had not been done before because it's such a harsh environment. Our Sherpa team carried a GPS device to the summit and remeasured the altitude. We also collected rock samples. Apparently, scientists didn't precisely know how old Everest is, so the samples helped determine that, and there were a bunch of other studies I didn't understand [laughs].

Of all my climbing accomplishments, I'm most proud of climbing Everest. I know that's a bit strange for a sport climber to say, because Everest is not considered a technically difficult climb. Physically it wasn't as demanding as other things I've done, but mentally it was the most difficult thing I've ever had to do. In terms of learning about myself and changing me as a person, it had the most profound effect. In fact, I'm still learning about the effects. It was a super eye-opening, interesting, amazing experience. I'm still realizing what a trip like that can do for you.

It is the most challenging thing I've ever done mentally, because it was so raw and real. I had never experienced mountains like that before. I'd been to Nepal and seen how big the mountains are there and how amazing and powerful they are, but I'd never climbed one. So Everest was my first big peak. In fact it was my first time over twelve thousand feet. In normal life you don't experience that kind of power and emotion in yourself, other people, or the environment. We experienced it for nearly three months. It was hard just to be up there that long with the same people and to be going through all this uncomfortable stuff in really cold, extreme temperatures. It was hard physically and, in a way, monotonous. And there were a lot of challenging occurrences this year (2012) in terms of deaths on the mountain. I'd never had to face that before.

It's the kind of environment that strips you down so you find out who you really are and who everyone else is. And the relationships that I formed with the members of the team are much stronger than the relationships I've formed with climbing partners on other climbs.

In comparison modern life is easy, comfortable, and indulgent. I guess that's why mountaineers love to *suffer* [laughs]. I finally figured it out!

Climbing Everest is basically walking up a big hill, but we had some of the best athletes in the world there. Out of nine of us, only six summited. Those aren't great odds. It was pretty amazing to feel the effects of the altitude and how much your body gets worn down just by taking the next step. Literally walking just ten feet was hard. I've had a lot of personal challenges in my life, and Everest is right at the top. Maybe I found it a greater challenge because of the extended period of time we were there, all the personal things I was going through, and all the drama between different team members that was happening on the mountain. Sure, it was a big adventure, but people don't realize that big adventures of this type can also involve spending a good part of two months sitting in a tent. When I arrived at base camp, I had a chest infection that didn't go away for two weeks, and I stayed in the tent the entire time! I didn't eat, and I didn't really sleep. I was at 17,500 feet. My body was truly struggling, and this was only the very beginning of the climb! I thought, I can't even walk to the bathroom. There's no way I'm going to be able to

Emily Harrington rides The Great White Behemoth (12b) Ten Sleep.

climb this mountain. Looking back it was a great adventure, but while it was happening, it wasn't great. It was miserable. Definitely not fun.

STRENGTHS

I think when it comes to climbing, my greatest strength is the confidence I have to be able to accomplish or succeed in something—whatever it may be. Simultaneously, I'm able to keep things in perspective and not underestimate or overestimate what I'm trying to do. A good example is Everest. I knew I could do it. I knew I was capable of it, but in no way did I underestimate how difficult it would be. This ability to keep things in perspective and maintain confidence helps me, whether I'm working a sport route or climbing a big mountain.

CAREER

If you want to become a professional climber, go for it. But also know that you've got to be in it for life. You have to *really want* to be a climber and that doesn't include only competition climbing. I'd encourage you to explore other aspects of life as well. Go to school and study and find out if there are other things you're interested in. Maintaining balance is important. You may find out in the end that yes, you want to climb, but you may also want to be a doctor. Life shouldn't be just about climbing.

THE FUTURE

Climbing is a lifelong activity for me. The great thing about climbing is that it's not boring. Sure, I got tired of competitions and switched to climbing outside. I got tired of that, so I started ice climbing. And after ice climbing, I went back to rock climbing. Climbing's easy to switch things up. I don't think I'll ever get bored of it.

RELATIONSHIPS

Is it better to have a boyfriend who climbs? That's a good question! I'm still trying to figure that one out, and I don't have an answer [laughs]. I could date someone who doesn't climb and doesn't understand climbing, but at the same time, climbing at a professional level requires total focus and intensity, and that might be difficult for a non-climbing partner to understand. So I don't know. Balance is hard to find. But in a way that's the challenge of all relationships.

I think I want a family. I don't know [laughs]. Yeah. I do. I want a family and kids, but that's really in the distant future.

OTHER PASSIONS

Outside of climbing, I enjoy running and skiing. I like doing things outside and being outside. I've gotten into surfing a bit, even though I'm really bad. In fact I'm terrible. But I enjoy it. As for nonsports activities, I really enjoy writing. I find it to be cathartic and meditative. I like taking pictures with my iPhone. I like reading. Just normal stuff. Socializing. I'm really social. I like being around people and being with my friends.

Emily Harrington connects the dots on School's Out (10d) Ten Sleep.

How do you psych yourself up for a hard route?

I don't psych myself up. In a way I psych myself down, because I don't like to get too nervous. I tell myself it's just a route. It's always going to be there, so it's not a big deal. I look at it as an opportunity to perform well and do my best. When I start putting pressure on myself and getting nervous, I say to myself, "Why are you even doing this if you're not enjoying it?" Life's too short to do things that aren't fun.

What's your favorite place to climb?

My favorite place to climb is Rifle Mountain Park in Colorado, because I started climbing outside there. It's where I've had my most important sends in sport climbing. I love Rifle because it's really complicated, and you have to figure things out. It's like a puzzle.

My favorite routes are all the ones at Rifle that took me the longest to figure out. The routes where you get on and think, "Wow, I can't do this move! I don't know how to do this move!" Then slowly, you whittle away at it. That feeling you get when you begin understanding the sequence, when things start to click, is truly what makes climbing worthwhile for me and what makes project- ing worthwhile.

If you could offer one essential tip to other climbers, what would it be?

Try to keep things in perspective and see the bigger picture. Always be true to yourself, and don't let anyone else tell you what's right for you. In climbing and in life, follow your own path, because I've done things based on other people's opinion and it never turns out how I want. So that's what I've learned [laughs].

How do you train?

I train to increase my power, because I'm naturally better at endurance—that is, hang- ing on for a long time. I've figured out a good method for maintaining endurance, and I don't necessarily need to train for it anymore. As long as I'm strong and have power, I can do harder moves easier, and therefore I don't need as much endurance. So I focus on doing a lot of pull-ups and big-muscle exercises to get stronger physically.

When I'm training, I don't climb every day. I'll climb two days on and one day off, for about a week. Then that will be too exhaust- ing, and I'll take two days off. I listen to my body. I avoid climbing too much when I'm doing a lot of finger workouts, because I'm scared of getting injured. I have not been injured ever, and I'd like to keep it that way! So rest is important. If I ever feel tweaky or anything other than simple muscle fatigue, I stop and rest.

LISA HATHAWAY

I want to be Lisa Hathaway when I grow up. I don't know anyone more stoked about life or more beloved by her friends. When I spend time with Lisa, I feel like I have a personality deficiency—as though I'm lacking in the essential daily vitamins and minerals of *joie de vivre*.

Lisa is the climbing ambassador of her hometown of Moab, Utah, where she welcomes all the strays (human and otherwise) who stop by to visit. In her book, *Learning to Fly*, Steph Davis describes Lisa as "a six-foot tall, blond . . . wildlife biologist, [who] was the heart of Moab's climbing social scene. She lived surrounded by her dogs, friends, and visitors, in a remodeled hen house she called the Bird Shack. Her door was literally always open, which meant there were typically at least three random climbers to be found on her couch at any one time, sometimes to her chagrin."

At night Lisa wanders the canyons calling for the owls and raptors that she studies. She plays guitar in several different bands and spends her days climbing and bouldering. She's made the *only known* female ascent of Aesthetics (5.13) and the first female ascents of the Mossacre and MossD (both 5.13), the Flying Elvises (5.13), Reckon So (12+), Slice of Ice (13b,) the Black Mamba (12+), and Hot Stuff (13-). These are all sport climbs located in Mill Creek Canyon in the La Sal Mountains above Moab, and as anyone who has climbed in Mill Creek knows, it's not a place for the faint of heart. The ratings are stout, and the runouts are thought provoking.

When it comes to bouldering, Lisa made the first female ascent of the Chaos (v8), the Hueco

Left, Cover girl Lisa Hathaway high above the canyons of Southern Utah. Above, Climber and lead guitarist Hathaway jams with her band in Moab, Utah.

Traverse (v7), the Hell Belly (v8, standing start), and the Black Angus (v7) problems at Big Bend outside Moab. And some of her favorite trad first ascents include Kiss of the Spider Women (12-), Chasin' Skirt (11+), Full Moon Apology (11), and Superfly (12-).

Lisa is a strong advocate of giving back to the climbing community by establishing new routes, mentoring young climbers, and helping to preserve America's climbing heritage. She's a member of the board of directors of Friends of Indian Creek, an advocacy group serving as a liaison between climbers, landowners, and the land and wildlife managers who administer public lands in southern Utah. Lisa's good humor and background as a climber and biologist make her an ideal bridge between the different interests.

ROOTS

My name's Lisa Hathaway. I was born in Yarmouth, Maine, in 1965, and I grew up in Maine. During my junior year of college, I did a biological field survey in the Mojave Desert. After college, I felt compelled to return to the desert, so I made a drastic lifestyle change by moving from the lush East Coast to hot, stark, Moab, Utah.

The first time I went climbing was when I was still living back east. I'd been asking friends who were climbers to take me, and a friend from high school agreed. I was intrigued when I heard them talking about going to North Conway and Cathedral Ledge in New Hampshire. So I said, "I want to go!" And they said, "You're a girl. We're not taking *you* climbing." But eventually I talked them into it. And I was *instantly smitten.*

I'd been working at the clothing company L.L.Bean in an area called the Knife Island [laughs]. The Knife Island had a TV for playing videos. So whenever I worked, I'd put on *Masters of Stone,* a video series of rock climbers in action in locations around the world. I'd watch those videos, and knew I *had* to try climbing! I saw Lynn Hill, Ron Kauk, and Dan Osman in those videos, and I was completely infatuated with bringing climbing into my life.

So I decided to take a volunteer position with the US National Park Service in Moab. I told everybody in Maine that I was going out west to be a climber [laughs]. My coworkers gave me some climbing gear and an old pair of EB climbing shoes as going-away presents. I resoled the EBs with stealth rubber and moved to Moab. I thought, "Okay, where do I meet climbers? I *want* to go climbing!" Really. I was that naive [laughs].

Since that time I've viewed climbing as integral to my life. I spend gobs of time doing it. I consider myself an advanced recreational climber, but one who spends an *exorbitant* amount of time being advanced. Yes, I can imagine a life that doesn't involve climbing, but would I want that life? No.

CAREER

In college I was a biology major with the intention of one day magically becoming an orthopedic surgeon. In fact, I worked for some orthopedic surgeons. Then one day one of the doctors sat me down and said, "Are you sure you want to do this? Because you seem like the kind of person who wants to have a life, and if you go to medical school, that's going to have a significant impact on living the life you seem you might enjoy."

Lisa Hathaway "crushes" Crush the Skull (12+) Mill Creek Canyon, Utah.

He had a point, so I shifted my focus to wildlife biology, and I loved it. I loved the backpacking, camping, transecting small mammals, and identifying plants. I enjoyed studying birds of prey, and I am still doing that work to this day.

ENJOYING THE SPORT

I love everything about climbing. I like the beautiful places, the physical exertion, and the problem solving. I'm drawn to an intricate, rather than *thuggy*, style of climbing. I like seeing things come together. As a kid, I participated in figure skating. That's a sport in which you build a skating routine for yourself move by move. You build your skill set, and in the end, you have a *project/program* you're trying to *send*.

That same approach carried into my climbing, especially when I discovered *redpoint climbing,* which climbers call *projecting.* I really like the whole process of starting out feeling useless [laughs], then building something that comes together as you learn one move on top of the other, until you can *redpoint* an entire route.

But ultimately I love being active outside, where you can have your friends and your dogs. It's like the Saturday picnics many of us enjoyed as kids, but you get to do it *all the time.* And you get to go *climbing,* which is *totally cool.*

DESERT CLIMBING

Moab is a challenging place to learn, because most beginner climbers learn what's called *face* climbing, which is more natural, like climbing a ladder of holds on the *face* of the rock. When I first came to Moab, I was told I was going *crag* climbing, and I said, "Okay. I've done some of those *crag* climbs on Cathedral Ledge, you know."

Then I get to the base of a *desert* crag, and I see there are just these pure *splitters,* that is, cracks *splitting* the rock. Not much else. There are these cracks, or fissures, and that's where you place various body parts, primarily your hands and feet, for upward progress. They range in size from just big enough for a fingertip to the width of a body. Aside from the cracks, the rock's *really* smooth, and there are few features to hang from or step on. For me it wasn't intuitive to put my hands and feet into cracks and wedge them in various ways in order to create a handhold or

foothold. You're using a lot of friction and body tension to stay on the rock rather than simply hanging on to a face hold.

CHROMOSOMES

I've been asked if women approach climbing differently from men, but I feel there are more differences between *individuals* than between genders. When I started, there were no indoor climbing gyms. Sport climbing wasn't widespread. It existed, but it wasn't the norm. Same with bouldering. In those days it was considered appropriate for a beginner to become an *understudy* to a more experienced climber. You would follow routes. In that way, you'd learn slowly but surely how to place gear. When you did lead, you began on a route you knew, because it wasn't considered good style to fall or hang on the rope. It was a slower approach. But it was that way for everyone, not just women. Nowadays I think young girls and guys are on more equal footing, because most start in a gym at a much younger age.

RELATIONSHIPS

When it comes to relationships, I don't think having them as a climber is any harder than it is for other people. But that said, I think maintaining a relationship is one of the hardest tasks humans, with their big brains and opposable thumbs have to contend with. Look at every other mammal species, and it seems so simple. They eat. They sleep. They reproduce, and sometimes they kill each other. I guess it's the same with us, except we have this alleged higher consciousness that causes us to ponder everything and then totally screw it up.

Climbing is a really selfish activity. But crocheting can be selfish too if you're so into crocheting, you'd rather be crocheting than be with
your friends. And yes, climbing can be that way.
I admit there are times (probably about nine out
of ten), when I'd rather be at the crag than having dinner with my friends. Absolutely.

But you should always have enough space
in your life to have a cup of coffee with a friend.
And that goes double for your family. Relationships are like a garden. You have to tend them.
Sometimes you have to weed! You have to water.
Neither gardens nor strong relationships happen
by accident.

RISK

I've been fortunate, because the climbing I do
is relatively safe. One time, however, I nearly
fell when my belayer lowered me off the end
of the rope. That situation was 100 percent my
responsibility, because I had a less-experienced
climber belaying me, and I should've tied a knot
in the other end of the rope before starting. The
onus was mine to ensure the safety of both us.
Yet the universe gave me a get-out-of-jail-free
card, because I grabbed a tree branch just before
I watched the end of the rope slide through the
belay device and out of my belayer's hands.

One other close call was the time a big block
came my way during a first ascent and took a big
chunk out of the rope, but it didn't take a chunk
out of me. Thank goodness!

LOSS

I have lost friends to climbing. When Micah
Dash and Jonny Copp died, that was the first
incident that really hit home. You realize your

Lisa Hathaway on Crush the Skull (12+).

friends are not coming back. They're not coming
to Moab in the fall to climb with you. Micah and
Jonny were a big loss for the climbing community and for me personally. Sue Nott is another.
Losing friends drives home the fact life's short,
so you better make the most of it. I'm sad to
lose my friends. I'm happy they were doing what
they loved, but it's a big price to pay.

FEAR

When you go climbing, you always have two
companions with you, and their names are *fear*
and *anxiety*. That's part of leaving the ground,
and it's part of the human experience.

I went through a phase in which I was rather debilitated by fear. Then I realized it wasn't fear of falling or fear of heights, it was fear of losing control. I also realized that fear is what keeps us alive. Fear is what keeps us from walking off the cliff's edge. Fear is *life preserving*. So I learned it's important to acknowledge we have fear and why then look at it rationally. As climbers, we need to ask: Do I really have something to worry about here or am I just making it up?

These days I let fear come, and I try to let it go. And if I can't let it go? Well, hopefully, I'm not sixteen pitches up some alpine climb in a random valley in Pakistan, and I can just pack my bag and go home!

Sometimes you're in situations in which your fear could literally hurt or kill you, and you need to accept that and say, "Okay, I'm terrified now. I'm thirty feet above a crappy piece of gear, but my only choice is to go up, so calm down, and get this done."

Some people say they never get scared. Personally, I think they're not being honest. But if *saying* they don't get scared helps them *deal* with their fear, then that's great. Everybody has their own way. The fact is if you want to be a climber, then you need to face the fact that you're going to get scared and try to deal with it rationally.

PERSONAL GROWTH

Climbing has probably changed me in many ways I don't even recognize. I've modified my life quite a bit in order to enjoy climbing. At one point I realized I was already in some sort of early semi-retirement, and that meant when I actually reached retirement age I would probably have to get a job and start working *really*

Lisa Hathaway does the twist on The Bleeding (14-) Mill Creek Canyon.

hard, [laughs], because I took this youthful path of enjoying myself as much as possible.

Climbing has also probably given me confidence in situations I don't even recognize. It's natural it would do that. Climbing gives you a sense of purpose. When I've gone through low times in my life, climbing's been my refuge.

STRENGTHS

I'd say my best asset is my finger strength, which is a bit of an oddity for someone my size. Relatively speaking, I'm a large climber (six feet tall). I have a really *low* strength to body weight ratio, which is a distinct *disadvantage* for the climbing I enjoy, such as sport and bouldering. But luckily, I have good finger strength. If I can get my little fingers on something, I usually hold on.

I also have good flexibility. When I've had injuries limiting my flexibility, my bouldering ability drops about six V grades because I can't high step or stem.

And finally, *psych* is one of the least talked about, but most beneficial, things a climber can have. People always try to attribute excellence in climbing to diet. Or training. Or genetics. Obviously all those things play a role, but if you really look at the best climbers in the world, their *psych* for climbing, their motivation and determination, is what makes them stand out. Of course people wish they were *smaller*. People wish they were *taller*. People wish they were *more flexible,* but ultimately if you get out of bed in the morning and you *really want* to go climbing, if you are *driven* to pursue your passion, that's going to be the biggest factor and the biggest strength anyone can possibly have.

LESSONS

Climbing is a constantly moving lesson that we carry over to the rest of our lives. You learn about frustration, and that makes you learn patience. You learn about pushing your limits. You learn to work with others. Mostly you learn about composure, confidence, and the ability to get things done. Climbing teaches that if you just take one small tiny step at a time, then you can achieve enormous and lofty goals.

There's so much to be learned. Sometimes it's obvious things like, hold on loosely, but don't let go! And sometimes it's something simple like,

"Take your foot off that nubbin, fool!" Let your body go where it wants to go, then you can do the move.

I constantly have to learn not to allow self-destructive thoughts like, "Oh I can't do this. It's too hard." Sometimes when climbing, you have to deal with self-defeating thinking on a move-by-move basis. And at the same time, recognize there's going to be negativity. There's going to be challenges. Good days and bad days. Ultimately what I learn from climbing is how fortunate we all are to be living in this place and time and to have the freedom to indulge in the activities we choose to do.

ACCOMPLISHMENTS

Many people assume that a climber's most important climbing experience is their hardest climb. But I'm definitely a social creature. A lot of my most important moments in climbing have more to do with who I was with or where I was.

For example, early in my climbing career I was with friends in New Hampshire. We canoed across a lake, looking for an obscure Jimmy Dunn cliff (of which there are many). We were determined to find this wall, and eventually we did. The route was supposed to be 5.9, but in New England 5.9 can mean anything.

I don't know if we succeeded or not. I have a feeling we didn't. Then we canoed back across the lake, hunted for wild mushrooms in the dying light, and made our dinner in a backwoods cabin in the forest.

To me that memory encapsulates everything climbing's brought to my life. The actual movement over rock is part of the package, but it's not the be-all and end-all of the trip.

CHALLENGES

Sometimes I'm devastated because I can't do a route. I come home and my friends say, "Poor Lisa, you feel like a failure because you didn't do your project today. Boohoo! Do you realize you do stuff other people only dream about? How cool is that?" I think that's a really good perspective to have. Overall, I try to treat challenges as something to be grateful for and as opportunities to learn, as opposed to something that's knocking me down.

MUSIC

Playing the guitar is another thing I love. It's also something I don't think I'm good at. I came to climbing late in life, and I'm a late-in-life musician as well. But I really love it! Just as with climbing, there's always a new challenge. Because you know, I'm pretty much a *5.10 guitar player,* but I want to be a *5.13 guitar player!* The difference is that in climbing I can see logical steps to get better: If I need to get stronger, then I'll do pull-ups. But with music there are so many factors. When you climb, you want to make things flow, but you can get by if they don't. But when you're playing music, you really want things to flow and sound good.

ADVICE

If I could offer one piece of advice, it would be to do what feels right for you, not what feels right for someone else. My parents have always been pretty supportive of everything I do, but they were definitely *not stoked* about climbing. But at the same time, they trusted that I needed to do

what I enjoyed. So yeah, maybe I'm *not* going to graduate school *ever.* But if I change my mind, graduate school will still be there. Climbing as hard as I want to climb, however, will not be possible forever. I believe you've got to pursue the dream you believe in and realize you will have to sacrifice other things. That sacrifice might be a good job. So if the job's the most important thing, grab it. Climbing will still be there. If you really love climbing, do it because it brings you joy. As the Stephen Stills song says, "if you don't have love in your heart, then Baby, you ain't got no right to do it at all!"

THE FUTURE

Given the way my life unfolded, I missed out on the whole road-tripping thing—living out of the back of a truck and climbing. So I find myself dreaming of spending a whole delicious year on the road, going to Yosemite National Park in California, to the Black Canyon of the Gunnison national park and to Estes Park in Colorado, and to all the other great places I haven't had a chance to properly enjoy. Seriously, for the amount of time I've spent climbing, I'm probably the least-traveled climber on the planet!

Beyond that, I'll be the old grandmother who gets wheeled out to the boulders in her wheelchair, shouting beta at the young upstarts. "Hey you! Young whippersnapper, spot your friend better!" And, "You there! Brush that hold when you're done" [laughs]. So even if I can't actually be out there doing those problems, I'll want to go everyday to encourage or scold the upcoming youth.

How do you psych yourself up for a hard route?

Some people like to get amped, get their Grrrr on. But I find it better to seek calmness through preparation. I've always been one of the 20 percent for whom visualization doesn't work very well. For me it's better to know I have done my homework, feel prepared, and have a game plan.

What's your favorite place to climb?

I'm so fortunate to live in Moab and to have access to beautiful red rock towers and crags. Then I started climbing in Millcreek in the La Sal Mountains. If you ask anybody where they think Lisa's favorite climbing area is, everyone will say, "Oh, Millcreek. Hands down." And absolutely, if I had to pick one climbing area, it would be Millcreek. But Kentucky's Red River Gorge would be a pretty close second, if you could move it to Moab [laughs].

As far as favorite routes, there's a Millcreek route I've climbed probably a thousand times. It's called Techno Christ (5.12). It's my baseline. My litmus test. Sometimes it's my warm-up and sometimes it's my project, but it's always home base. The thing you tag, then you're safe.

How do you train?

I've heard people say, "Oh, I don't train," or "Training's bad." I hear people say that Chris Sharma never trained. Well, hellooo, he went to the gym every single day! Essentially, if you're doing something more than three days a week, then you're training, and training's something you have to do if you want to get better.

If your goal's simply to climb at the level you're at right now—for the rest of your life—and you'd enjoy that, okay fine. But if you want to improve, then you've got to take measures to improve. And the first thing is take stock of where your weaknesses lie, and then work on those weaknesses. And personally, a lack of strength is my weakness. So when I train, it's going to be strength based. And that might be doing hang-board sets or climbing on steep plastic, basically doing things that make me feel uncomfortable, such as thuggy moves and open-handed moves. Believe me, I am not drawn to these activities, but I force myself to pursue that type of training.

How do you prepare for a climb?

Before I start a project, I evaluate it. Does it favor my strengths? Does it favor my weaknesses? I tend to be drawn to routes that target my weaknesses. Then I begin training, both on the rock and off, to develop those weaknesses into strengths. For instance, when I train for pinch strength, I work on routes that are pinchy and ask friends, "What would you do to get better pinch strength?" Then when pinch comes to shove, I have a plan.

LYNN HILL

We call Lynn the sorceress because she magically finds a way through any sequence no matter how hard.

—LAUREN LEE MCCORMICK

More than any other individual, Lynn Hill has been called a hero, a mentor, and an inspiration by the other climbers featured in this book. I first met Lynn in 1994 in Yosemite soon after she'd free-climbed the Nose in a day, and I was struck by how thoughtful she was. In my experience most climbers simply put on their shoes and jump on the rock, but not Lynn.

Regardless of what she is climbing, whether she is working out the intricacy of Yosemite's Midnight Lightning or a run-out 5.10 slab, she takes her time. She looks, analyzes, and previsualizes before committing to the moves. In fact, in all the years I've been involved in climbing, I've never known anyone who thinks more deeply or speaks more clearly about the technical aspects of the sport than Lynn. Optimizing performance, both on and off the rock, is the guiding principle of her life.

As a climbing beginner in Southern California, Lynn's natural ability caught the attention of some of the best climbers of the day—John Long, John Bachar, and other *stone masters* who were pioneering modern free-climbing in America. Lynn's background as a high school gymnast gave her insight into the benefit of systematic

training and rehearsal of movement, which seems common sense today but which was a radical rethinking of the prevailing style and ethics for climbers in the seventies.

Perhaps Lynn's most important asset and the key to her lasting significance is her ability

Left, Lynn Hill soars on The Bird in the Ak-Su Region of the Pamir Mountains, Kyrgyzstan. Above, In her natural element, Hill relaxes on Hang Em High (12c) Rifle Mountain Park, Colorado.

to maintain an open mind. While many of the best climbers of the eighties were pushed to the sidelines or gave up the sport entirely because of rigidly held beliefs, Lynn embraced sport and competition climbing when they appeared. She went on to excel in both, becoming the first woman to *on-sight* 13b. In 1991 she became the first woman to climb 5.14. During her competitive career, Lynn won more than thirty international competitions, including placing first at the Rock Master Festival in Arco, Italy, five times.

But it's Lynn's first free ascent by any climber of the Nose on Yosemite's El Capitan in 1993, followed by her one-day free-climb of the same route a year later, that are her defining achievements, and they remain pivotal accomplishments in climbing history. The Nose is the most-famous big-wall climb in the world, and Lynn's accomplishments created an entirely new paradigm of what's possible. It dramatically ushered in the era of modern free-climbing still unfolding today. As of 2013, Tommy Caldwell is the only other climber to repeat Lynn's feat of free-climbing the Nose in a day.

Today Lynn lives in Boulder, Colorado, with her son, Owen. Her memoir, *Climbing Free: My Life in the Vertical World*, is an engaging, behind-the-scenes look at three of the most interesting and formative decades in climbing history. The book opens with a description of a ground fall from the top of the Styx Wall in Buoux in the south of France that came a hairbreadth from ending Lynn's life. Anyone who's climbed at Buoux shakes their head in astonishment that someone could fall from the top of Styx and survive.

Currently, Lynn's hard at work on yet another monumental project. This time she's putting her thirty-five years of experience into an instructional video. I've seen some of the footage, and once again, Lynn has the potential to set the standard for the way people think and practice climbing for years to come.

ROOTS

I'm Lynn Hill. I was born in 1961, and I began climbing in the mid 1970s. I'm a well-rounded climber, because I started by doing traditional climbs, figuring things out, and taking responsibility for myself, for where the route goes, and how to place protection. This background allows me to climb on just about any rock formation in the world. When I started, I did plenty of bouldering, multipitch routes, and the occasional big-wall climb. On trips to Yosemite I bouldered in Camp Four, did many of the classic free routes, and climbed El Cap, Half Dome, and many of the shorter big walls. I thought of these adventures as a kind of *vertical retreat,* a pilgrimage into the unknown to experience a real adventure. The bigger the wall, the greater the chance of something unexpected happening. That can be uncomfortable, but I think hardship builds character and the ability to adapt. This was a great foundation for me in learning how to adapt to many different kinds of rock and how to get along with other people.

Because I started climbing in California, I learned the values of the *stone masters'* generation. That is, you start from the ground and free-climb without using any aid from your equipment for upward progress. You don't preview the route from the top, nor do you *top-rope* the route before trying to lead it, although I did occasionally top-rope some routes on overhanging

Lynn Hill explores Outer Space (10b), the Bastille, Eldorado Canyon, Colorado.

faces that were not possible to lead using natural protection. I approached each climb as if I was standing in front of a mountain like Mount Everest. If you want to climb a mountain, you can't just run around to the top and throw a rope down. You have to figure out each step from the ground to the top. I embraced that *ground-up* approach as a style of *fair means.* Simply getting to the top was *not* my goal. I wanted to get to the top using the *purest style* possible.

In 1983 I moved from California to the Shawangunk Mountains in New York, and it was a turning point in my climbing style. I suddenly found myself on increasingly difficult routes that offered little protection.

At that point, I began questioning the strict "traditional style." I was a kid of the sixties, and even though I wasn't old enough to protest the Vietnam War, the liberal spirit of those times influenced me. I grew up believing that nature is our best teacher as opposed to some artificial set of rules. Climbing was a means of interpreting nature in my own way. And I had to. I'm a small person, and the methods used by the men I climbed with didn't work for me. When I started climbing, I was fourteen years old, and I learned to listen to my own sense of intuition about what felt right. I think that's part of the beauty of climbing: We all have our own unique style and personal expression.

So I didn't like the idea of rules, but the fact is, climbers *were* all following rules, and they were pretty strict when it came to the idea of not hanging on the rope. For instance, if you fell, then you'd be lowered back to the ground to start again. It was considered cheating to rest on gear to figure out the moves.

During that same period, climbers in Europe were developing what we now call *sport climbing.* This was before the Internet, so I didn't really know much about what was going on in Europe. It was rare for American climbers to have enough money to travel to Europe. I'd heard stories from Russ Clune, who went on climbing trips there and had even participated in the first international climbing competition in Arco, Italy, in 1985. Though I didn't know much about the style of climbing on limestone, I did know the Europeans didn't follow the *no hang dogging* ethic, which was a very controversial issue at the time in the United States.

This issue came to a head at the annual American Alpine Club meeting in 1986. I was invited to participate in a panel discussion concerning the issues of *hang dogging* and rappel-placed bolts. The panel included climbers from across the United States: Henry Barber, John Bachar, Ron Kauk, Todd Skinner, Christian Griffith, Randy Vogel, Alan Watts, and Rob Robinson. I was the only woman, and I literally sat in the middle of this group of men with conflicting opinions on both sides.

Since I have a gymnastics background, it was easy for me to understand the logic of how practice and repetition are the best way to optimize technique and improve as a climber. It seemed this disagreement over one's choice of style was turning into an ego war, and that's not what climbing is about for me. I believe that as long as you're not taking something away from others in terms of damaging the rock or ruining the experience for others in some way, then everyone should be free to climb in whatever style they choose.

For me the point is to *get better.* I like to be challenged, and it was really exciting to learn and evolve as a climber by working through the grades and mastering all the necessary skills involved to progress to the next level. It was exciting to go climbing in Europe and see all those overhanging limestone faces that were perfect for bolt-protected face climbing. You couldn't use traditional gear to protect those routes. You had to use bolts—bolts placed on rappel.

So I enjoyed being part of the transition from *trad* to *sport,* and sure, at times it was difficult to go against longstanding traditions. I still respect those fundamental values, and I'm grateful I learned to climb traditional routes in the purest style possible. Learning how to take responsibility for myself is an invaluable skill. I think we should all take responsibility for ourselves and then some. We're all connected.

DEFINITIONS

I don't like definitions. People ask me what my favorite climbing area is, and I don't have one. And I don't have a definition of what kind of climber I am, because that's not the way I think. As a climber, I like to do everything—bouldering, sport, and big walls. But *free-climb*ing is my main passion.

Diversity is what I like most. But when the gym is my only alternative, I'm happy to go there. I wouldn't say it's my favorite, but it's what I do most often, because I have limited time due to my role as a mother, along with everything else going on in my life.

PHILOSOPHY

I consider myself a spiritual person but not a religious person. I've studied formal religions a bit, and the religion that interests me most is Buddhism, because it's more of a philosophy. It's not a set of rules. It's an attitude based on an understanding of humanity. I find that interesting. That's been my greatest teacher, the combination of looking at my life through the lens of Buddhist thought and climbing as the exercise or practice.

Climbing's a moving meditation that's good for my soul. It's my medicine. If I don't climb, I don't feel good. I suppose I could replace climbing with another activity, but climbing's brought me closest to what I call my natural state of being, closest to a connection with *what is.*

I believe there's a higher order. You can call it God. But it's a kind of universal order that we all respect in order to function in the world. I try to be conscious, and climbing is one way to practice that. It's also my way of reflecting. I don't just think about how to do a move. My mood and ability to climb are influenced by my underlying motivation. When I look at a climb, I may get excited to climb it because it's beautiful, and aesthetics are important to me. That's why I like to climb outside.

TECHNIQUE

Sometimes there's an inverse relationship between the aesthetics of the place and the aesthetics of movement on the rock. For example, Rifle Mountain Park in Colorado is not an ugly place, but if you look at the rock, it's very shattered, and sometimes big chunks fall off, including formations with bolts in them. So it's a bit scary from that standpoint, but it's also really fun, challenging, and interesting, because it's so featured. Limestone has all these pockets and tiny features, so, particularly if you're small, there's

Lynn Hill makes Just Another Boy's Climb (12a) look easy, the Flatirons, Boulder, Colorado.

some little nubbin that can help you push in the right spot to keep your body in balance. This type of featured rock can help develop awareness of your center, your *still point* of balance, and also how to use *momentum,* so you arrive at a particular hold in a certain body position.

In order to climb this way, I use a lot of visualization, a skill I've developed as I've progressed and over time become more conscious of. That's why I'm producing an instructional video, because I find this type of visualization so

helpful. When I'm climbing, I'm able to imagine the space nearly 360 degrees around me—like a sphere. I see the geometry and the physics of movement; it's become second nature.

I think this spatial awareness began when I was a gymnast and through simpler activities, like climbing trees. It always felt natural for me to climb. But when I was a kid, I had no understanding of what rock climbing was. I'd never even seen a picture. So I climbed our light pole. I created this clamping technique with my knees, and I figured out how to create friction through opposition. It just came to me. It wasn't like, *"Oh, how do I do this?"*

In gymnastics you learn how to break movement into basic steps. So if you're learning how to do a back layout, first you learn how to do a cartwheel, and then you learn how to do a round off back handspring. Once you have that wired, you do it again, jumping as high as you can so you get enough height to do a back layout, or a layout with a full twist, or a double backflip. You have to believe your brain will carry out what you've mentally programmed it to do. And so I learned a lot about what to focus on during the learning process.

When I was trying to figure out the hardest moves on the Nose, I looked at the situation in a similar way. I'd see the angle of the holds. It's a bit like a game of *Twister*. You've got to have one hand *here,* one foot *there,* and you've got to maintain this precise position, even as your body's moving. You can't let those angles of force change, or you'll lose purchase and fall. Unless you're jumping dynamically, most of the time you have three points of contact with the rock, while either reaching or stepping to the next hold. You go from one tripod position to another. You have either two hands and one foot or two footholds and one handhold, but you're always reaching or stepping into the next tripod. I've been consciously aware of that process for a long time.

Not too many people think about climbing in this way. I asked Chris Sharma about it, and he doesn't seem to have a conscious approach at all. He just looks at the rock and instinctively knows how to move. There's one move of Sharma's that

fascinates me. It was a famous jump he made on Las Puntas, a stone arch in Spain. I believe it took him several seasons to successfully make the move. When you watch him jump, it's clear it's not just about strength. It's about Chris's body position at every moment from when he leaves the rock until he arrives in precisely the right body position with his hand on the hold. So to determine the proper angle, you draw a line perpendicular from it. Then you calculate the amount of force with which to jump. Too much force and you overshoot. Everything depends on where you're coming from and where you want to go next.

I can usually figure out the mechanics of movement by looking at the situation, but then I need to feel it in my body, too. I try to gauge the amount of force that is going to get you to that precise point on the rock in exactly the right position. When I find myself way above the ground, this is not just a concept, I rely on those visualization skills I learned in gymnastics.

Let's take Midnight Lightning for example (one of the world's most famous boulder problems located in Yosemite's Camp Four). There's a move on Midnight Lightning where I'm coming from underneath a steep bulge, and I have to jump to the "lightning bolt" hold and grab it so that my elbow is aligned at precisely the right angle. Everyone, even if they're taller, needs to end up with their elbow at about the same angle. The difference is if you're taller, you have better leverage between the two holds, whereas I have to jump and use a lot of force to stabilize my body as it swings out into space.

Once I catch it, my fingertips are totally extended and barely maintaining contact. All of this has to be timed perfectly with proper body tension. So it's timing and body tension, and obviously you have to have the strength to propel yourself upward and hang on. I enjoy the process of figuring out how to coordinate all these different factors. That's what's interesting. It's not just a matter of brute strength.

I'd say the first rule in climbing is not to fall. Right? When I first started climbing, I took that seriously because I didn't know how to place gear very well. I remember one of my first leads. I didn't want to stop to try to place protection, because it was so strenuous. I didn't know how to find restful positions that would help recover strength. So I kept climbing until I got so far out that I knew I had to stop and place some pro. For me, at that time, it wasn't an easy decision. Do I just keep climbing and not fall? Or should I stop and possibly get really pumped trying to place a solid piece? But you need gear. If not, why bring a rope?

So in that way I learned to take calculated risks. And later on those skills became more important, because when you're doing a first ascent and you don't know what's ahead, you don't want to use all your strength then risk falling where there may not be protection. You've got to figure out how to be really creative and rest whenever possible.

Let's say you're getting pumped. You know, the red light's going off, and "BEEP! BEEP!" The alarm's ringing. You just have to take a big breath, look at the situation, and say, "*Okay, I've got to get to that next hold. How's my body position? How can I make the next move?*"

Sometimes it helps to imagine what the geometry of the situation would look like from the perspective of an observer. I'll mentally draw a plumb line from the next handhold and then figure out where to look to find a foothold, I imagine what my body position will look like once I get my hand or a foot on the next hold. I usually anticipate one to two moves in advance.

When preparing to climb a challenging route, I mentally practice going through the moves. I remember how it feels when my body is in the right position. Or when trying to on-sight a hard route, I pay attention when "*it doesn't feel right,*" since I can "see" that I may come up an inch shy of the hold. I wait until I'm ready, and if I feel like I might be missing that one inch, I try putting my foot a little higher onto something that may not be as good, but might be in a better position once my hand arrives on the next hold.

OTHER PASSIONS

If I wasn't a climber, then I suppose I'd be involved with something that involves movement, music, or the martial arts, some sort of practice like that. Maybe yoga, but yoga's missing a few elements that climbing offers. I like the vertical, three-dimensional aspects of climbing. I don't know of any other activity that offers as much as climbing.

And, in my opinion, being in nature is always the best place for any activity. Going to the most beautiful places in the world, the most pristine natural environments is such a privilege!

RISK

My closest call was falling in Buoux. I fell over seventy feet, because I got distracted and forgot to finish tying my knot. I got distracted talking to someone. I didn't see the knot was unfinished, because it was hidden beneath my jacket. And the climb was easy, so I didn't feel the fear of falling that I might have felt if the climb were more difficult. My partner was also distracted by talking while I was climbing. This kind of situation is all too common in modern sport climbing.

When I got to the top, my belayer was still talking, so I thought I'd just pull on the other side of the rope to take up the slack before leaning back to be lowered. Instead, when I pulled on the rope, it slipped through my harness, and I fell seventy-two feet to the ground! Luckily, I didn't land on my head. I remember using my arms to keep myself from rotating backward. I also happened to hit a tree branch, which dislocated my elbow and slowed my fall. Then when I hit the ground, I landed on the flat part of my butt (my gluteus maximus), which absorbed the impact. I actually bounced about three feet in the air, and then landed face down in the dirt between two boulders. I was *very* lucky. If I'd hit one of those boulders, then I would have died or suffered more serious injuries. Most people don't fall that distance and walk away. I didn't exactly walk away, but three days later I was able to walk out of the hospital.

But that's part of life isn't it? That's part of the adventure, because we all have unexpected things happen, and sometimes we die as a result. Some people would say, "*Well, your time was up.*" After a close call like mine, some might decide to quit climbing and say, "I'm going to do everything I can in the future to avoid risk and no longer do anything dangerous."

I could have stopped then, but it never really occurred to me to quit climbing. Some may decide to quit if they have a near-death experience, but to me, this accident was like pulling out into traffic without looking, because you weren't focused. These types of things happen every day. It's not limited to climbing.

So I didn't think this accident was a good enough reason to stop climbing. *I love climbing.* Climbing *gives* me life. And perhaps one day it will also take my life. I don't know. But if that happens, I've already lived a great life. I'm fifty-one, and I'm happy I've made it this far. So I consider that day in Buoux to be my second birthday.

No matter what happens, you have to look at life and say this is what's meant to be. This is my path. This is what I need to learn. Say you broke your leg today, or discovered you had cancer, or you walked under a cliff and got hit by a rock. These things happen. So I just try to avoid *unnecessary* risks, and at the same time try to be very aware and conscious about the risks I choose.

For example, some days I feel totally comfortable climbing long *runouts*. Some people might say I'm being irresponsible. "*You call yourself a careful climber and a mother and say you try to avoid risk.*" I haven't fallen up to this point, but I suppose a rock could have hit me in the head or a hold could suddenly break at an inopportune moment. That's true. Even so, I don't usually risk taking ground falls. I try to remain within a certain range of risk and where I feel comfortable.

In comparison I wouldn't *free solo* like Alex Honnold does. He has no backup against unexpected things occurring, like rock fall or a bird flying out of a crack. But he feels comfortable doing that. That's his level of acceptable risk.

Lynn Hill isn't scared of Blocky Horror Show (12d) Rifle.

But for me, as a mother, I wouldn't consider that style of climbing.

I've developed the ability to be aware of where I am, and if I fall, I'm confident I will instinctively keep myself upright.

EQUALITY

Overall as a woman, I've felt primarily acceptance and support from the climbing community. In the beginning there weren't that many women, and guys really like having women around, so they welcomed me. But I remember once early on, after I'd done a hard boulder problem, I heard some guy say, *"Gee, I can't even do that move."* I think he assumed that because he was a man he could climb better than me.

But why would he think that? I was strong and flexible and very aware of my position on the rock. If you watched me climb, you would say, *"Wow! That's impressive."* Instead, he naturally assumed that a girl couldn't possibly climb better than a grown man.

That sort of chauvinistic attitude is limiting, because even now we're not even close to the maximum ability in climbing—for men or women. Years ago, I said, *"Someday people are going to be warming up on 5.13,"* and now that's true. I think if we adopted the training methods of gymnastics and applied them to climbing, standards would rise. Even twenty years ago, when I freed the Nose, I saw that climbing was still a young sport and that people weren't close to achieving their maximum potential. What I saw was that people were limited by their minds. I saw that having a rigid mindset is a detriment, not only when it comes to gender but also when dealing with the world at every level.

It's obvious women have a different approach to climbing than men. Like the classic story about the muscle-bound guy who can't get off the ground and the little girl who runs up the route because she's using balance and shifting her weight over her feet. She's not really pulling with her arms when she doesn't need to. The guy assumes, "I need to be strong to do this," so he wastes energy pulling himself up the rock instead of approaching the situation with a different attitude.

As climbers, we need to see *possibilities* instead of *limitations.* In that way, I think women

are the perfect complement to men. We complement each other in the style of climbing we're good at. And given the opportunity, women can now do the most physically demanding climbs, climbs that were previously reserved for the fraternity *of men.*

I believe each person should do his, or her, part whether on a climb or in a partnership of any kind. We need cooperation. We don't need to conquer anymore. That's an outdated mentality. For everyone to advance and progress and to find harmony and balance in the world, women should be included, heard, and given an equal chance. And I think climbing is a great way for women and girls to develop their confidence, their abilities, and their creativity in figuring out how to do a problem, how to work with others, and how to step outside the *me* focus and help everyone attain their goals.

Women don't need to play by the boys' rules. We need to honor our uniquely feminine style and approach. We should be more supportive of each other, rather than backstabbing one another. Haven't we had it hard enough? Why would anyone want to sabotage another person? To stand on top of the victory podium? *Really?* What's the meaning of success if it wasn't achieved honestly or with the right intention?

RELATIONSHIPS

I would *love* to be a housewife! I think it would be a great job [laughs]. But not if I wasn't free to climb! It would be great to be supported and to have the job of running the house.

I like being capable of taking care of myself. I also enjoy sharing my life with others. Men and women are on equal ground in the sense that we must all take responsibility for *ourselves,* regardless of marital status. If you find a great partner, then there's nothing wrong with getting married. Figuring out how to support each other and share good times together is an ongoing process that evolves over time.

As for roles, if one person happens to be good at cooking and it happens to be the man, great! If that's what they do best, then the other person can do the dishes. Of course, it's nice to have a partnership, but partnership is not on a piece of paper. It's not in a bank account, and it's no longer based on the traditional roles of the past.

ATTITUDE

I try to be open-minded in all aspects of life. In climbing that means being aware and paying attention in a certain way. I'm sure I see the rock differently than most people. When looking at the relief on the surface of a rock face, I see the shapes and angles of potential holds.

You have to be humble and get ego out of the way to see things openly. Let's say you're in a climbing competition. You think to yourself, "*Oh, I'm getting pumped. I'm going to fall! I'm not going to win!*" Or you think, "*Whoops! My foot slipped! Oh my, I'm climbing so badly!*" Your thoughts can carry you into panic if you believe them. Okay, your foot slipped, but you're still on the wall, and you can keep going if you don't freak out. Just put your foot *back on the wall and keep going.*

I shoot for the ideal, because it inspires me to go the furthest. My efforts may not lead me where I thought I was going, but they get me further than if I never tried. For example, I didn't climb El Cap without falling. That's what

I wanted to do. But I fell *way* up high. So the ascent wasn't my *ideal.* I had to accept that it was my best at that time. I'm still very happy I was able to free-climb the route in a day.

I don't see things in black and white. For example, someone might appear as a threat and an ally at the same time. Let's say you are a competitor in a climbing competition. Typically people think of the people against whom they're competing as adversaries, obstacles that get in the way of what they want—to be Number One. But, in fact, your fellow competitors are a necessary part of the experience, since if it weren't for them, winning the competition would have no meaning.

Being in a competition, or climbing before an audience, can enhance your performance. I still remember the roar of the crowd from some of the comps. I could tell they really wanted me to win. That gave me extra energy.

At the same time there's the energy from your adversary, the competitor who doesn't want to see you do well because *she* wants to win. It would be more enjoyable if everyone could watch objectively, and say, "*Wow, she's climbing really well. Good for her.*" And be truly happy for the other competitors. It's also good to remind yourself that you're not *always* going to win. That's a given. On any given day you could be the best competitor, the most fit, or the most qualified, but you're not able do what it takes to win. Most often, this is because people feel too uptight and concerned about results. If we can't accept the idea of failure, then that resistance can be a huge distraction during crucial moments of difficulty.

Again, take the Nose. I knew I was trying something that was a huge step forward. But I felt I could rise to the challenge if I gave my best effort. Even if I didn't do exactly what I set out to do, I knew if I gave my best, I'd be satisfied. I developed psychological skills from all those years of competition that were helpful during those crucial moments. When they call your name in a comp, it's time to go out and do your best, even if your stomach hurts. That's just the way it is. It doesn't have to get in the way of what you're there to do. If you're free to simply do your best, then you'll have a better shot than if you're imprisoned by ideas like, "*I must win.*"

This kind of thinking also messes climbers up when they're trying to *send* a project. They fall off at the very last move, because they don't believe they can do it. They don't follow through to the end. Somewhere inside they've accepted the idea that they're not strong enough. Instead say to yourself, "*Okay, I'm tired, but I'm going to grab that hold and hold on.*" If you focus on thoughts like, "*Oh I'm pumped. I don't have enough strength to do it,*" most likely you will fall off. But believe me, you can do a lot more by sticking with it. That's what's great about competitions and pushing yourself in general. You can surprise yourself by following through and doing your absolute best.

MOTIVATION

The thing that keeps me motivated is that I love to climb. Even though you might think I'd get tired of climbing, I don't, because there's so many different levels of enjoyment, and it's so integrated into my life—my friendships, the places I've been, and many beautiful experiences in the world.

And it feels good, just like the medicine of yoga or any other kind of daily practice. It keeps my body feeling good. I'm still flexible and

connected. It's what I call *my time,* when I can tune in and let go of all the other stuff that's not that important. There's this lightness of feeling beyond words. If I've gone climbing, you can see it in my face. You can see I feel better.

It's natural that as you get older you appreciate doing more with less. In some ways it's the same mentality I started out with as a climber at the age of fourteen. I strived to do more with less and I still do, but I also appreciate different aspects now. For example, I really enjoy doing easy routes (that is routes that are relatively easy for me). I find a lot of pleasure in creating an efficient flow of movement.

But I also like going to a place like Rifle and *picking a climb to try that feels really hard.*" At first, I might think to myself, "*Oh my God. Will I ever be able to do this?*" Then little by little, I make progress. That's fascinating. And every route's different. Even when repeating a route, sometimes it occurs to me that I may not be doing the moves in the most efficient way. Over time this natural optimization happens. As climbers, we're always learning, and I like learning.

REFLECTION

I've tried meditation, and perhaps in the future I'll have more interest in that. At the moment I don't spend much time doing *Om Mani Padme Hum*, but I do like taking baths. I'll lie in my tub, and that's a form of meditation because I'm not moving. I'm comfortable in warm water. I'm able to relax and reflect. I come up with a lot of ideas that way. It's not meditating as much as it is reflecting. But I think reflection is something we're not doing enough of in today's world, because we have so many choices and so many demands with constant phone calls, texts, and e-mails. Taking the time to disengage from all those things and reflect is important for our growth and our understanding of things that we're not paying enough attention to. It happens when I'm climbing too. Sometimes I don't listen to that little voice saying, *don't* put your hand *there* (where I think it should go because it's got chalk all over it), but my subconscious knows better.

DETERMINATION

Whenever I have a goal I'm trying to accomplish, I just focus on it. What do I need to do in order to get the job done? In the climbing sense, you're not thinking about much else. If you are, you're probably not climbing at your highest level.

So *determined* is definitely a word that describes me. I'm a Capricorn. We're slow but sure. Writing my book, *Climbing Free,* took me a long time, because for years it was just an idea. I had to let it incubate. I had to write notes and sometimes little stories that never went anywhere. But that process made me consider what I really wanted to say. So it was important to take my time. I never gave up on the idea I was going to finish the book, even though lots of people made jokes. "*Oh yes the book, hahahaha.*"

They didn't understand that I had every intention of finishing it. Just as in climbing, I won't make the move until I'm ready.

MORE WITH LESS

When I free-climbed the Nose, I was at the height of my career. I had just retired from competitions. I wanted to utilize all the skills I'd learned throughout my career and try doing something important, noteworthy, and meaningful. It was

a statement. I didn't even have to speak about it because the act spoke for itself. That *we* can do it—as women, as human beings. It wasn't just for women; it was a statement that everyone should follow their own vision. Believe that you can, then work *really* hard, and surprise yourself. Everyone can do that at his or her own level.

So determination was probably my greatest strength at that time, but now it's more psychological—trying to do more with less. For instance, I have less time. I can't train as much. I still maintain a high level of climbing performance, perhaps an even higher technical level than when I was climbing full time. But I was young then. I was learning. I didn't have the refinement of movement I have now. At the same time, however, I'm not as strong now, and I'm not as flexible, because I haven't been stretching as much. Flexibility helps. It makes you more efficient, because you're more fluid and relaxed.

So in the video I'm producing, I talk about what I call the *contact vector.* If I think about pulling in a particular direction on a hold, I can direct the forces and move my body more efficiently than if I simply pull blindly on the hold. So the process of making this video and watching myself and others climb in a variety of situations has helped me understand and see sequences faster than I could in the past.

VISION

The first time I climbed the Nose on El Cap was in 1979 with Mari Gingery and Dean Fidelman. At that time I wasn't thinking about freeing the route, but there were plenty of sections that I was able to free-climb, and I did. But when you're up high on a big wall and you're aiding,

Lynn Hill finds the solution to Filibuster (13a), Rifle.

standing in *etriers*, it becomes really hard to step out of them and start free-climbing again. You're looking at the rock from a totally different perspective. You've got tons of gear, and the *etriers* are dangling down, getting in your way. You're just trying to get up the wall. You're tired, and the move ahead looks hard, so you put in a piece and stand up on the *etrier*.

Even back then, I remember people were talking about the possibility of freeing the Nose. In fact around 1983 Ron Kauk, Werner Braun, and Beverly Johnson went up on the Nose for a television show called *Sports Watch*. They got all the way to the Great Roof. Ron was trying to free-climb it, and he was only wearing a swami belt! Watching that footage, you can tell the times had not yet evolved enough. It's not just the gear but also the style and approach. For one thing hang dogging wasn't permitted. So when Ron slipped and got back on the rock, I thought, "Wow, he got back on the rock!" But that's totally understandable isn't it? He'd just climbed two thousand feet to get to that point. After he slipped, he wanted to try again. But then he cut himself and was bleeding. You could see his strategy on the lower layback section wasn't working, and he was out of strength. But nobody was doing anything close to that kind of climbing in those days. Ron was at the leading edge, and he was up there thinking, "*Oh my God. This is too much.*"

So, yes, there were many climbers who tried to free-climb the Nose. There were Americans Ron Kauk, John Bachar, and Jim Bridwell. Then international climbers started coming over, including Stefan Glowacz, Jerry Moffatt, Yuji Hirayama, and many other people I didn't even know.

But, of course, there was a *lot less* interest after I succeeded. I put the bar up high, and I'm a woman, so after that it was probably harder for a man to accept the possibility of failure. After my success, there was a lot of talk about how I was able to do it because of my small fingers.

Yes, it helped to have small fingers in certain spots, but Tommy Caldwell freed the Nose too,

and he only has nine and a half fingers (due to a table-saw accident).

EVOLUTION

When I look back over the twenty years since I free-climbed the Nose, climbing has changed a lot. Sure, some things are the same, such as some of the reasons people are attracted to climbing in the first place: the challenge, the opportunity to get to know yourself better, and a way to build confidence.

But climbing is far more specialized now. Take today's boulderers: Many have never used a rope. If you watch the style of climbing in competitions, you see people jumping, doing double-lunging dynos, and inverting themselves feet first. There are climbers who only go to Utah's Indian Creek and others who only go climbing in Kentucky's Red River Gorge.

The point is that most climbers have only developed part of the skill set necessary to do something like free-climbing the Nose. I had the background because I'd done plenty of slab and crack climbing. I'm a well-rounded climber, and it took all those skills to free the Nose. With the exception of people like Tommy Caldwell and Alex Honnold, there aren't many people today with that kind of background, who've mastered all the skills.

THE FUTURE

I started thinking about making an instructional video even before I wrote my book. I wanted to give climbers tools to help optimize their skills and enjoyment of climbing. But it wasn't the right time. You might say I was still doing the R&D. In my book, I wanted to tell stories and give readers some history and a few lessons. I wanted to create something entertaining. I knew if I wanted to *teach climbing,* a video would be better, because if I wanted to talk about technique, I needed to show it.

In the future I'd like to move toward more interactive teaching, helping to develop climbing structures that reinforce efficient movement patterns, strength, and flexibility. I've thought long and hard about what I want to put my time into, and I believe people would benefit most from me sharing my experiences through interactive teaching. And, of course, I also expect to learn from them, so again I'm constantly trying to get better at whatever I'm doing.

For thirty years I've thought about creating a system that would help climbers build three-dimensional body awareness. And I'd like to offer it to the widest possible audience, from children to adults, because climbing is a great activity, and each individual can decide where they want to take it. I'd like to make it affordable. When you look at the history of climbing, it was born in the Victorian era, practiced by wealthy people who hired local farmers to guide them. Today you still have to have money to go climbing. A child cannot be on a climbing team without parents who can afford the time and money to pay for it. It's not cheap and I feel bad about that.

So I'd like to turn things around and again do more with less. Personally I have less time these days, and I know lots of people feel that way. Wouldn't it be nice to go meet your neighbors at the park and climb on some nice looking boulders? It builds community when people play together. It's healthy, and I believe it should be accessible to everyone. So that's one of my goals, and it's a big one.

Primarily what I'm most interested in is having a rich life, exploring the world, getting to know myself better, and feeling a sense of harmony in my community. It's an ongoing process, but I'm happy with the way it has worked out so far.

If you could offer one essential tip to other climbers, what would it be?
Eat good food, and I mean fresh, organic food. And take care of your body. Do your stretching. Consistent cardio exercise is good. Try practicing a variety of sports in order to stay balanced, because climbers tend to have rounded shoulders from overdevelopment of climbing-specific muscles. Most of all have fun! Don't take it all too seriously, because we all need a sense of playfulness in our lives. Climbing's not just about feeling good about yourself because you did a certain route; it's about being supportive of others, being part of a community, and connecting with the peace and beauty of nature.

JC HUNTER

have infinite respect for all the climbers profiled in this book, but in many ways I'm most
in awe of JC Hunter. As a parent myself, I
know that dealing with bad *pro* and sporty
run-outs is child's play compared to juggling the
demands of a family and a full-time job. And
JC not only climbs 5.14, but she's also a full-
time nurse and a mother of *four children.* What's
more, she and her husband, Mike Hunter (also
a nurse), do it all with patience, grace, and good
humor.

I was privileged to accompany the Hunter
clan one Easter weekend on a climbing trip
to southern Utah. First off, let's get one thing
straight: *No one* packs a minivan better than
JC and Mike. Upon arriving at the crag, I was
astounded by the sheer amount of gear, toys,
food, and other essentials they fit inside, along
with all six members of the family. As soon as
things were unpacked, the boys took off exploring on their mountain bikes, while the girls set
up housekeeping with their dolls. It takes a special talent to climb 5.12 while fielding questions
concerning lunch, the Easter Bunny, and every
parent's favorite, *when are we leaving?* But JC
and Mike managed it flawlessly. At one point,
without a drop of frustration, JC lowered off a
project in order to comfort a crying daughter.
And when the climbing was done, I witnessed

one of the most enthusiastic Easter egg hunts
imaginable. While the kids pretended not to
watch from the van, JC and Mike expertly hid
all the eggs, including the very special *golden
egg,* among the rocks, dry washes, prickly pear,
and rabbit brush of the Sonoran Desert. I was

*Left, JC Hunter keeps a clear head on Sniffing Glue (13d), the Black and Tan Wall, near St. George Utah. Above,
Hunter with daughter Olivia (age 7) in St. George, Utah.*

relieved when no one found a rattlesnake guarding one of the prizes.

JC's sponsored by prAna, Maxim, and La Sportiva. Her most notable first ascent is Fantasy Island, a 5.14b sport route in Utah's American Fork Canyon. She's climbed Dead Souls (13d/14a), also in American Fork, and made the first female ascents of Breaking the Law (14b; at the Black and Tan Wall in Saint George, Utah), and Body Count (13d, American Fork). When bouldering, she's climbed numerous problems ranging from v9 to v10, with some standouts being an on-sight flash of Three Weeks (v9) and the first female ascent of Jitterbug Perfume (v11), both in Joe's Valley in Utah.

JC's living proof that taking seven years off from climbing to have four kids does not have to scuttle your climbing career. She talks with characteristic honesty about what can be accomplished when families work together to make climbing an important part of their lives—even if the kids aren't climbers. She offers invaluable

JC Hunter finds her rhythm on Banana Dance (11d), St. George, Utah.

advice and perspective on balancing the demands of being a working mother and a climber and talks about dealing with the guilt all parents (no matter how skillful and dedicated) feel when trying to balance their own needs with the needs of their children.

And last, but not certainly not least, JC earns a special commendation for being the only climber profiled here who took on the task of writing her own profile, a challenge she accepted with the same grit and determination she brings to climbing 5.14.

ROOTS

My name's Jacinda Hunter, but everyone calls me JC. I was born at home, delivered by my father, in Wenatchee, Washington, in 1978. I don't think my parents were hippies so much, as they were just cheap. I grew up playing in the hills and orchards of my small town without a lot of parental supervision. I rode my bike everywhere—across town, to the candy store, and in the foothills. In fact, when I was growing up, I spent nearly every spare moment outside. My dad inspired my love for the outdoors by taking the family on backpacking trips in the Cascade Range. I remember skinny-dipping in a high Cascade lake when I was four, seeing a porcupine for the first time and standing inside a hollow evergreen trunk. I loved adventure and the feeling of freedom the mountains gave me.

I moved to Utah at the age of ten, following my parents' divorce, and even though she had little money, my mom always made sure I had the opportunity to ski, hike, camp, and enjoy the outdoors. In high school I ran track and field, which helped keep me out of too much trouble. I was

a state champion hurdler, but I quit running my senior year, forfeiting a full-ride university scholarship in order to spite my parents. I went back to school in my early twenties and got a degree in nursing, which I am *still* paying for!

A friend introduced me to climbing when I was eighteen. I first climbed in the Virgin River Gorge (VRG) near Saint George, Utah. When I started, I couldn't even top-rope a 5.9. I met my future husband, Mike, in the VRG and fell in love with him and climbing simultaneously. I took seven years off from climbing while we were creating a family. Mike and I now have four children, ages seven to fourteen. Looking back at that period, my life is so much easier now! Having babies and taking care of lots of little ones is exhausting! It constantly felt like I either had a child in my belly or one on my breast. *Uuugh!*

Most of my climbing experience is in sport climbing. One of my lifetime climbing goals is to climb Yosemite's El Capitan, except that first I need to learn how to climb cracks! The few times I tried crack climbing, I really sucked, so it might be awhile before I check El Cap off my bucket list.

EVOLUTION

When I look back over my career, I'm most proud of my first ascent of a route I named Fantasy Island. It's a 5.14b sport route in Utah's American Fork Canyon that was first bolted around 1992 but never successfully climbed. It's certainly not the most aesthetic climb in the world, but it took huge heart and soul for me to stick with it and make the first ascent.

When I reflect on my first experiences climbing, all I can say is I'm so glad there weren't any

JC Hunter on her signature climb Fantasy Island (14b) American Fork Canyon, Utah.

major accidents! I remember an early climbing partner yelling up at the top of a climb about how to thread the chains and clean the route. I'd never done that before; yet there I was, seventy feet off the deck trying to decipher instructions from a belayer I couldn't see and could barely hear.

At that time climbing was still relatively small, and there were far fewer indoor gyms. Nobody I knew took a lead climbing or safety class. You just kind of learned on the spot and hoped for the best.

When I consider how my approach to climbing has changed over the years, I can say that I now have a greater appreciation for the limited amount of time I have to pursue the sport. But I've always kept the same attitude, which is that I constantly want to push my limits. I've always been a big dreamer.

I've never really had a climbing mentor. I just always did my own thing. In fact, if anything, I got a lot of criticism initially for my approach. I started *skipping grades* and jumping on climbs way beyond my redpoint level. In other words, I didn't follow the conventional wisdom of slowly progressing up the pyramid of climbing grades, and I still believe that way of thinking holds a lot of people back. I never cared what something was rated. I just loved the challenge. Besides, who cares if someone gets their ass kicked on a climb? At least they tried!

ENJOYING THE SPORT

What I love *most* about climbing is the feeling of accomplishment. I love *projecting* routes, and I like being a little scared. What I like *least* is freezing temperatures. But I will endure frigid conditions if it means working on my project. I've trekked through snowstorms—literally through snow up to my thighs on a twenty-five-degree

JC Hunter campuses the crux of Fantasy Island.

day—just to give my project a try. I know it sounds obsessive, but I only have so many days to get out, so I have to make the most of the time I have. I once drove two hours in horrible weather in order to give my project three tries before we were snowed out and had to drive home. That was the day I sent Resident Evil (v10), a boulder problem I'd been working on in Joe's Valley.

STRENGTHS AND WEAKNESSES

For me, anxiety is one of the most difficult mental aspects of climbing to deal with. I have more anxiety worrying about whether I'll *complete* a project, than I have fear of being injured. I climb best when I'm able to be completely focused and relaxed, with no worries about the outcome. In order to climb my hardest, I need to calm my mind and set aside all my expectations. It can be very challenging to wipe out all the external pressure I create for myself. In fact, my best performance usually happens when I'm least expecting it. Somehow having fewer expectations because I'm not feeling well that day or I'm climbing poorly is when I surprise myself and unexpectedly

Whew, glad that part's over! JC Hunter exits the roof on Fantasy Island.

send a project. I wish I could harness the ability to clear my mind in this way every time I go out. When I'm focused and calm, it makes me feel euphoric. Maybe that's what keeps me going back.

My biggest asset is my finger strength. I'm not sure if it was from all the pull-ups I used to do on my parents' doorjamb when I was a kid, but my *crimp* strength has definitely helped me most when climbing. My greatest weaknesses are *slopers, dynos,* and *deadpoints.* I really don't have good hand-eye coordination. Honestly, it's good I found climbing, because I'm pretty terrible at most other sports. In fact, I was devastated when I was cut from the high school soccer team. I was having so much fun in the tryouts. I *really* wanted to play soccer, but my sloppy coordination let me down!

WOBBLERS

My biggest pet peeve is when someone throws a *wobbler.* It's bad enough outside at the crag, but it's especially ridiculous in the gym. Of all places! *Seriously,* did the Green Route mean that much to you? Also, I can't stand most dogs brought to the crag. And, *yes,* this is different than bringing children. Although I agree that some children can be far more irritating than any dog, they are also the future of our sport. Those kids will likely have a great impact on future access issues, crag development, and the preservation of climbing in general. So, while I dislike obnoxious undisciplined children as much as the next person, I see more reason to tolerate their presence. And hopefully by the end of the day, they haven't gobbled up your food, peed on your pack, or chewed up your shoes.

FAMILY

The biggest challenge I've had, in climbing and in life, is juggling a full-time job, a husband, four kids, and time for climbing. It's a constant balancing act. Sometimes I feel like a failure at climbing, and sometimes I feel like a failure at parenting. The best times are when I feel I'm doing a pretty good job at both. When it comes to my husband, he is a climber as well, so we've had our own roller-coaster ride, pursuing the sport together. There are times when we have the *greatest* time together and other times when we've taken *all* our frustrations out on each other. But overall, climbing has really helped us grow and enjoy our lives together.

The Hunter clan. JC and Mike Hunter with their four children.

One year we took the kids out of school and homeschooled them. We spent every other week in a Saint George motel and went climbing. Of course we had to entertain the kids, so we ended up with a great collection of throwing knives, Chinese stars, and walkie-talkies for the boys and an immense assortment of Barbies for the girls. They played all day long in the hills, rode bikes, and had time to just be kids—while we climbed. Sometimes they chose to climb, but I have *never* forced climbing on them.

There were a few days, however, that were so cold the kids refused to even get out of the car. They holed up inside watching movies. By the end of each day, the inside of our car looked liked a band of homeless persons lived there. There were food crumbs everywhere, garbage in every possible crevice, and dirty clothes, pillows, and tired whiny children bursting out of the seams. Needless to say, our nonclimbing days consisted of a lot of hikes, trips to the swimming pool, museums, or whatever the kids wanted to do.

Many of our holidays are spent at the crag. Our best Easter egg hunt ever was at the Black and Tan crag in the Utah hills after a day of climbing. Before we hid the eggs, we counted all of them to make sure none would be left behind as inadvertent *litter*. Even so, it took at least an hour to find the last one, because Mike and I couldn't remember where we'd hidden them all! That day, my youngest found the *golden egg,* which had a special gift inside, and even though her older brothers were disappointed, the kids still ask if we can spend Easter in Saint George. So I guess we're doing something right.

Raising our kids in this way—without television, video games, or even a lot of extra friends—I believe they have gained independence and the ability to entertain themselves and use their own imaginations.

If I could change one thing about myself, it would be my patience—I wish I had more. Believe me, dealing with *four* kids can really test your patience! If I get to a point where I feel like I'm failing, it's usually when my fuse is short. I see a clear correlation between my kids' attitudes and the way I respond to their needs. If I'm patient, then at the end of the day, everyone's *happier.* But if I'm short and irritated, that negativity ripples through the entire family. I struggle every day to make my attitude better than it was the day before.

GUILT

One of the other things I struggle with is feeling guilty. It's challenging to find time for myself, but when I do, I often end up feeling guilty and wondering if I should be doing something for someone else. Mike's great in supporting and encouraging me to take time to go climbing. Even if it's only for a short period, I'm always glad I went. I truly believe that maintaining personal fitness, no matter what type you pursue, is important for your happiness. I've met plenty of other moms who also struggle with feelings of guilt when doing something for themself. I think this is why so many parents end up in a rut, focusing solely on what their kids are doing. I also believe children learn by example, so by taking time for my own personal and mental well-being, I feel I'm teaching my kids a valuable lesson.

PHILOSOPHY

When it comes to my philosophy of climbing, I feel it's not about *overcoming the climb itself,* but rather *overcoming something inside of us that doubts what's possible,* the part of us that doesn't believe we really can climb as hard as we are able.

In addition to climbing, nothing brings me more happiness than watching our children grow and develop. I *love* watching the girls dance ballet, and the boys play basketball, run, ski, and play instruments. That being said, I also have a lot of friends (married and single) without children. I don't think a person needs to have children in order to have a happy fulfilled life. Having children just happens to be the path my life took, so I've consciously chosen to make it fulfilling. There are plenty of unhappy, unfulfilled individuals out there, who are raising kids.

THE FUTURE

I definitely see climbing as a lifelong activity. Even if my abilities decline, I'll always enjoy the movement and the mental aspects of the sport. Having new projects keeps me motivated. When I think about the future, I worry about my kids' future more than my own. If I can raise my children to be happy, healthy adults, I will not need anything else.

To be honest, I really don't know what kind of person I would be without climbing. It's brought me a lot of joy and satisfaction. I can't imagine life without it. The biggest gifts climbing has given me are health, fitness, and mental happiness! I don't have any regrets at all, just wishes for more of the same in the future.

If you could offer one essential tip to other climbers, what would it be?
Don't let anyone tell you that you can't do something (unless you're doing something stupid and dangerous; that's different). Attempt what seems impossible, don't give up, push your limits, and don't take any of it too seriously. It's just climbing after all!

How do you train?
I try to get to the gym two to three times per week. I like to climb three routes in a row for endurance. If I can climb twelve routes in a session, that's great, but I usually only get in six to ten burns. For power training I boulder every now and then, usually for a couple hours. Bouldering is nice, because I don't need a partner, and I can usually get in a pretty good workout in a short period of time. This is great for a working mom in a hurry!

FAME

As for the vicissitudes of fame, every once in a while someone will recognize me at the crag. One day in Utah's Maple Canyon, I was about to get on a route when I heard one of the other climbers say to his girlfriend, "Get ready to see some amazing climbing." I ended up *dogging* the route bolt to bolt and bailing three quarters of the way up. So whoever you were watching that day, sorry to disappoint!

LAUREN LEE McCORMICK

It's easy to get lost in numbers. Who climbed 5.14 this and 5.15 that. Who on-sighted this and redpointed that. But when you're in the presence of a climber like Lauren Lee McCormick, all the confusion drops away. Lauren is one of the most naturally gifted climbers I know. Watching Lauren climb rock is like watching dolphins swim in the sea. She makes you want to jump in and swim along, which is about the time you discover how completely outclassed you are.

The first time I saw Lauren climb was at the Chuckwalla Wall in Saint George, Utah. As a warm-up, she was running effortless laps on the crag's three–star, 12a, Second Coming. The next time I ran into her was in 2010. I was photographing the Sport Climbing Series National Championships at the Momentum Indoor Climbing gym in Salt Lake City, Utah. Even though she hadn't competed for several years, Lauren took second against America's rising generation of young superstars, being bested only by golden girl, Sasha DiGiulian.

A year later Lauren's life made a radical shift when she and husband, Nate McCormick, himself a dedicated climber, decided they wanted to become parents. In 2011 their daughter, Lydia, was born, and now Lauren tackles motherhood with the same commitment and unshakable self-confidence that she applied to climbing.

Having lived through the sometimes-harrowing experience of trying to blend the demands of an active outdoor lifestyle with having children, I have nothing but admiration for those who get it right. Lauren and Nate are exemplary in the way they've fully committed to working together, honoring and supporting each

Left, Lauren McCormick remembers the moves on Lost and Found (12b) Rifle Mountain Park, Colorado. Above, McCormick with daughter Lydia (age 1) and family pooch at home near Glenwood Springs, Colorado.

other's and the baby's needs, no matter how challenged and sleep deprived they become.

Lauren's fourteen-year evolution from a young, midwestern girl who loved to party to the 5.14-climbing mom she later became was never assured. It took years for her to fully commit to the climbing lifestyle, but when she did, she immediately stood out. In 2003 and 2004 she entered thirteen bouldering competitions and either won or stood on the podium in all but two. Her tick list of sport climbs rated 5.13 to 5.14 spans four pages of single-spaced type, with the standout climbs being the Present and Half Baked Half Broken in Saint George, Utah, and Roadside Prophet in Rifle Mountain Park in Colorado. They are all 5.14.

When the weather's warm Lauren, Nate, and Lydia are weekend fixtures at Rifle Mountain Park, an hour's drive from their Glenwood Springs home. Unlike many climbers who never return to their hardest projects for fear they can't repeat their success, Lauren returns to Roadside Prophet whenever she can. These days, she's running her warm-up laps on the 5.13s in the Ruckman Cave with the same happy, effortless nonchalance I witnessed in Saint George years ago.

ROOTS

My name's Lauren Lee McCormick. I was born in 1980 in Cincinnati, Ohio. In high school I was a cheerleader, a gymnast, a soccer player, and a runner. I've a brother who's sixteen months older, and I was always trying to keep up with him. My dad's house was near a nature preserve, so my brother and I would run around there with our dog, just having a good time and growing up.

My dad liked rock climbing, and his house was five minutes from a gym so he would take my brother and me. My brother was good, and I was decent. To me climbing seems to be an inherent ability that just needs to be nurtured.

I didn't take climbing seriously until my first year of college. Even then, I can't say I was disciplined. It was just something I liked to do. I was supposed to be going to school, but I wasn't. I had to move out of the college dorms, because I wasn't attending classes. I got an apartment with some friends, and my life revolved around dancing and partying. I was a bit lost, and my father was concerned about my future. He wanted to connect, so he showed up one weekend and asked if I wanted to go to the gym. When we arrived, it was closed for a local competition. Not to be deterred, my dad said, "What the heck, it's only fifteen dollars to enter. Let's try it out." So we both entered in the lowest possible category. I think I took last place in the beginners division.

But that day I got to see people who *really* knew how to climb for the first time. Suddenly, climbing became more interesting and aesthetic. I realized climbing was probably more constructive than my fun-filled nights dancing. I was growing weary of the party grind anyway, so maybe it was simply time to find something new.

At the time I was working at an outdoor shop, and some of the employees took me on my first climbing trip to Kentucky's Red River Gorge. It was awesome! Then I got invited on another trip, and my boss wouldn't give me the weekend off. So I told him I was going away to look at colleges with my father. In reality, I was climbing with friends at Seneca Rocks in West Virginia. While I was gone, my dad stopped by the store and totally blew my cover. I came home to discover I was unemployed.

But I still didn't feel a deep connection to climbing. I was still being pulled in different directions by various groups of friends. Sure, I liked my climbing friends. I liked being outside. But I didn't have a strong desire to climb full time. Dancing was what I was still most passionate about. None of my dance friends had any interest in climbing, so it was something I had to pursue on my own. I continued to climb when it was convenient.

However, the soul connection did come, but it wasn't until I was in my midtwenties. At that time I moved to Saint George, Utah, in order to work with the photographer Jorge Visser. The influence of Jorge and the local Saint George climbers enlightened me. It is said that you meet the right people at the right time in your life, and that seems to have been the case for me. It was the combination of the desert, the climbing community, and the lessons you can only learn in nature that brought home the beauty and the essence of climbing that I'd been missing.

Today I love sport climbing; however, that wasn't always the case. My first love was bouldering, and it took me a long time to overcome my fear of falling when roped climbing. But I'm so glad I did.

ENJOYING THE SPORT

It's hard to put a finger on what I love most about rock climbing, because there's so much. A big part of it is that I can share climbing with my family. My husband enjoys climbing immensely, and we both want to expose our daughter to the things we're passionate about.

Another aspect of climbing I love is the challenge. When you're at your limit, you never know how things will turn out, whether you're going to make it to the top or come screaming off. I find that limbo of not knowing intoxicating. I love putting out maximum effort and experiencing the climb as it comes together.

EVOLUTION

My approach to climbing has always been a bit chaotic. I enjoyed climbing, so I climbed. I tried hard, observed others, and did what I could to improve. I never imagined I'd be where I am now, climbing at the level I am. At first, I liked the social aspect of competitions. Comps were an easy outlet to gain exposure and be around friends. One of the first big comps I did was in Salt Lake City called the Boulder Blast. All the best climbers were there; all the people I'd seen in magazines, such as Beth Rodden, Stephanie Forte, Brittany Griffith, Tiffany Levine, and Lisa Hathaway. All these amazing female athletes were there, and I ended up taking second place.

After that, I was approached by the climbing industry. The first companies I worked with were Prana, Five Ten, and BlueWater Ropes. It was what I thought I'd always wanted—to be published in magazines, books, and calendars. Up to that time my climbing was more about creating images than creating a plan for how I could progress to the next level. I felt dependent on my boyfriend at the time. I looked to him for everything: to be my climbing partner, to choose where to climb, and to be my photographer. This ended up being a huge strain on our relationship and ultimately led to our demise. That breakup

Rifle is famous for inverted knee bar climbing. Lauren McCormick shows why on Rendezspew (13a).

was a tipping point for me and a big wake-up call to take control of my own life.

I kept bouldering—inside and out—which helped my climbing immensely. And I competed. I was on (or near) the podium in almost every competition I entered. It was an exciting time. You would walk into these events, and you could feel the energy buzz. Just by feeding off that ambient energy, you felt you could do anything.

last one I entered was the Sport Climbing Series National Championships held in Salt Lake in 2010. I took second, and I haven't had the desire to compete since.

I believe climbing taught me boundaries. It's made me want to explore. I've seen different parts of the world. I've met different people. I've experienced different things that I'd never have been exposed to if not for climbing. I think these experiences gave me a more realistic perspective. It allowed me to grow up and see how other people react to situations and how other people do things. I wouldn't say rock climbing has changed me, but all the things that come with climbing certainly have.

STRENGTHS AND WEAKNESSES

Competitions aren't necessarily the best measure of how good a climber you are. Everyone has good days and bad days. Some days the route setters set something that speaks to your strengths, and some days they don't. Maybe competition climbing is really all about your weaknesses. I don't know.

My greatest strength is my ability to improvise. I can pretty much climb the same crux of a route differently every time I tie in. I'm no longer debilitated by fear when I step off the ground. I'm able to allow myself to enjoy the climbing rather than focusing on what I cannot control. When I first started sport climbing, I was so insecure about my abilities that I'd rehearse the climb until I knew success was assured. Now without an overwhelming fear of falling, I can climb and the outcome no longer matters. Ultimately, what's important is everything between the first move and the chains—trying hard, failing,

But eventually my interest in bouldering dwindled. I lost my enthusiasm, so I switched gears, started sport climbing, and I never went back. After I began focusing on roped climbing, I entered three or four sport competitions. The

Lauren McCormick defies gravity on Return To Sender (12a) Rifle.

Lauren Lee McCormick on her way to a second-place finish in the 2010 Sport Climbing Series Sport Climbing National Championship at Momentum Climbing Gym in Salt Lake City, Utah.

questionable moves. He'll rehearse the troubling sequence until he's ready, and then he'll send the climb on his next attempt.

CHROMOSOMES

I don't really know if women approach climbing differently than men. I think men and women have different strengths. Everyone addresses climbing in different ways and those differences are more about you as an individual rather than your gender. One can say that typically men are stronger and prefer a steeper style of climbing, and women are better technical climbers. In some ways, there are more differences between the generations than between genders. I think smart young climbers today focus on how to make themselves better. All the things the previous generation did have helped raise these kids to a new level. The older generation made the climbing gyms. They made the holds. They made all the videos that teach and encourage. These kids have taken full advantage of these things, and the results are in their accomplishments.

succeeding—whatever it is, I want to *celebrate* and enjoy it. I don't want to know what's coming next. I want to be surprised. Not knowing gives me the opportunity to dig deep and to be creative.

My biggest weakness is not being able to remember difficult sequences. I'm often strong enough to do cruxes in several different ways, but I'm not patient enough to sort through all the possibilities before trying. Dave Graham, however, is a climber who will try a route, and if he doesn't do it the first go, he figures out the section where he's having problems, making sure to link the rest of the climb with the

RISK

Becoming a mother has changed how I deal with risks. I take very little risk these days. I'm concerned about getting everything right before I start climbing, making sure I've finished my knot and checking my belayer to ensure everything's squared away on his end. There are times when I'll even hang on the rope in order to reassure myself everything's good. Having our daughter with us at the crag is also a concern, because there's a lot of chossy rock. I find myself looking up for anything that might become detached. This isn't just paranoia. When Lydia was five months old, we were in Rifle during the spring thaw. A rock the size of a trash can crashed into the bed of our friend's pickup truck while we were talking to him. If we hadn't been there, he might have been in the back of the truck unloading gear and gotten hit.

INSPIRATION

I've climbed with a lot of inspiring people. Definitely Lynn Hill—she's an amazing inspiration. I've also climbed with Chris Sharma, Dave Graham, Nate Gold, Obi Carrion, and Lee Sheftel. Anyone in your life can be an inspiration. You just have to be able to appreciate what they offer and that takes maturity. When you're around greatness, it's important to try to understand what makes that particular person special, then try *in your own way* to emulate those gifts. No matter what you do, if you're trying, you're improving.

ACCOMPLISHMENTS

I'm proud of all my climbing accomplishments and the fact that I grew up to be someone comfortable outdoors, even when conditions aren't in my favor. All my bouldering and sport-climbing accomplishments mean a lot, but ironically the climb I'm most of proud of is Moonlight Buttress (V, 5.12+, trad) in Utah's Zion National Park. I climbed it with Hilde, a girl from Norway who I met in Utah's Indian Creek, and her two friends. Her friends didn't want to climb Moonlight Buttress in a group of three, so Hilde asked if I was interested partnering with her. At that time I'd led a grand total of ten traditional climbs and climbed nothing close to the difficulty of Moonlight Buttress.

But I figured Hilde's experience could bail me out of any dicey situations that I couldn't resolve on my own. So we went for it, and there were times when I wanted to rappel down— *right now!* But Hilde was determined. It was her only shot at the climb, so we saw it through. She insisted I do the two hardest leads, which was okay, because she did all the other pitches that would have been absolutely terrifying for me. Completing such a difficult climb made that day memorable.

FAMILY

I've been immensely challenged being a mom. I'm fortunate to have a great husband who's so helpful and a daughter who brings us so much joy. Lydia's love for the outdoors helps us stay connected, but it's still a challenge trying to understand how to meet all of my family's needs instead of being focused solely on my own.

When we got together, Nate and I decided we wanted a baby. It was an experience we wanted to share. We were friends and climbing partners, and the decision to have a family seemed to be the only thing we were missing, even if we needed to make sacrifices to allow our love to evolve in that way.

So we had this great little baby, and it was exciting, scary, fascinating, and mind expanding. It was like flying a spaceship into an *event horizon,* where we were swallowed whole. After becoming a father, Nate didn't have to give up his career. But for me, becoming a mom meant I had to let go of being a professional climber. But as time passes, we've been regaining the lives we had before. I'm not the sort of person who likes to do something half assed. For me it's got to be all or nothing. Since I was committed to the journey, I just bobbed along with the ebb and the flow, allowing all the things we love to gradually float back into our lives.

And now, a year after Lydia's birth, I don't feel I lost any momentum as a climber. Sure, I don't have the time I did before, but I find the same pleasure in climbing that I always did. I'm sleep deprived and miss being outdoors, but the rewards outweigh the sacrifices.

The time I had available to train when I wasn't a mom was infinite; now I have limited time and energy. Sometimes that means redirecting my energy into something other than climbing, so when I do climb, I still have a reasonable level of fitness. Knowing the demands of parenthood, I make sure to fit in time for a yoga class or a short training session on our garage climbing wall. If I'm lucky, I'll find time for a bike ride, while contemplating how to keep a clean house, make nutritious meals, and balance it all with the activities we love.

Lauren McCormick on Rifle's Return to Sender

PHILOSOPHY

My personal philosophy is to keep things simple. So many people become enslaved by the things they want, things that aren't really important. They pursue all these things without stopping to realize how cumbersome their lives have become. I believe that if you simplify, if you *need what you have and have what you need,* life can be really beautiful.

THE FUTURE

Climbing's a lifelong activity for me. I recognized that when I was younger, even before I knew I wanted a family. I want to be a strong role model for my daughter. I want her to see that accomplishment is always possible, even if the road is long. I want to be a good mom, and I think that by showing Lydia the things I love, she'll be able to understand me, as well as her own life, better.

RELATIONSHIPS

Luckily for me, I have a great partner in Nate. We understand and respect one another. We knew all the components we needed to start a family, and we prioritized. We decided that having a baby was important to both of us and that we both love climbing and cycling. So how do we make this work? If I have a climbing partner (or even better, *two* climbing partners), I'll go climbing once or twice during the week, and our weekends are reserved for family climbing. Generally, family climbing involves a good friend who doesn't mind the family mix. With a baby along there's a lot more to strategize and manage, but it's all worth it because it brings us together to do something we love.

GIFTS

The biggest gift climbing has given me is my husband. If I wasn't a climber, then I wouldn't have him in my life, and without Nate I wouldn't have Lydia. So they are the two biggest gifts I've received.

Lauren on her all time favorite Rifle climb, Roadside Prophet (14a)

How do you psych yourself up for a competition?

The most important thing I do when competing is to take good care of myself. I eat well and get enough sleep. Then I relax and enjoy the experience. During competitions, you can be in isolation for what seems like forever, especially if you're performing well. You've got to wait your turn and that can mean a lot of time hanging out. You have to keep restlessness at bay and feed your body the necessary resources it needs. You're also going to have other competitors trying to psych you out. Comps can be a minefield of weird emotions

My approach is to just enjoy what the route setters have created. I believe it's important to put the emphasis on appreciation, rather than focusing on beating someone else. My advice is to enjoy the experience and try to let go, losing all thought, agenda, and expectations. Surrender to that unique moment when you can put all your energy into trying your hardest.

What's your favorite place to climb?

Southwestern Utah, the area around Saint George and the Arizona Strip. That's where I cut my teeth. Those cliffs have seen me through a lot of good times and plenty of hard times. That desert has seen me change. I can go back there and tap into those moments in my life that were pivotal. The climbing's excellent, and the weather's good too.

One of my all-time favorite routes is Roadside Prophet (14a sport, Bauhaus Wall) in Rifle Mountain Park. When I first redpointed it, I told myself I would climb this route every time I go to Rifle. As I was lowering off one day, I said to Nate, "This is like true love!" I was beaming as though I was shooting off rays of complete and utter happiness!

If you could offer one essential tip to other climbers, what would it be?

Find what makes you happy and then nurture it. Things that make you happy aren't always things that come easily. So understand the process of getting what you want from your efforts and realize there will be sacrifice and challenge involved.

ALISON OSIUS

Alison Osius has had a profound influence on the way Americans perceive, practice, and talk about climbing. She is not only a climber but also the executive editor at *Rock and Ice* magazine (and a senior editor at *Climbing* magazine before that). She has written articles about climbing that have been published in magazines, such as the *Washington Post Sunday Magazine, Outside, Backpacker, Skiing,* and *Self,* and in newspapers, such as the *Denver Post,* the *Wall Street Journal,* the *Independent* (London), and the *Boston Globe.* She's the author of *Second Ascent: The Story of Hugh Herr,* a biography of a New England climber who kept climbing despite losing both feet to frostbite. Excerpts of her work have appeared in eleven anthologies, and in 2007 she received the American Alpine Club Literary Award. Alison's husband, Michael Benge, is also in publishing. He is the editor of *Trail Runner* magazine.

But Alison's no *armchair* mountaineering writer. She's climbed all over the world from sport routes in Europe to big walls in the United States. In 1984, along with Neil Cannon, she made the first ascent of the Labyrinth Wall (III, 5.11) on New Hampshire's Cannon Cliff. After Lynn Hill and Barbara Devine, Alison became the third woman to free-climb Supercrack (12d) in the Shawangunk Mountains in New York, and she was prominent among the first generation of American women to embrace competition climbing. From 1988 to 1995 Alison competed in local, national, and World Cup competitions, winning three national championships along the way.

Left, Alison Osius invests in Fistful of Dollars (11c) Rifle Mountain Park, Rifle, Colorado. Above, Executive Editor Osius in the offices of Rock and Ice Magazine, *Carbondale, Colorado.*

Alison cares deeply about climbers and climbing, having introduced hundreds to the sport through teaching and guiding for companies in Great Britain, California, Washington, and New Hampshire. As an editor, she's guided an equal number of novice writers and interns through the equally dicey *highball* maneuvers of finding and trusting their own voice. And somehow, between the demands of parenting two teenage boys and the relentless monthly deadlines of magazine publishing, she found time to serve as the first woman president of the American Alpine Club. American climbers owe a debt of gratitude to Alison for helping illuminate and shape our world.

ROOTS

My name's Alison Osius. I was born in 1958 in Oakland, California. I grew up in Maryland and went to college at Middlebury in Vermont and grad school at Columbia University in New York. I've moved around a lot during my life, but now I live in Carbondale, Colorado, with my husband and our two sons.

I've been climbing since 1977. I started completely by chance. When I went to college, I wanted to write for the college newspaper. I saw a notice for a meeting for students interested in the paper and I attended. At the meeting the editor had a list of suggested topics. I signed up to write a piece on dance.

At the end of the meeting, the editor went down the list again, and no one had signed up for a piece on ice climbing. "I'm surprised," he said. "I thought this one would be interesting." And in that instant I unknowingly changed my future. Impulsively, I held up my hand and said, "I'll take it."

The editor gave me a list of names, and I walked around campus interviewing those people, and eventually they all became friends. I ended up writing a two-part story—the first on ice climbing, the second on rock climbing. I ended up going with several of the people I interviewed to these little top-roping cliffs at Vermont's Lake Dunmore, which is a really beautiful place. Those first climbing partners and I became lifelong friends.

When my older son, Ted, started college at Middlebury, I saw all these same friends again. We went back to Lake Dunmore and had a wonderful day. So now it feels like things have come full circle.

When I started climbing, I was instantly hooked, and it was funny going back to Lake Dunmore and looking at the short, slabby, polished (they've been climbed a million times) routes. It was really fun just to be there, and I thought, *this is where it all started!* I still remember coming home after that first day years ago, thinking the experience had been really important and meaningful and perhaps a bit overwhelming.

I competed in World Cup climbing competitions from 1988 to 1993, the year Ted was born. And for several years after that I still did a few comps a season, with one or two international events, plus the X Games, which is held in the United States. During those years, I did local, national, and World Cups. Then Roy was born in 1996. I didn't compete after that. After you have two kids, it's harder, and at the same time I was asked to serve as president of the American Alpine Club. So I didn't have a lot of time [laughs], and the time that I had was going to something different, which offered different satisfactions. It was nice to help the climbing community and be part of something bigger, something with a history that reaches back a long way.

These days I'm into climbing for fun and convenience. I began as a trad climber, which took me all over the world to some beautiful places. Sport climbing is what I mostly do now. So I go out and practice my sport and get a workout. Of course I can still get hurt, but overall it's a lot easier mentally, and less committing, than trad. So I can still test myself. It's interesting but not scary.

WRITING AND CLIMBING

I was a bookworm as a kid, so from an early age I thought about being a writer. For a senior project in high school, I did an internship with a local newspaper. I wrote two articles with a byline, and I think they even paid me! I was thrilled [laughs]. I don't know how many bylines I had by the time I started college, but as I said, I wrote for the college paper, and eventually I became one of the editors. I also wrote articles for the *Baltimore Sun* as a freelancer, and at one point, I did a nightlife column for it. And eventually I started writing for US climbing publications and went back to school and got my graduate degree in journalism.

I think that climbing and writing both aid in developing focus. Sometimes I think of them as complementary, because they provide balance. Let's say I'm writing something or I'm proofreading all day (by the end of the day, your eyes are twitching, and you're totally sick of it), and I think, "Won't it be nice when I'm done with this, and I can go climb a bit this evening?" So they complement each other that way. People think, "Oh you people at *Rock and Ice* must go climbing all the time," but actually we're at our desks. Being an editor is a regular job. The way I've come to think about it is that I never climb *a lot,* but I never *don't climb.* Sometimes in winter I might go six weeks without climbing. But usually I don't. But in autumn it's usually one day outside on the weekend and one evening at the gym, or if I'm lucky, at a local crag. And I still take road trips. I try to take at least one trip every fall.

When it comes to discipline as a writer and editor, I don't have a problem sitting down and doing the work. In fact, I feel better when I get it done. I try to get things done ahead of time, because I don't like feeling nervous, and I want to do a good job. I learned that in college, especially grad school, because you have a lot to do, and it's easier to plan it out and get it done instead of stressing over it. And if you care about the quality of the work, then you want to put the time into it. I suppose that's a fault of mine. I get obsessive about going back, *and back,* and fixing it, but at some point it's time to just hand it in.

FAMILY

Our kids don't climb. They say it's boring. They say it wouldn't be so bad if you didn't have to wait so long for your turn. Which is *true!* They do other things, which is fine. They both ski and compete in downhill mountain biking. They both play team sports. In some ways it's a relief they don't climb, because I always thought it would be hard not to be scared to see those little bodies so far off the ground! I remember feeling that with Ted when he was little. I tied his knot myself, and I probably rechecked that knot eight times, but I was still scared. So I suppose a part of me was relieved when they chose not to climb, but they did choose downhill mountain biking, and that *really* scares me! Over time more and more of us climbers are having to face the fact that we probably did things that scared our parents, and now our kids are scaring us. All you can do is hope they do it right, have good coaching, have good role models, and learn the techniques well.

MOTIVATION

It just keeps hitting me how much fun climbing is! Of course it works better when you've been climbing regularly, because you have that sense of momentum, and that's important. I always tell people, if you haven't been climbing recently, it takes three days. The first day you don't feel so good. You have that weird *twangy* feeling in your muscles. The second day you're feeling better, and the third day you might not be fit—but you're comfortable and having a great time. You get that sense of momentum back, where you're not standing still between moves, you keep moving, and you're flowing from one move to the next. You're outside in a beautiful place. You're with friends, talking and laughing, and the movement is so much fun! Climbing is always satisfying, because it takes a lot out of you. It's hard! But when it works, it feels *so good.* The most important things I've learned from climbing is to keep a cool head and keep making the moves. You don't know if each one is going to work, but somehow they keep working! It's magic when that happens.

LOSS

I've probably lost twenty-five to thirty friends to climbing accidents. There have been a lot over the years, certainly more due to the increased dangers of Himalayan and alpine climbing but also in backcountry skiing.

Kevin Bein was one of the first, and he was a really dear friend, someone I was always delighted to see. He lived in the Gunks, and he always asked, "What did you do today?" He was more stoked about what you did than what he had done. He was like the ultimate host.

Catherine Freer's death really shook me, because Catherine was a role model for me. I didn't know her well, but I'd been around her, and we had a nice connection.

Alex Lowe was such an intelligent person. He was fun to be around, and he had more energy than God. He was such an incredible climber!

These are terrible losses for the people left behind. Another reason the death of other climbers shakes me is because it makes me realize how easy it would be for something similar to happen to me.

RISK

I think the climbing I do is pretty safe, but I realize I'm playing the numbers. Not too many people get killed doing what I do, but I hope I'm with the majority.

For example, a few years ago I was at Thompson Creek, our local climbing area. The climbs there are twenty to thirty feet tall. It's just a really fun crag. But on this day a group of young men showed up, somehow got off the normal hiking trail, and ended up hiking above us in a gully. At

High above the autumn trees, Alison Osius cruises the ultra-classic Feline (5.11) at Rifle.

A raven's eye view of Alison on Feline.

first they were just enjoying the view; then one young man started scrambling in an area where no one goes, and he pushed off a rock. It was huge! I was sitting, eating a sandwich, and everyone started yelling, "Rock! Roooock!"

I tried to hide under the cliff, but it wasn't very steep. I remember looking out, trying to see where the rock was going, but the sun was in my eyes. Suddenly I saw this thing, spinning through space straight for me. There was a little tree about three or four inches in diameter nearby, and I tried to hide behind it.

I remember thinking, well this is how it happens. Then the rock hit the tree and a portion of the cliff simultaneously and broke into pieces. One of the pieces hit me, sending me flying down the hillside. I was cut and bleeding. I twisted one ankle badly in the fall, and it's never been quite right since. But I think, "Well, at least my head didn't get crunched in!" So there you go. It's a beautiful day at a local crag, and the last thing you think as you leave the house is "I may not come home tonight."

But I would say that a bigger risk is human error. I've tied in to the rope thousands of times. It would not be hard to do it wrong once. So when I go climbing with my friends, I try to ask with every pitch, "How's your knot?" And I double-check my own knot and my belay, and I say it out loud. You try to safeguard yourself and your partners as best you can.

Over time the kinds of things that bring me satisfaction while climbing have evolved, and this has also lowered the risk I face. There was a time when it meant more to me to do a scary 5.10 or 5.11. That was fine then, but I don't want to do that anymore. When I take a climbing trip to West Virginia's New River Gorge, I don't want to do a *scary* route; *I want to do a great route!*

STRENGTHS AND WEAKNESSES

I think my biggest strength is my ability to figure the moves out. Sometimes I make the moves on the fly. At other times I have the patience to find a rest, milk it, step up, study the sequence, step back down, rest, and step up. I'll wait until I've figured things out, then go.

I also believe I've got a good variety of skills. I've climbed all over the world and on all kinds of rock. I've never been in a place where I thought, "I don't know how to climb this."

I suppose my biggest weakness is not climbing enough. But that's okay; it's a conscious decision. People will ask me, "Oh do you still climb?" And they'll say, "A lot?" And I'll say, "Oh about once a week." And they'll say, "That's a lot!" So to some people once a week is a lot, but to me it doesn't seem like it. My main weakness is how *weak* I am! But of course this is something all climbers struggle with. I've definitely been stronger in my life, but really, does anybody care except me? No.

CHROMOSOMES

I have an intern named Gentry Houghton. After attending some sort of climbing gathering, she commented to me how nice it was to climb with women because they climb so differently than men. I accepted her statement without question at the time, but now I can't really think of ways in which women climb differently. I don't feel like I climb that differently than men.

When I started climbing, not that many people climbed, *especially* women. I had no idea if women could climb hard or how hard any of us could ever aspire to. Now, of course, there's a million images of female climbers in books, magazines, and videos. Today there's no shortage of role models for women climbers.

EVOLUTION

Climbing gyms *have changed everything* by making climbing a mainstream sport. And for the most part, I think that's good, because it's important that people get some form of exercise! Everyone should choose a type of exercise that makes them happy.

I think we're currently witnessing another huge shift in perspective as all these little kids start doing really hard climbs. As Sasha D. pointed out in her foreword, Ashima is climbing hard 5.14 at eleven years old as this book goes to print. Look at what difficult routes and problems she is able to climb! What's she going

How do you psych yourself up a hard route?
It's important to be smiling and laughing before you start. I've read the act of smiling does something physiological to relax you. It's also important to trust your belayer, to exchange a few words, and to smile. That starts things out right.

What's your favorite place to climb?
Rifle Mountain Park. I really like the steep rock there and the limestone techniques. As for specific routes, just go to Rifle. They're all good!

If you could offer one essential tip to other climbers, what would it be?
Be smart. Learn as much as you can from peers, coaches, and books. Even though it was published in 1993, Performance Rock Climbing, written by Dale Goddard and Udo Neumann, offers useful information for young climbers. Neil Gresham writes a column for Rock and Ice magazine about how you should train during different periods of your life. For instance, how old should you be before starting to use a campus board? Or when are you too old to dyno or boulder as much? There's plenty of great information out there, and the more you know, the more you're going to be able to climb. Become a good partner so people will want to climb with you!

If you could offer advice to young people who'd like to combine their passion for climbing with journalism, what would it be?
Good! We can always use more people to write and report on climbing, whether they're just starting their career or have an entire lifetime of experience they'd like to share.

to be able to do in the coming years? Ashima has a really good coach in Obe Carrion, and you can tell he really cares about her. There are other kids like Ashima, who are coming along without preconceptions and who have lots of talent and dedication. If climbing ever becomes an Olympic sport, then more children than ever will become interested in climbing.

Look at Sasha DiGiulian and how well she's done. She had a number of factors converge in a very fortuitous way. She found the sport when she was young, and she had climbing gyms nearby. She had good coaches and parents who were supportive and willing to get her where she needed to go. And finally, she's very talented and has an *incredible* work ethic.

ANGIE PAYNE

Three of the climbers profiled in *this book* were born in Ohio: Dawn Glanc, Lauren McCormick, and Angie Payne. The Midwest tends to produce people with practical, down-to-earth personalities. No bull, no spin, and no affectations. They are people who are open and authentic, humble about their achievements, and honest about their limitations. Angie's no exception. She never considered herself a particularly gifted or talented boulderer until she started entering comps and found herself standing on the podium alongside the acknowledged best in the world.

At this point no one else doubts her talents. She's made the first female ascent of twenty-five boulder problems ranging from v9 to v12. In 2010 she climbed the Automator in Colorado's Rocky Mountain National Park, becoming the first woman in the world to climb a confirmed v13. Her competition record is equally impressive. In 2003 she was the Professional Climbing Association overall female champion. She's won the American Bouldering Series National Championships three times, along with making the podium in fifteen additional competitions. In the following pages Angie describes the combination of discipline and commitment (qualities she refers to as *stubbornness* and *obsession*) required to boulder at the highest level.

ROOTS

I'm Angie Payne. I was born in 1984 and raised in Cincinnati, Ohio. I'm a midwesterner through and through; at least I think I am. I started climbing when I was eleven. Not too many rocks in Ohio, so I started in the gym. I moved to Boulder, Colorado, when I was eighteen to attend the University of Colorado. I came to Boulder for school, but I also came for climbing.

Left, Angie Payne works the moves on Freaks of the Industry (v13), Chaos Canyon, Rocky Mountain National Park, Colorado. Above, Payne rests between boulder problems in Chaos Canyon.

When I started, I was primarily a gym rat and sport climber. I'm still a gym rat, but I'm no longer a sport climber. I boulder almost exclusively. I started out as a competition climber, and I still compete, although I've gone through a lot of transitions. Competition no longer defines me, but it's still a big part of my climbing. I guess I'd describe myself as a gym rat who's engaged in a series of love affairs with real rocks. I'm not ashamed to admit that I'm still a gym rat at heart but one who has discovered the joy of climbing on rock as well as on plastic.

By the time I was eleven, I'd played just about every sport in existence. I tried everything—even football! I was the first girl at our school to play on the boys' football team. I also tried soccer, basketball, karate, diving, swimming, golf, skiing, gymnastics, and dance. I wasn't very good at any of them. I was a dedicated athlete, but I couldn't find a sport. Then my older brother went to a climbing gym with a friend. I have a vivid memory of being in the car that dropped him off. I'm sure I was jealous that he was getting to do something cool because he was older. The next time he went was after one of my basketball games. The game ended, and my dad and brother said we were going climbing. And I remember thinking that sounded fun. I was small, so I scampered up a 5.6 slab. And somebody said, "Hey you're pretty good at this."

I liked that I was *finally* good at *something,* so I kept going. My dad signed us up for climbing lessons. My brother was pretty good too, but I remember there came a day when I did a move he couldn't. And he said, "Ange, how did you do that move? I can't do it."

And being an eleven-year-old little sister, I was not helpful. I said, "I don't know. I just do it." And he stormed off. I'm pretty sure he didn't climb after that. He was done. But I kept after it, and the rest is history.

During the first five years that I climbed, I didn't do much bouldering. I competed in sport climbing competitions until I got burned-out. I needed something different. This was around the time I got my driver's license, and there was another gym in Cincinnati, so I started going there, probably because I wanted to assert my independence—both as a climber and as a teenager! So I started going to that gym, because I didn't need anyone to go with me. But the gym didn't offer roped climbing, so I was forced to boulder. And I was horrible! It was really hard for me, but I wanted to do my own thing. So I just kept at it, and I got a little bit better, but slowly, *very slowly.*

It took several years until I felt that I was any good at all. Then I started going to these Professional Climbers Association competitions in Salt Lake City, Utah. That was the first time I realized that I was okay at this bouldering thing, because I got fifth at one comp, and Lisa Rands was there. She's a *really* strong boulderer, so I thought, "Hmmm, I must not suck that much" [laughs]. So at that point I realized I wasn't such a horrible boulderer after all, and I've never stopped doing it.

ENJOYING THE SPORT

I think what I love most about climbing is that it's hard and challenging. It gives me something to focus my stubbornness on. I don't get much satisfaction out of something easy to achieve. I

Rocky mountain high. Angie Payne illuminates The Autobot (v5), RMNP.

like the frustrating aspect of climbing, because it teaches me more about myself.

And I really like the movement. It's my creative outlet. I love trying to refine the moves and make them as close to perfect as possible. I love that there's always a new challenge. You're only on top temporarily. You're never going to do everything. There's always something else to try. And I like that you can't get complacent. It keeps you trying *hard* all the time.

And I like that I'm good at it. I know that's one reason why I've pursued climbing as much as I have. I feel like I'm mastering a skill. It's

rewarding to put time and effort into something you're good at it and enjoy doing it.

And the other thing I love is that climbing never fails to humble me. Every single time I think I'm getting better, or stronger, or the least bit smug, there's some boulder problem that shuts me down. Climbing's like that. As soon as you think you've achieved everything you can, an experience comes along that says, "Nope, you're not there yet. Try harder!"

There are so many variations and so many possibilities that *no one* will ever do every move. It's so cool that there are moves the strongest person in the world can't do, and there will *always* be something they can't do. That's what drives the sport forward. I suppose climbers must love frustration, because we just keep trying, even while knowing there's always something harder ahead. It's human nature to keep trying to achieve something that's ultimately unattainable.

The challenge is maintaining your confidence, while knowing that at some point you're going to fail. That's hard, because as I said, as soon as you get overconfident, climbing puts you in your place.

In competition bouldering you have to trust that you have built up a certain skill set and understand that the problems are set for the ability level of the field that day. So in that way, perhaps it's easier to have confidence during competitions because of the human element of the route setters. They gauge the ability of the competitors, and they're not going to set up something impossible. If you know where you stack up against the rest of the field, you know you have a relatively good chance of succeeding on the problems presented.

Outside, however, it's a different story, because for me, bouldering outside is a delicate balance between confidence and skepticism. It's important I have confidence in my ability, but I also have to maintain some level of doubt. When I think I can do a boulder problem, I sometimes become overconfident about success. That's when it becomes the most challenging, because as soon as I realize it's possible, I don't try as hard.

That's the thing about bouldering, even if you *can* do it, it's *never* going to be easy. *Climbing's always hard.* And if you're going to climb at the upper edge of your ability, it's going to be

really hard. As soon as you get overconfident and think you can breeze through, you get a reality check. I struggle with that a lot, because I spend a lot of time *projecting* outside, and that's always a defining moment in the process: When I realize I can do something, it suddenly becomes a mental challenge.

That's why going back to problems that really challenged you in the past is a dangerous game to play [laughs]. I've done it but rarely. In fact, the only time I did was when I was filming a problem at Colorado's Mount Evans. I'd worked on it for something like five to seven days then finally sent it. It was hard for me, but I went back to film it. My parents were visiting, so they came along. And the cameraman said, "Okay, I just need you to do the first two moves." So I did the first two moves, and then I thought, "I'm just going to do a couple more." Then, possibly because my parents were watching, I kept going, and I did the whole problem.

But that's probably the only time I ever repeated something I'd spent more than a few days working on, because it's *really* scary to go back and try to do something that was hard for you. You have the feeling that there was that one magical moment when you did it and that moment is so precious and fleeting you don't want to mess with it. Once a project is done, it's like closing a chapter in your life. Just let it be what it was, and don't get too cocky about the fact that you did it.

I think the thing I like least is not really about climbing, but what climbing brings out in me. I tend to get *really obsessive,* and there are so many things in climbing to obsess about! There are so many subtleties. That's one of the things I love, but it can also drive me crazy. It brings out this *obsessiveness* that I have to fight to control. That's been a real battle for me—to care enough, but not care so much I can't think about anything else. I think a lot of climbers are that way, because climbing has so many variables you can change and tweak. You can't stop thinking about how to do it better.

And climbing definitely attracts people with obsessive personalities, and bouldering perhaps even more so, because it has fewer moves, but they're all difficult. You can obsess so much about trying to do four moves! Okay it's *only* four moves, but I've put in *thirty* days trying to do those four moves!

Yes, there have been times in my life when I've done that, and you know, you've got to have a bit of crazy in you to do that. And *I do.* I do have that craziness in me [laughs].

Angie Payne dials the exit moves on Freaks of the Industry.

PROJECTING

Since I've moved to Colorado, I've fallen in love with the process of projecting boulder problems. Sure I love going out climbing a lot and getting to the top of different boulders. That feels good. But I also love the process of picking something I want to do and going back and working on it until it's done, however long it takes. And honestly the longer the process takes, the better I feel. It's much more rewarding if I've put thirty days into it.

I know it's just a boulder problem! It's not like sending it is going to change the world. When I was younger, I thought, "Oh, if I just do this problem my life will be so much better." Now I see that it's not climbing boulders that changes anything. My life has changed because of the time and effort I put into climbing and what I've learned about myself through the process.

At times I like bouldering by myself, and other times I like being with people. At work, at school, and even at home, there's somebody else around most of the time, and that's great. But I don't give myself enough time to be by myself, so going up to work on a boulder problem alone can provide that space. I'm going to this beautiful place, and I'll just sit in front of the boulder and study it. It's peaceful. Maybe I'll be frustrated by the end of the day, but in the meantime I enjoy the peace and solitude.

STRENGTHS AND WEAKNESSES

I would say my greatest strength is perseverance. I stick with whatever I start until I succeed. In other words I'm stubborn. If I set my mind on something, I don't let go.

My greatest weakness is tunnel vision. I'll set my mind on something, and that's it. That's what I'm going to do, and how I'm going to do it. In climbing tunnel vision can be detrimental, because there are often other options. For some reason, my mind often latches on to the first option that occurs to me.

For instance, in comps you have to think really quickly. If you don't do something on the first try, you must immediately change your approach. But I have trouble thinking outside the box. Sometimes I'm not as open to other options, and I get stuck. So in situations like this my tunnel vision can set me on the wrong path, and my stubbornness keeps me there. I need to be more willing to mold myself to the problem that's presented and to keep myself open to all the options available.

LESSONS

Climbing is such a metaphor for life. It's like life itself is a *project.* Climbing has taught me to look at the big picture. It's taught me a lot about priorities. It might sound cheesy, but climbing reminds me what my priorities are. For instance, when I go to competitions, there's a part of me that says, "Oh, you didn't win." Then I realize, *I just got to go to Paris!* I got to be with my friends in Paris! When would I ever do that if I wasn't climbing? And it's taught me a ton about myself, such as how I approach problems, how I deal with success and failure, and how I approach relationships. Everything in my world is now related to climbing in some way.

I just got to go to Greenland. And I would never have gone to Greenland if I had just gone straight through school as I'd planned. I'm sure I'd still be happy, but I wouldn't have gone to Greenland. So climbing puts my life in perspective and helps me remember how lucky I am and how cool my life has been because of it.

MENTORS

My first coach was at the climbing gym in Cincinnati. Her name was Lynette Miller, and she was a close friend of our family, so close that she was like a big sister to me.

Angie Payne slaps Tommy's Arete (v7) RMNP.

Then there was Margarita Martinez and Rene Keyzer-André in Dayton, Ohio. I would go and take lessons at their home climbing wall every few weeks. Just being around those people taught me a good attitude toward climbing because they have a really good positive outlook on everything.

Once I moved from Ohio I did my own thing, and I haven't had much coaching since. On my own I started working on being more dynamic and putting more structure in my training, and I've had friends who've helped with that. It helps to climb with people who have different strengths, and that's common in bouldering. In fact, a lot of my weaknesses are things that most boulderers are pretty good at. I've always been weak at dynamic movement and thuggy, powerful sequences. And a lot of people are attracted to bouldering specifically because they're good at that kind of climbing.

For a long time I tried to ignore those weaknesses. I didn't really want to work on them, but I've been forced to, because the women I compete with are getting *really* good at dynamic moves, and I was falling behind. So in that way, I'm happy I'm competing. It forces me to improve my weaknesses. That really comes out in a comp, where it's like, "Oh yeah, I would have done that move if only I knew how to jump!" It really puts it in your face. Then, because I'm competitive, I have the motivation to get better. So these days a lot of my *coaching* comes from my peers.

ACCOMPLISHMENTS

There's this boulder problem called European Human Being (v12). It's up in Rocky Mountain National Park. I spent a couple of years working on it on and off. It's only four moves long! I would go up and work on it in the evening, after school and after work, and finally I did it. That was a proud moment. It's not a beautiful boulder problem. It's not the coolest problem, but it was a personal victory, after putting so much time in. At the time it was the hardest problem I'd done, and no other woman had done it. And I like doing first female ascents, trying to open the door of possibility for other women.

The Automator is actually the hardest problem I've ever done, and when I did it, I was the first woman in the world to climb a confirmed v13. So I suppose people would say that accomplishment is more impressive because of the rating, and I'm definitely proud of doing it. But I didn't put as much time into it, and the problems I spend the most time on mean the most to me.

One of the things I'm most proud of is my trip to Greenland. It opened my eyes to the opportunities that climbing can provide for me and the places it can take me. I didn't do any really hard problems in Greenland, but I want to do more trips like that. Greenland reminded me: "Oh yeah, I really do *love* climbing! I don't just love doing the hardest boulder problems, I also just love to climb."

CHROMOSOMES

Yes, in general, there are differences in the way men and women climb. To be at, or near, the top of the field, a woman can go out and repeat v12 boulder problems. They don't have to do first ascents. They don't have to go find the problem, scrub it, and establish a v12 boulder problem to be recognized as on the cutting edge of female bouldering.

I think it's awesome that people develop boulder problems for other people to climb. It's a hard job. But women don't do it as often. There's no pressure on them to do so. To be leading the field, a woman doesn't have to be putting up *first* ascents, just first *female* ascents. So in the past it's been easy to simply repeat what men have already done.

If you can climb v12 and be respected for it, that takes away some of the incentive to go and find a new v12. Then there's the matter of credibility. You can't just go establish a problem and call it v14, if you've never climbed v14. No one's going to believe you. So you've got to prove yourself by repeating test pieces.

So males still dominate the exploration and development of the sport. Why is that? It's weird. Maybe it does have something to do with differences between men and women. Or is it because women approach climbing in a way that's shaped by tradition? Is it because men have more of a competitive streak, a drive to nab first ascents? Have you ever heard anyone describe an ascent as the first *male* ascent?

It's a big question. And I don't know the answer. I don't know why women approach climbing differently than men—or even if they do. In the past there haven't been as many women climbers, but that's certainly changing. Perhaps as more women enter the sport, they'll become a bigger force in its evolution.

One thing I notice is that, on the whole, guys seem more obsessive. There seem to be a lot of guys who project things for a *loong* time, and sometimes I feel like I'm part of the minority when it comes to women doing that.

CHALLENGES

One day I took a bad fall in the gym and hurt my ankle. I had to have surgery, and I was out of climbing for eight months. That was a challenge because since the age of eleven, I'd never been without climbing. But in the end it was good, because when I came back I appreciated the sport on a whole new level, and I came back stronger. In the end it *helped* my climbing.

Since then, I've injured the other ankle twice but not as badly. I'm lucky. I've gotten away with *only* three ankle injuries in fifteen years of bouldering! Knock on wood!

OTHER PASSIONS

I love animals. That's why I considered pursuing veterinary medicine. I worked at an animal clinic for six years. I love dogs. I think they're the coolest.

I like writing. It's hard for me, but again that's part of the appeal. It's a bit like bouldering in that I'm trying to find that perfect flow.

THE FUTURE

I believe I'll climb for the rest of my life. Early on I had my doubts. I thought climbing was just a phase. I'm sure my parents thought that too [laughs]. But now I can't imagine life without climbing.

I'd like to keep pushing as far as I can, get stronger, and perhaps explore different aspects of the sport. It's possible I'll eventually return to sport climbing, because I haven't even scratched the surface, and it would be cool to explore that.

I always thought I'd have a family someday, and I still think that's something I'll end up doing, but I try not to put a time line on it. I

How do you psych yourself up for a competition?

I try not to think about it! I've learned I do better if I don't overthink. You can't let yourself think the comp is the most important thing in the world, because as soon as you do, you put too much pressure on yourself to do well. So I try to find the right balance between being casual and saving the psych for precisely the right moment. "Okay, I need to get psyched right now in order to do this move and win this competition!" So what works best for me is to stay calm 99 percent of the time and bring out the psych for the 1 percent of the time I really need it.

How do you calm down?

When I was nineteen, I was doing national comps. I was doing well, and I won a few. But that put even more pressure on me to keep winning! So I started painting pottery! On the day of the finals, I would go to a pottery place and paint, because it calmed my mind. It gave me something else to focus on. I could

think "I want to make this look cool," instead of "I really need to win tonight!" Now I have this little collection of pottery that I painted during those years. It's cool. I like having it.

What's your favorite place to climb?

Probably my sentimental favorite is Horse Pens 40 in Alabama. It was one of the first places I bouldered outside. The rock is amazing, the climbing's really fun, and the people are great.

The classic problem at Horse Pens is Millipede (v5). It requires slapping slopers and climbing sandstone bubbles. It's perfect. I really like that problem. And to the left of it, there's a problem called Bum Boy (v3). It has some of the coolest slopers I've ever seen. You're wrestling with the rock, but it's some of the best rock I've ever touched.

And my other favorite is Rocky Mountain National Park. The boulders aren't the prettiest. The rock isn't the best. But the place is special because I've spent so much time there. It feels like home. At the same time the

used to put a time line on things, but I learned that life's unpredictable. I used to be stuck on a certain plan, but now I'm trying to be open

to all my options. I suppose my hope is to achieve a certain level of contentment but not complacency.

weather can be volatile. It can be gorgeous and sunny one moment and stormy the next, literally sending you running for your life!

My favorite Rocky Mountain boulder problem is the Warm Up (v1) in Chaos Canyon. I'm not sure of the rating or if it has another name. I love it. I do it every time I go there, because it's so fun, and the view from the top is awesome. Then there's another one in Upper Chaos called Skipper D (v8). It's hidden in the talus, but it's worth finding.

If you could offer one essential tip to other climbers, what would it be?

Climb for yourself. If you're frustrated, if you're failing, and even when you're succeeding, remember why you're climbing. That's hard to do. I struggle with it all the time. There are all these numbers. The sport's full of numbers, and people want to achieve a certain level, climb a certain grade, but in the end don't climb for numbers—climb for yourself.

How do you train?

The truth is I don't really have training methods. I've always been one of those people who think the best training for climbing is climbing. Nothing really makes up for learning what I've heard people call your vocabulary of movement on different types of rock. Don't get me wrong. I've done my fair share of training. Lately I've been targeting my weaknesses, doing more dynamic moves, lots of jumping, and lots of falling, a whole lot of falling!

A lot of training I do for competitions is focused on on-sight training, trying to flash problems and having boulder problems made up for me then pretending I'm in a comp and trying to send them in five minutes or less. It's important to get used to the format in which you're competing. But as far as ongoing, regular training, I don't have any tried-and-true method. I play around with a lot of different things.

ALEX PUCCIO

Alex Puccio is a natural competitor. She has won the American Bouldering Series National Championships seven times. She's won the Bouldering World Cup and is a Teva Mountain Games bouldering champion, a Mammut Bouldering Cup champion, and a Unified Bouldering Cup champion, winning each competition twice. Alex currently lives in England with her fiancé, Chris Webb Parsons (also a Bouldering World Cup competitor), and travels the world to compete and seek out new problems. She's hoping to move back soon.

I first met Alex in 2010, and like everyone else who sees her climb, I was immediately impressed by her unique combination of power and beauty. Power is her secret weapon, one that allows her to dominate women's bouldering competition in this era of dynos and crowd-pleasing acrobatic maneuvers. And she doesn't just crush it on the climbing wall. After comps end, Alex is known for crushing the pride of any man in the bar foolish enough to challenge her to arm wrestling.

Outdoors she's climbed more than fifty v9 to v12 boulder problems. Some of her most notable sends include the first female ascents of Centaur and A Maze of Death (both v12; both in Bishop, California); Tequila Sunrise (v12) at

Hueco Tanks in Texas; and Trice (v12) on Flagstaff Mountain outside Boulder, Colorado.

ROOTS

My name's Alex Puccio. I was born in Rochester, New York, in 1989. I grew up in Dallas, Texas. After high school, I moved to Boulder, Colorado,

Left, Alex Puccio sends Unshackled Low (v11), Lincoln Lake, Mount Evans, Colorado. Above, Bouldering champion Puccio.

to pursue my climbing career. I lived in Boulder for four years, and now I live in England. Traveling, competing on the World Cup bouldering circuit, having fun, and expanding my horizons is my life.

I've been climbing since I was 13 years old. My favorite style of climbing is bouldering. I've done a bit of route climbing here and there. In fact, I started as a route climber but quickly realized bouldering is more my thing. I prefer bouldering because of the power required. I don't know why I like power climbing more than endurance or technique. I guess the pure power of trying a few hard moves has always interested me. If climbing was just technique, such as climbing slabs or vertical walls, I'm not sure I'd have stayed with it. But I really enjoy giving everything I've got on a few really demanding moves.

In my family my mom, Kim Puccio, was the first to start climbing, and she's now a climbing coach. So she got my sister, my brother, and me all involved. At first my little sister, who is younger than me, was better than me. She could climb to the top of this twenty-foot wall, and I couldn't. When I saw that, I knew I *really had to do it!* That competition between my sister and me really motivated me.

Then my sister was asked to join the climbing team at the local gym. And I'm thinking, "I want to be on the team!" To make things worse my sister didn't even know if she wanted to be on the team or not.

So I trained on my own. I started climbing v5 and v6 boulder problems, and pretty soon the kids in the gym were saying, "Hey, you're good. Why aren't you on the team?" And I said, "Well tell your coach I really want to be on the team."

The coach thought I was a bit too old. Perhaps he thought he couldn't mold me since I was thirteen. But eventually he came round and said, "Okay, I see your dedication. You can join." And I've been hooked ever since.

My mother still climbs, and she coaches about forty kids on a team near Dallas. She tries to come to all of my competitions, at least when they're in the United States.

I participated in tons of sports when I was young. I think the first was T-ball. I remember telling my mom that it was too hot and I didn't like it. Maybe the real reason was I couldn't hit the ball off the T-stand. I participated in gymnastics. Beside climbing, gymnastics is the sport I was most involved with. The problem was I wasn't very flexible or good at floor exercises. I was scared to do a backflip. After gymnastics, I tried figure skating, then basketball, and finally I did some acting. I wasn't very good at any of those things. So it's *a good thing* my mom found climbing!

ENJOYING THE SPORT

What I love most about climbing is traveling and meeting new people. If I wasn't a climber, I doubt if I would have this crazy lifestyle. You go to a World Cup event, and you meet people from Asia, Europe, Africa, and America. It's amazing. You end up with friends all over the world, and that's cool.

What I like least about climbing is that sometimes people are too competitive with each other. Everyone says there's too much drama, especially in Boulder, Colorado, since there are so many professional climbers living there, but there's drama in every sport. And climbing's still

Alex Puccio bouldering on Flagstaff Mountain near Boulder, Colorado.

small. It's big in the sense that it's global, but it's still tiny compared to other sports. But, of course, that doesn't stop people from getting worked up about it, so maybe that's one of the biggest cons.

But I don't have many bad things to say about climbing. Sure it frustrates me at times. I'll be working a boulder problem, and I'll get frustrated. I'll sit down, just look at the climb, and think how crazy am I? I'm getting angry at a piece of rock! You know, if a nonclimber walked by, he'd say, "Hey you know there's an easy way to the top of that boulder on the other side" [laughs]. You try so hard just to get to the top of this tiny piece of stone. I realize this is a crazy sport.

But it's the sense of achievement you get when you finally solve the puzzle and climb the problem that makes this sport great. That's why I do it, and I suppose why other people do it as well. You set a goal for yourself, and it feels *really* good when you succeed.

INJURIES
I have not had any *bad* injuries—knock on wood! I've torn my LCL (lateral collateral ligament). But I was able to climb again three days later, although I had to wear a knee brace for six months. I actually fractured my ankle spotting someone. That wasn't fun! For boulderers finger injuries are most common. In fact, I hurt the pulley tendons in my fingers fairly often. I have three minor injuries right now, and my fingers don't like it when I crimp. I'm a bit lazy when it comes to doing rehab—you know, icing your fingers or applying heat and massage. But I'm noticing that as I get older

my injuries last longer. They used to be gone in a week, and now it's more like three to five months. So maybe I need to get more serious about doing rehab.

My fiancé, Chris, had to have surgery on his shoulder a few years ago. He tore his labrum. After listening to his stories about recovering, I don't want to experience that kind of injury. I can't imagine going down so many levels in climbing then having to gain it back again.

TRAINING
This year, 2012, is the first year Chris and I have followed an actual training program. We've never had a strict schedule before, and to tell the truth, I think we got this one a bit wrong. I definitely felt stronger last year, when I was just going to the gym and climbing and not following anything specific. If you go climbing and just have fun—but try your hardest—you're definitely training. Previously we went to the gym when we felt like it. If we didn't feel like it, then we didn't go. Some weeks we climbed three days, and other weeks it was six days in a row. So now we're trying to make it more scientific, so we can control when we peak, etc. It's our first attempt, and I'm thinking we don't have it down. I don't know if a specific training regimen is for me or not. After all, when your body's tired, it's telling you not to train that day. And when you feel good, it's telling you to try harder!

ANXIETY
When it comes to climbing, I experience the most fear and anxiety when I'm competing. I get *really* nervous. I feel like I have to pee very five seconds. A lot of my friends say, "Oh you must

get less nervous the more comps you're in," but to me it feels the other way around. The more comps I do, the more nervous I get, because when you start doing well, people expect more from you, and you start expecting more from yourself. No one wants to do worse! You always want to keep achieving and improving. I've had people come up to me and say, "All of my money is on you to win today." I know they're kidding, but that's a lot of pressure to deal with.

In order to calm down I'll listen to music and do some breathing exercises. Sometimes I'll close my eyes and try to get focused. Sometimes in a comp it feels like my brain is going a million miles an hour. That's one thing that Chris says I need to work on. This last competition I listened to music on my iPod, and I tried to calm my heart rate before going out on stage. As far as competitions go, the bottom line is that you have to stay calm, forget about everything else, and focus on the climb itself.

As far as fear of falling and being injured, I'm not a big fan of *highball* boulder problems. I don't do a lot of highballs. If it's a slab, I won't do it. If it's vertical or slightly overhanging and it's got some holds I can grab onto, I might give it a go.

But generally I'm more scared when route climbing, even though I have a harness and a rope. With bouldering you know you are *always* going to take a *ground fall,* so I only go as high as I feel comfortable. When you're route climbing, the first three bolts are the most dangerous section of the climb, but that's when I feel *safest,* because I know if I hit the ground, I'm not going to die. But the higher I get, the more I worry about something breaking. What if the rope breaks? Or the harness? If I did more roped climbing, I'm sure I would get more comfortable. It just takes time.

RELATIONSHIPS

Yes, having a significant other who also climbs and competes helps. Having Chris share this aspect of my life is really cool. But it also has its bad points. For instance, it makes me even *more* nervous when he goes first in the qualifiers. I know how bad he wants to place, so I become more nervous for him than I am for myself. In one comp he was one attempt too many from making it into the finals, and I wanted to cry. I felt so bad. So I don't just have to worry about my own performance. I worry about his too. It's nerve-racking having to deal with anxiety for both of us.

STRENGTHS AND WEAKNESSES

My greatest strength is my power. Most people who follow the World Cup say I have the most power of all the women competitors. But every competitor has different talents. For instance, I'd say Anna Stöhr is a more well-rounded climber. Maybe I have more power, but she's plenty strong, and her technique is *a lot* better than mine. The thing about competitions is that winning often comes down to the types of problems the route setters create. It's not always the strongest or most technical climber who wins. There are many different factors, and probably the biggest is the style and type of climbing the course setters emphasize at that specific competition.

My biggest weaknesses are footwork, technique, and balance. All those things you encounter on a climb when you can't just grab and pull

Alex Puccio dynos an unknown problem in Colorado.

your way through. Living in England gives me the opportunity to become a better technical climber. In England boulder problems are primarily technical, demanding really good footwork. Watching British climbers on gritstone is phenomenal. There are problems graded pretty easy that I can't even do. I've seen climbers in their seventies who *hike* these things, and I'm thinking, "How do they do that?"

CHROMOSOMES

I believe personal differences are more important than whether someone's male or female. Okay, maybe if I see a guy do a problem, then I might feel less motivated to try it than if I see a girl. If I see a guy climb something, then I think, "Oh well he's a guy. He's stronger and more powerful." It's an excuse. But if I see a girl do it, then I think okay, I can do it too. I know it's possible. But there are other times when I like to try to *burn off* the guys. One time I was in the gym, climbing with a lot of guys. We're all working this problem and getting close, but I sent it first. One of my friends was watching, and he said, "Wow Alex, you were really motivated to show up the guys." It's not that I'm trying to prove something. It's just a fun achievement, because not too many women can do it. I thought it was funny, but *absolutely* it was motivating as well.

LESSONS

The most important lesson I've learned from climbing is how to interact with other people. And the biggest lesson I'm *still* learning is be more thoughtful before I speak. I have a strong personality, and I say things I shouldn't. Through climbing you meet many different people and

experience many different cultures, and this forces you to learn how to handle different situations. You have to learn to adapt. Not completely change yourself, but definitely respect others.

I've learned to treat my body better, and I've learned to focus. I could go on, because there are so many different things, but just thinking about how many things you learn from climbing makes you realize it's not just a sport, it's a lifestyle. I live it and breathe it. It's everything I do.

CAREER

Turning climbing into a career is stressful. I have friends who are good enough to be pros, but they don't go that direction because they don't want the added pressure. They prefer a job outside climbing, because they want climbing to still be fun, and they believe that turning pro takes the fun out of it.

For me, being a professional climber doesn't take the fun out, but it definitely adds some pressure. For example, every contract with a sponsor has a contingency clause that states if you get injured, and after so many months you can't climb or you're not at the top of your game, the company can cancel the contract. That's standard industry practice. But it definitely adds pressure. This is how I make my money. If I get badly injured, it will change everything. I haven't gone to college yet. It's important to have something to fall back on, so I still want to go to college at some point.

THE FUTURE

I'd like to climb my entire life. It's a good way to keep healthy and fit, and I enjoy it more than other fitness programs. So even when I'm

Alex Puccio traverses a problem on Flagstaff Mountain.

no longer a pro, I'll still climb. And I want a family. That's one of my biggest goals. I've even said I want a family before I turn thirty, but then every year I think, "Whoa thirty's getting closer!" But I think it will be amazing to introduce my kids to climbing, just like my mom introduced it to me. Climbers who have children and still climb hard, like JC Hunter, are an inspiration to me. There's another woman named Cecile Avezou who competes for France on the World Cup circuit. I believe she's forty, she's French, she has three kids, and she made the finals in the Munich World Cup last year. And there's Robyn Erbesfield-Raboutou, who has two kids.

How do you psych yourself up for a hard route?

It's primarily mental. I have to be in just the right mindset.

For example, I remember when I had a project in Colorado. I was really close to sending it, so I took a rest day and came back, but I couldn't get off the ground. And it was a long boulder problem too, something like fourteen consecutive moves. And I can't even get started, so we packed up our stuff and started hiking out. Then after fifteen minutes of hiking, this amazing motivation suddenly appeared. I thought, "Man I wish I'd tried harder." And I said to Chris, "All of a sudden I'm feeling really psyched." So he said, "Well then, we should go back." And I said, "No, we're already hiking out, and it's really a long hike." But we went back, and I ended up sending the problem. That was interesting, because I thought I was too tired. That experience showed me that everything is really about your mental attitude. Sometimes you can't force it. You have to let it come.

What's your favorite place to climb?

The Magic Woods in Switzerland. It's in a forest by a river, and it's beautiful. The rock is fine, green granite. Beauty and great rock—everything you want in a bouldering destination.

In the United States one of my favorite areas is Hueco Tanks in Texas. The bouldering there is really powerful (which I like) and really fun. Another favorite place is Joe's Valley in Utah. I love sandstone, and Joe's has amazing sandstone.

If you could offer one essential tip to other climbers, what would it be?

Enjoy it! Have fun and don't let other people pressure you. Make sure whatever you're doing is because you want to do it, not because other people said it would be cool. I have a friend who's a competitor who always says that whether you're doing good or bad in competition, the first thing to ask yourself is "Am I having fun?" If you're not, then maybe you shouldn't be there.

ACCOMPLISHMENTS

I think my proudest accomplishment was winning the 2009 Bouldering World Cup in Vail, Colorado. In 2011 I came in third overall. And in 2011 I came in third for the entire Bouldering World Cup circuit. I'm 99.9 percent sure that no American has ever achieved that before in bouldering, so that's a good achievement.

LISA RANDS

L isa Rands doesn't like to be called a *boulderer*. Not that she has anything against bouldering, it's just that she loves all kinds of rock climbing and doesn't like to be boxed in by labels. The problem is that bouldering is one of her favorite forms of climbing, and she's one of the best boulderers in the world, so the term kind of sticks in people's minds when they think of her.

Lisa and her husband, Wills Young, have a sweet deal. Living in Bishop California, their *backyard* is the Sierra Nevada. One of the world's most revered bouldering areas—the Buttermilks—is only a fifteen-minute drive from their back door. The sport-climbing mecca of the Owens River Gorge is about the same distance to the north, and the entrance to Yosemite National Park is little more than an hour beyond that.

Lisa makes the most of her location. She's famous for extremely difficult, and often dangerous, boulder ascents, including the first female ascent of the Mandala (v12) in the Buttermilks and This Side of Paradise (v10), an ultrahighball prow of rock nearby. When she feels like roping up, she calls her neighbor, legendary rock climber Peter Croft, for adventures like the Venturi Effect (5.12) on the Incredible Hulk, one of the Sierra's largest backcountry crags. Or she and Peter hike into the remote Merriam Peak, where in 2012 they established two new routes, the Flying Buttress and the Gargoyle, both 5.11.

When it comes to clipping bolts, Lisa has climbed up to 13d on sport routes worldwide,

Left, Lisa Rands defies the gravitational force of Black Hole (12b) in California's Owens River Gorge. Above, Climbing couple extraordinaire, Rands and husband, Wills Young, on the threshold of their Bishop, California, home.

and she cross trains by trail running and peak bagging in the foothills above Bishop.

Lisa's husband, Wills, a world-class boulderer in his own right, who literally wrote the book on bouldering in Bishop (*Bishop Bouldering*), serves as her trainer. Theirs is a unique relationship, one in which they've learned to respect one another's talents and work together to further their respective careers.

The results speak for themselves. Lisa was the first American woman to win an international bouldering event. In fact, during her first year of competition, she won two World Cup comps, and in 2002 she was ranked number one in the world. Lisa also won the Phoenix Boulderblast, the world's biggest outdoor climbing contest, three consecutive years in a row, and in 2004 she won all three open events at the Triple Crown Bouldering Series.

With her ascent of High Plains Drifter in the Buttermilks in 2001, Lisa became the first American woman to achieve the grade of v11, and she's made the first female ascent of many other problems as well, including Haroun and the Sea of Stories (v11/12) and Xavier's Roof (v11), both in Bishop.

But to climbing's cognoscenti, Lisa's most impressive achievements may be her *on-sight* and *headpoint* ascents on Great Britain's gritstone, technically difficult, run-out climbs, where ground falls are a real possibility. She was the first woman to on-sight a gritstone E6, and when she climbed the spectacular and dangerous End of the Affair (E8) at Curbar Edge in 2004, Lisa became the first woman to climb a traditional E8 (roughly equivalent to 13c-14a). But *please,* don't call her a boulderer.

ROOTS

My name's Lisa Rands. I was born in 1975 and grew up in Southern California. I attended Cal Poly Pomona (California State Polytechnic University, Pomona), and as soon as I graduated with my geology degree, I got a job and moved to Colorado. But it didn't take long for me to realize I was not cut out to live in the snow, so I moved back to California. Now I live in Bishop, and I spend my life climbing.

Within the sport I define myself simply as a *climber.* I don't like to pigeonhole myself as a particular type of climber. I grew up doing all types of rock climbing from bouldering to multipitch, traditional climbing. I happen to excel at bouldering, so people tend to categorize me as a boulderer, but I enjoy all types of climbing.

I've always loved athletics. I grew up competing in gymnastics, and in high school I competed in cross-country running and track and field. I also spent a fair bit of my childhood on roller skates. I was a little tomboy. I ran around the neighborhood, jumping fences, and climbing trees. In high school I had a boyfriend who was a climber, and he introduced me to the sport. In those days having a boyfriend was how a lot of women were introduced to climbing. When I first went climbing, I just watched. Maybe I was a little bit afraid, because it was bouldering. We didn't have crash pads back then, so if you fell, you hit the ground. But as soon as I tried climbing for myself, I loved it.

When I first learned how to climb, it was at a time in my life when I'd stopped running for the season, and I no longer did gymnastics. It was my junior year of high school, and I felt stagnant. I didn't know what to do with my future.

Lisa Rands shoots up Chocolate To Morphine (11c) Owens River Gorge.

But the reality was that in order to stay happy I needed something athletic to focus on. As soon as I tried climbing, it filled that void. The challenge of trying something that was completely new, that engaged muscles I'd never used before, and that I wasn't particularly good at opened up this whole new world for me.

Another appeal was that climbing took place outside. I grew up in a modest house that was not my favorite place to be, especially in sunny California. There were no climbing gyms, so to climb you had to go outside, and I loved that. Having a reason to get into nature was a big draw.

ENJOYING THE SPORT

Climbing fills many needs for me and keeps me happy. It fills the athletic niche, the need for mental and physical challenge, and it's taken me to places all over the globe I never thought I'd see in person. It's helped satisfy a curiosity about how other people live by allowing me to get to know climbers around the world. It's been very fulfilling.

What I like *least* about climbing is that you have to warm up carefully [laughs]. I've always wished I could jump right on my project and have a great day. I find the whole warming-up aspect of things a bit tedious.

EVOLUTION

My initial climbing experience was bouldering, so maybe that's why it's my first love. After that, I spent time going roped climbing in places like Joshua Tree, Tahquitz Rock, and Suicide Rocks, all in California. We taught ourselves to climb, and I was never really sure if I was placing the gear correctly. As a result, I didn't push myself as much when I was roped climbing.

At one point, I spent time learning to aid climb, partly because I wanted to learn how to place better gear. So I did some clean aid routes in Utah's Zion National Park, not pounding pitons, but aiding on nuts and cams. During one climb, I had an epiphany. I looked over at a party climbing next to us, and here were these older guys, pretty overweight and out of shape, and they made me realize that aid climbing was *not* what I should be doing at that stage of my career. So I went back to focusing on free-climbing.

When I was in college, it was easier to stay in shape bouldering than route climbing. Then I moved to Colorado, and I was working full time. A friend had a climbing wall in his garage, so we'd go train bouldering sessions after work.

One day I decided to enter a national bouldering competition—and I won. That victory opened up a whole new world of opportunity—competition climbing. In fact, I'd say that's when my bouldering career really started. On weekends I went to places like Joe's Valley and Ibex (both in Utah), and I started to climb harder outside as well.

Eventually, because of a knee injury (and I suppose I was getting a bit bored with just bouldering), I started climbing with Peter Croft, who also lives in Bishop, and he got me interested in alpine style climbing. I'm very fortunate that Peter has had the patience to climb with me. Climbing with him was a great outlet just when I needed something new. The whole package of hiking up into the Sierras and climbing a long route was very rewarding.

Once I was injury free and back at a good fitness level, I began thinking of dedicating myself to bouldering again. I have goals I want to achieve for myself, before it's too late. I'm not always going to want to take big falls. I know a lot of people (in fact many friends, who are not even that old) who've stopped because bouldering takes a toll on your body. One bad fall can take you out—permanently. So the evolution of climbing for me is participating in these other areas of climbing, so I can stay in the sport for the long haul. Being a good climber is all about staying psyched and healthy.

OPPORTUNITIES

Climbing has changed me a lot over the years. When I was growing up, I was painfully shy. Climbing forced me into more public situations, and it made me more confident. It's given my life more structure and more goals. And most importantly, it's given me the opportunity to travel and meet new people. It's made me more humble and helped me to realize California is *not* the center of the universe. It's made me appreciate the opportunities I've had: I grew up in a comfortable household, I always had enough to eat, and I had clothes on my back. I also had the opportunity to go to college and earn a degree. Climbing brought all that to me. In a sense it's forced me out of my shell to learn about the world.

COMPETITIONS

I attended the first US national bouldering championship, and I don't think the organizers knew what format to use, so they patterned the comp after route climbing competitions. Although competitors had something like *seven minutes* to climb each of the problems in the finals, you were allowed *only one* try. I didn't grow up climbing on plastic, so I wasn't overly familiar with indoor climbing holds. I walked up to the problem and grabbed the first hold the wrong way. Immediately I was stuck. I couldn't move. I tried everything I could, then basically I just stepped off.

So then I had something like six minutes and forty seconds remaining on the clock to just stand there and stare at the audience. And they stared back [laughs]. I wanted to shrink until I was an inch tall and crawl into the padding. The organizers realized pretty quickly that was *not* a good format.

One of the things I love about bouldering is that it's very physical. It's gymnastic. You need explosive power for short periods. Yet, when I first went to compete in Europe on the World Cup, they were still setting delicate problems. I was a powerful climber, and I would misread sequences and overpower everything. The route setters wanted you to be a *beautiful* climber. I've seen that change over the years, especially in the United States. The problems became more powerful and more dynamic, and now the comps really love *dynos.* The routes and the walls became taller. Whoa! You've got to have some good padding these days, because you're just *flying* off these problems. The comps are faster paced, and they're a lot harder on your body, because quite often you're jumping for holds at the top of the climb.

And the competitors are taking the competitions far more seriously. They're training and dedicating themselves to competitive bouldering. We always did it more *cowboy* style. When I was competing, training for me meant going rock climbing. Looking back on it, I guess I climbed in a way that simulated training, but all of my training was done on the rock. In the week before a competition, I'd travel to a climbing gym to try to get used to plastic. Although my training was pretty effective and I was winning, I see a lot of things I could have done differently. In fact, at this point, I'm pretty interested in training and have been doing a lot of studying about training and the human body.

CROSS TRAINING

I like to say that my husband is my trainer. Actually, between us, it's a small joke, but it's also true. Wills is an amazing climber, who has impeccable technique. He has nicknames like *the Wizard* and *the Technician, given to him* by a number of top climbers. Wills has been amazingly patient with me and has dedicated years to traveling and climbing with me. In terms of climbing, it was very one-sided. It was always a question of what does Lisa want to do? Now we have reached a compromise by climbing on alternating days. We take turns climbing and spotting each other.

When you look at competitive climbing, climbers from other countries have full-time trainers and coaches. They show up at comps with a physical therapist and a coach, who makes sure they're warmed-up properly. Wills has tried to train me in a similar way. He sets boulder problems for me in the gyms we visit, and he tries to simulate competitions.

What I'm seeing now for the first time is the importance of balance through cross training. Wills told me for years that I needed to cross train. I've always loved running, so in the past that was my cross training and when my shoulders would start to feel rickety, I'd do a few rotator cuff exercises. But I never really dedicated myself to building a support structure, so my body could handle my overdeveloped climbing muscles. I think that's what held me back most. My pattern was to get really strong then all of a sudden crash and burn because of an injury. So that's where I want to focus in the future, trying to rebuild everything in a balanced way.

I'm still trying to figure out the best way to do that. I'm doing research about balancing opposing muscle groups, trying to do it in a fun way where it doesn't feel like training. And now there's a motivated group of us in Bishop who are doing our workouts together. I just modify mine so I feel I'm getting maximum climbing benefit.

RISK

I've had a few close calls but fortunately nothing major. Climbing tall *(highball)* boulder problems can be quite dangerous, but if things don't feel right, I back off. If the weather doesn't seem right, I don't go. The few close calls I've had are kind of silly. For instance, I'd been doing a lot of easy soloing while peak bagging in the Sierra Nevada, where I live. I felt very comfortable on that type of terrain. Then once, when I was down climbing a section and feeling totally relaxed, my foot slipped. My body *barn doored* away from the rock, and for a moment I thought I was going to fall. I swung back into the rock, regained my balance, and continued, but I remember thinking how frail I felt, how one moment of lost focus can lead to a fatal mistake.

INJURIES

I've had some sprained ankles. One time I was starting up a tall boulder problem, when I slipped only three feet above the ground. I rolled

*While Wills spots,
Lisa powers up on
The Seam (v10),
Mammoth Lakes,
California.*

my foot on the edge of the crash pad and had to be helped back to the car. So sure, bouldering can be dangerous, and you don't have to be high off the ground to get hurt.

The worst injury I've had was a torn hamstring tendon, but I kept on climbing. The doctors initially could not figure out what was wrong, so although I had a lot of pain and I was really struggling to use my leg properly, I did not want to stop my athletics. Then one day I was heel hooking, and something popped behind my knee. Initially I thought it was going to be a career ender. But after proper rest, it healed, and now I can take bouldering falls and go running like I used to.

LESSONS

The most important lesson I've learned from climbing is patience. I've had to have patience with injuries, patience with training, and patience with people while traveling.

The amazing thing about life is that you never stop learning. There's so much more for me to learn about climbing, and I hope I never stop. I think the minute you stop learning you limit yourself.

STRENGTHS AND WEAKNESSES

My greatest strength is my determination. And my greatest weakness is probably that it doesn't take much for me to lose my confidence. When that happens, I have to immediately address the problem and build my confidence back up. It's a constant battle. Confidence is an interesting thing. If you're feeling good, your confidence rises naturally, but if you're feeling bad, it's tough to get it back. Usually my husband or a close friend will put me back on track. They say, "Lisa, what are you thinking? You're being silly."

CHROMOSOMES

Ten years ago I would've said that women approach climbing differently than men. In the past women had more limitations imposed on them in terms of what they were supposed to do in life and what they could do physically. Even though I grew up in the seventies and eighties, on the heels of the women's liberation movement, I felt I was not supposed to be better than men. So I limited myself. Female climbers were not that common. That's changed a lot. Now it's accepted that women can be as strong as the guys, pushing themselves and their athletic ability. Women are not expected to have a family at an early age or to be a great cook and housekeeper. Today young women don't approach climbing any differently than men do. They don't feel any limitations, and that's awesome. It's taking women's athletics to a whole new level.

ACCOMPLISHMENTS

When I'm asked what I'm most proud of in climbing, it's always difficult to answer, because I never feel *content* with what I've accomplished. However, I'm proud I was able to spend time in England working on the mental side of my climbing. Although I won a number of major bouldering competitions, including several World Cups, I never felt comfortable competing. I was such a nervous wreck in comps that I decided to travel to Great Britain to climb on gritstone in order to become a better competition climber. Gritstone climbing is notorious for being scary and dangerous, so my reasoning was

Sequence of Lisa Rands climbing the high ball boulder problem Drunken Chicken (v6), Way Lake Boulders, California.

that by learning to climb it, I'd also be able to learn how to control my nerves. So I climbed, while controlling my fear and keeping my mind calm. I ended up loving the feeling so much, I dedicated several more trips to the gritstone just to keep pushing myself. Those subsequent trips were not for improving my performance in competitions but for the sake of being able to

Lisa Rands two steps on Flux Capacitor (12c), Owens River Gorge.

calm my mind while climbing in dangerous situations. During that phase, I *on-sighted* up to E6 and *headpointed* up to E8. Then I transitioned the skills I'd learned to *ground-up highballing* on tall boulders like This Side of Paradise (v10) at the Bardini Boulders in Bishop, and So High (v6) at Joshua Tree.

When I look back over my career, I also realize how exciting it was to be involved with the development of Rocklands in South Africa. I was fortunate to be in one of the first groups that went there and found whole new boulder fields to climb. I'd never been into putting up first ascents in the past, but suddenly I realized, "Wow! Here's this whole new playground! I can pick what I want and be the first to climb it." The Rocklands is an amazing area.

PHILOSOPHY

My personal philosophy is that you should get the most out of your life and enjoy it, because you only live once. I do that while also making sure that I'm not being selfish or having a negative impact on other people.

When I'm a little old lady, sitting on the porch in my rocking chair, I want to be able to look back and be content with my accomplishments. I don't want to feel like I failed to pursue my goals and missed out on all the experiences that were possible.

THE FUTURE

I always want to climb, and I want to be a professional climber for as long as possible. I'm also very interested in analyzing injuries and how to train to avoid them. I think a logical progression for me would be to train other climbers. I've

Lisa Rands on the Warm Up at Way Lake.

trained my entire life for athletics, and now I'm doing more regimented study to learn how to apply my experience and knowledge into training other athletes.

RELATIONSHIPS

When it comes to personal relationships, it's always been important to me to date a climber. I think it's important to have the same experiences, the same passion, and the same drive. But then there's *crag couple dynamics*. It's not always *pretty,* and it's not always *easy* to have your life partner also be your climbing partner. So I also think it's important to climb with other people. It's like taking your work home to your family. If you're taking your *climbing* home, the results can be *mixed*. So Wills and I climb with each other, and we also climb with other people.

OTHER PASSIONS

My interests and passions are always changing. Right now I'm spending a lot of time researching muscle groups, finding different ways to get the body balanced and healthy. And, of course,

I'm happy doing anything athletic. I really enjoy a mix of trail running and peak bagging. And Wills is into that as well, so that's been fun and good for our relationship.

And I enjoy cooking, partially because I'm finicky about maintaining a healthy diet. So I really enjoy cooking my own food and making Wills eat healthy too, because if left to his own devices, he will eat a lot of desserts. Luckily, I like cooking those too!

Lisa Rands demonstrates her championship precision and perfect form.

How do you psych yourself up for a hard route?

I don't have any particular routine. I remind myself that I'm prepared, and then I really work on calming my nerves. If I get too anxious or too excited, then I end up climbing stiffly. So for me it's about relaxing and staying focused.

What's your favorite place to climb?

If I only had one place to climb for the rest of my life, and assuming the weather was good all year long, then it would be South Africa.

What are your favorite routes or boulder problems?

I became the first woman to climb Thriller (v10) in Yosemite by unlocking a different sequence of moves at the top of the boulder problem, so I have a soft spot in my heart for that. High Plains Drifter (v7) is possibly my favorite boulder problem ever. On the gritstone in England, my first "hard grit route" was White Lines (E7) at Curbar, so it will always be memorable for breaking a barrier in my climbing. Another gritstone route Gaia (E8) at Black Rocks is a standout, because it is such a good-looking piece of rock. I love highballs and was psyched to get the fourth ascent of the stunning This Side of Paradise (v10). And, oh yeah, the Mandala (v12) (both in Bishop) is another favorite, because I grew up walking past that boulder before it even had a name, and no one was sure it could be climbed!

If you could offer one essential tip to other climbers, what would it be?

Always remember why you climb—which should be because you love it. Don't get wrapped up in focusing on grades and results. Climbing is about staying healthy and psyched and having fun!

How do you train?

At this point in my career, I'm approaching training in a way that builds my fitness at a slower pace in order to avoid injury. I've looked at what cyclists do. They spend a big chunk of time just spinning and building up mileage. In the past my approach has been to just get fit as fast as I can. But then I hurt myself. So what I'm doing now is building the whole base level at a slower pace so I stay healthy.

I love to run outside on soft roads. I've been doing a training circuit, walking and running in the mountains during summer. It takes three and a half hours. I go up a peak that requires some scrambling with easy climbing. I try doing that once a week. Everyone laughs at me, but I've been Rollerblading too. It's really good for my legs, plus it's fun. I'm always trying to find fun ways to train to keep motivated. I use a rowing machine, and I jump rope. I believe cardiovascular training is very important for climbing. And I have different strengthening exercises using lighter weights.

BETH RODDEN

Beth Rodden grew up pulling on plastic, but she came of age on the big walls of the world, first in Madagascar under the tutelage of Lynn Hill and Nancy Feagin, and then in Yosemite, the crucible of cutting-edge modern rock climbing.

Beth is a member of the first generation of American climbers who learned in the gym and then went on to excel in competition climbing. In 1996, 1997, and 1998, she was a US Junior National Champion. In 2004 Beth climbed the hardest sport climb in the world done by a woman at that time, the Optimist (14b) at Smith Rock State Park in Oregon.

But it's Yosemite where Beth chose to make her home, as well as her most remarkable ascents. In 2008 near Upper Cascade Falls, she established the hardest single trad pitch in the world climbed by a woman. She titled the route Meltdown, and it was subsequently graded 14c. When Beth successfully sent *Meltdown,* she *placed all gear while on lead!* To put that fact into perspective, it's important to point out that a very small percentage of climbers in the world today can climb 5.14 on bolted sport routes when all the quickdraws are *already* hanging in place and ready to clip. But it's far more heady and demanding to make 14c moves yet still have the power and endurance to stop and place gear that will safely hold a fall. Beth accomplished that remarkable feat by taping the protection required in the proper order on her thighs, ready to rip and place with lightning efficiency, giving a whole new meaning to the phrase *plug and play!*

Putting that level of skill and endurance to good use, Beth has free-climbed more routes on

Left, Beth Rodden makes the pilgrimage to the Mecca Crag, Yosemite National Park. Above, Rodden surrounded by the legendary big walls of Yosemite National Park.

El Capitan than any other woman, including the second free ascent of the Nose (VI, 5.14), the first free ascent of Lurking Fear (VI, 5.13c), and the second free ascent of El Corazon (VI, 13b). She has also made the first female ascents of cutting-edge traditional climbs, such as the Book of Hate (13d), Country Club Boys (13d), the Phoenix (13a, flash), the Stigma (13c), and Anaconda (13b).

Along the way, Beth faced her share of challenges. Taken hostage by a rebel group during an expedition to Kyrgyzstan in 2000, she and her companions were held at gunpoint for six days before overpowering one of their guards and escaping. The experience left Beth traumatized for years, uncertain about travel and ambiguous about climbing.

Since 2008 Beth has been plagued by a series of injuries lengthy enough to try the patience of Job. But hardship makes clear what the heart treasures, and these experiences only served to clarify and strengthen her love of climbing. When I spend time with Beth, she always reminds me of the healing power of the climbing life, a path that can provide the strength, courage, and grace not only to survive adversity, but also to transcend it.

ROOTS

My name's Beth Rodden. I was born in California in 1980, and I started climbing when I was fourteen. The first day I went to the climbing gym, it was love at first sight. I think that night I made my dad stay until closing, and from then on I was a permanent fixture at the gym.

Soon I began entering local climbing competitions. There weren't a ton of climbing gyms back then, only a handful in all of Northern California. I did local comps for about five years then progressed to national competitions and eventually to World Cups. The entire time I was in high school, I was traveling and competing. I was part of the first generation of American competition climbers, along with people such as Katie Brown, Chris Sharma, and Tommy Caldwell. It was a pretty cool time to be involved. We were just kids, having fun and competing alongside all these serious adults.

Then, after five or six years of competition, I fell more and more in love with climbing outside. I attended one semester of college and then decided to take *a semester off*. That turned into *a year off*, and eventually I was climbing full time, and that's what I've been doing ever since.

During that first year, I met and climbed with Lynn Hill. She invited me to go on an expedition to Madagascar with her, Nancy Feagin, and Kath Pike. At that time I was a sport climber. Then, at eighteen years old, I got to go to Madagascar and learn how to place pro and become a traditional climber.

After that experience, I came home to Yosemite, lived out of my car, and tried to hook up with people to climb and learn as much as possible about climbing in the valley. Ever since then, I've focused on harder traditional climbing, like free-climbing El Cap or difficult, single-pitch, trad routes. And, of course, I still mixed in hard sport routes from time to time.

ENJOYING THE SPORT

There are several aspects of climbing I love. The thing that grabbed me immediately was the movement. The movement of climbing is really fun. I also like problem solving, and climbing has plenty.

And I love the climbing community. Climbing's a social sport. You do it as an individual, but at the same time you learn from others. You climb together and figure out problems together. As you travel, you get to meet all these amazing people who you never would have met in any other way.

I also like to travel. Climbing lets you travel to places you might not normally go and meet all these amazing people you never would have met in any other way.

I suppose the thing I like *least* about climbing is the same thing I like least about any aspect of life: ego. I believe you can excel in climbing, or in anything else, and still be humble. When I see people who embody that, I respect them, and when I encounter the opposite (egotists), it really rubs me the wrong way.

Beth Rodden keeps her cool on Vikings In Heat (6c), Ton Sai Beach, Thailand.

KIDNAPPED

I haven't had many close calls. I think I'm actually pretty much of a pansy. When it comes to being bold, running it out on bad gear, or putting myself out there, I get scared. I much prefer to be calculated and prepared.

I did have an incident, however, when I was traveling to the Karasu Valley, a climbing area in Kyrgyzstan that was politically unstable at the time. Our entire team was kidnapped and held hostage for six days by a rebel group. It was a truly terrifying experience, but in the end we were able to escape. While this event is not what is traditionally considered a close call in climbing, it most certainly qualifies as a close call, and it did happen during a climbing trip; it was a result of geopolitical conflict in that region.

Before we went to the Karasu, we looked at the US State Department website, and it listed Kyrgyzstan at the same threat level as Northern Ireland and Australia during the Olympics. So we thought it was okay. You know, safe enough, but obviously we were wrong.

It took me a long time to get over that experience. I didn't climb much for a couple of years after. I guess I associated climbing with getting kidnapped. Of course, I'd go through the motions. You know, because I was a *professional climber,* I thought I should go climbing. But I didn't really want to do it.

I remember I had to be really patient with myself. I had to figure out why I started climbing in the first place, which was for the love of the sport and the community. I had to get back to my roots. It took a couple of years to get there again. Time is a great healer of many things.

Since that time, my experience in Kyrgyzstan has affected my travel choices. I've mainly wanted to go to Europe, South America, and safer places [laughs].

FEAR

If I get really scared while I'm climbing, I'll start singing to myself [laughs]. It distracts me. But I also try to think rationally. I remember the gear's good, and I've got a rope. I remind myself that everything's safe, and in that way I talk myself into calming down.

INJURIES

I've definitely had my fair share of injuries. I've had finger and ligament injuries, and I really suffered from a broken foot that I didn't take care of properly. The doctor said, "Don't put any weight on your ankle," and I interpreted that to mean that a three-mile hike was okay. So I've tried to learn from that. I've also had a shoulder problem, and I injured my hip. I've had just a litany of things.

I broke my ankle bouldering, when I was warming down at the end of the day. I slipped where there was this little ledge, and I landed wrong. I was probably only four feet off the ground, and it was literally the last problem I was going to do. So it happens [laughs].

Just another day in Paradise. Beth Rodden on the classic Lord of the Thais (7a+), Railei Beach, Thailand.

But I believe anyone can understand the frustration that goes into dealing with one injury after another. You achieve all this joy and sense of accomplishment from being a climber, then you are continually prevented from participating in the activity that makes you who you are. When you're unable to fully engage because your body's holding you back, it really pounds you down.

So it was hard mentally, because just as I was getting over one injury, another one came along. I'd start to feel good and want to go for it, then I'd get hurt and find myself right back to doing *nothing*. So I'd try and be patient all over again and wait it out. It was a vicious cycle that not only deprived me of climbing but also other activities, such as running and biking.

But I've realized, that for me personally, no matter what level I'm climbing—for example, when I couldn't climb for a really long time and then could only climb 5.8 and 5.9—it brought me so much *joy and happiness*. I realized okay, this is what I really *need*.

LESSONS

So I suppose the main lesson I've learned is to be patient. Well, I'm still not, and there are times when I'm so guilty of *not* practicing patience. For instance, I had a really good streak of climbing recently, and sure enough, I pushed too hard and reinjured my finger a bit. It's so difficult to climb below your level all the time. I've tried to learn patience. I've tried to learn why I want to climb. Is it to climb at the top level? Is it to put up the hardest routes in the world? Is it to just be a climber?

And I've realized that for me, the important thing is to be climbing at whatever level I can.

Climbing is *amazing!* If that wasn't the case, I'd definitely have given it up. It would have been too frustrating.

Perhaps the most important lesson I've learned is just to *have fun*. Enjoy climbing for the reason you had when you began—because you love it. *We all love climbing.* I've definitely been guilty of getting caught in other reasons.

And gosh, I still have so much to learn! Climbing humbles me. It teaches me good problem-solving skills. It opens my mind to all sorts of different people. It allows me to travel the world. It's a constant evolution.

TRAINING

Maintaining fitness through all this has been a juggling act. For a while I was running. I love to run. Then I hurt my hip, so I got into road biking. Recently I've been swimming. Before I discovered climbing, I was the runt of the high school swim team. I was horrible at swimming, but I really loved it. I guess I'm a pretty determined person so being horrible didn't deter me. Seriously, I was the slowest person in the pool *by minutes*. But I started swimming again recently and it's been really fun.

And of course, I try to do all my physical therapy exercises. And one thing I've found a lot of passion for while dealing with all these injuries is cooking. Cooking really good food using high quality locally grown ingredients. That's a big passion of mine right now, cooking and sourcing good food, and it's been awesome.

STRENGTHS AND WEAKNESSES

It's difficult for me to choose my greatest strength. I would say my strengths include my love of

Beth Rodden enjoys the world famous Buttermilk Boulders outside Bishop, California.

climbing, my determination, and my perseverance. For instance, if things aren't working out, I don't give up. I just switch it up a bit and try a different approach. I can also hold on *forever*. I've only fallen off if couldn't make a move or if I grabbed a hold wrong.

My biggest weaknesses are also my determination and my perseverance. Sometimes I can push too far and get hurt. Also, I'm not a very powerful climber. My arms are skinny, which forces me to rely on my feet.

CHROMOSOMES

Women approach climbing differently than men. For a lot of women, it's a more social activity. For example, I'll go to the crag or the gym, and I'll see small groups of women climbing together and really encouraging one another. You don't necessarily see that with guys. I mean they do go out together, but it seems a bit lighter with women.

And a lot of times I think women analyze the problem more than men, who may try just powering through. Obviously women are not physically the same, so we need to be more thoughtful. Maybe if I move my body this way or if I put my foot here or there and my hand here, it will make a difference. Since men are blessed with stronger bodies, they don't approach climbing that way.

I definitely see more women participating in the full-time climbing lifestyle than when I started. When I began, if you saw a full-time woman climber, she was usually coupled with a man. Now you see more women on the road by themselves doing the professional thing, but there are still fewer women pro climbers than guys.

Beth Rodden leads Wall Banger (10c), California's Owens River Gorge.

Maybe women are just smarter! Maybe they don't want to be living out of the back of their Honda Civic, eating cold soup for dinner every night!

Of course, there are definitely dirtbag women climbers out there, so maybe it's just percentages. There are more men than women climbers overall, so proportionally it's the same number pursuing climbing as a lifestyle. I don't know.

RELATIONSHIPS

When it comes to relationships, I think for some people having your *significant other* be your climbing partner can work out really well, especially if you work well together. You have similar goals, passions, and ideas. You see that working for a lot of people, and for me too, it worked great for a while.

But on the other hand, when you don't have that situation you've got to go out, meet new people, and explore. For instance, getting to know and climb with this current group of women whom I probably never would have had the opportunity to experience in the past. So it's opened up a great new avenue for me, and I'm able to climb with Randy as well (Beth's current husband Randy Puro). So there are always benefits to whatever situation you find yourself in. I don't know what's best. I don't know if there is a *best*. It's just, to each their own. [laughs]

PHILOSOPHY

I try to do good! I try to give back to the sport of climbing and respect the environment. I learned from my mentors, so I try to give something to young climbers as well. We all have this finite resource we enjoy, so we've got to learn to be good stewards of the earth as well as being good climbers.

THE FUTURE

My hope for the future is to continue on my path. If I can get out there and put up notable first ascents, then that would be awesome. If not, I'd love to work with young women and girls coming into the sport. I'd teach them why climbing can be such a wonderful part of your life and to respect our climbing resources. If we can do that, then climbing will be a great sport for many generations to come.

How do you psych yourself up for a hard route?

For me the potential of accomplishing something worthwhile justifies all the effort, even if that means months living and working a route on El Cap. And if it doesn't go? Oh well. I just try to learn as much as possible from the experience, regardless of the outcome.

What's your favorite place to climb?

Yosemite. Coming to the valley was a pivotal point in my career. I came back from Madagascar, and I really wanted to try Yosemite. It has so much history, and it's stout. It's a real challenge to climb well here. The valley has everything. There's world-class bouldering, sport climbing, and big walls.

My favorite El Cap route is either the Nose (VI, 5.14) or Lurking Fear (VI 5.13c). My favorite shorter route is probably Moratorium (11b, Schultz's Ridge) And my favorite cragging route is something on the Cookie I'm sure.

You've had a wholes series of home gyms. What's the secret to home gym success?

I think the secret to building a successful home gym is to create consistent, single, angles. For example, don't try to build a ton of different angles and walls meeting. It's nice to have just one consistent angle. And secondly, it's important to have friendly holds. Nothing too tweaky!

When you were competing, what did you do to get in the right mood?

Just the fact it was a comp would get me amped up. In fact, I'd usually have to calm myself down. All these other people are out there climbing really hard, so you know you have to too. So with comps sometimes I'd psych myself up too much, whereas climbing outside, it's just you. There's nothing else around, so it's up to you to dig deep and find the motivation.

What's your best advice to climbers dealing with injury?

Be patient! Of course, it's hard for me to follow my own advice!

KATE RUTHERFORD

We live in a data-obsessed society, one preoccupied with numbers and grades and those who attain them. Yet when I read Kate Rutherford's resume, I see Yosemite—the cut-glass water of the Merced River, the meadows and the whispering pines, and above it all, the cliffs rising. I hear the wind and see the clouds, streaming from Cerro Torre.

The name of a route and an attached number do little to conjure the hours of questing into the unknown, the uncertainty, the self-doubt, the cold, and the long nights that climbing big walls entails.

Kate's story speaks of all those things. It's a story that reads like a modern-day Jack London novel, complete with a childhood spent in the Alaskan bush. Kate's reputation and accomplishments are so impressive that before I met her, I imagined that she would be larger-than-life.

But the reality is far more charming. Kate is a soft-spoken, petite, slender blond, who, with the equally talented Madaleine Sorkin, is rewriting the playbook for hard-alpine and big-wall climbing by American women. Together Kate and Madaleine have free-climbed Free Rider on El Capitan (VI, 5.12+) in Yosemite. They gleaned the first female ascents of Moonlight Buttress (V, 5.12+) in Utah's Zion National Park, and the North West Face of Yosemite's Half Dome (VI, 5.12+). In the winter of 2013, during Madaleine's first visit to Chile's Torres del Paine National Park, they climbed Mate, Porro y Todo lo Demas on the North Pillar of Fitz Roy (900 meters, 11a) and the Red Pillar on Aguja Mermoz (450 meters, 12a). Along with her fiancé, Mikey Schaefer, and other partners, Kate made a number of notable first ascents in Patagonia, a region in South America, mostly in Argentina. These

Left, A room with a view. Kate Rutherford high above the Gunnison River on the Free Nose (12c), Black Canyon of the Gunnison National Park, Colorado. Above, Rutherford prepares to rappel to begin a day of climbing in the Black Canyon.

include the Washington Route on Fitz Roy (5.10, A2), Astro Choss (5.10, A2) on Aguja Saint Exupery, Tiempo Para La Playa (5.11, A1) on Aguja Rafael, and Hard Sayin' Not Knowin' (5.10, A2) on Aguja Guillaumet. Kate also climbed trad test pieces, such as the Optimator in Utah's Indian Creek and Yosemite's Keeper of the Flame and the Phoenix (all 5.13). In addition to Chile and Argentina, Kate's international climbing adventures have taken her to Armenia, the Ukraine, Croatia, Slovenia, Greenland, Namibia, Venezuela, Vietnam, Laos, and Canada. On rest days Kate fashions handmade jewelry from natural materials she discovers during her journeys.

ROOTS

My name's Kate Rutherford. I was born in 1981 in a one-room schoolhouse in Roundup, Montana. My parents had been living in Alaska, working in a gold mine, but they didn't feel comfortable giving birth to a baby at a gold mine in January, so they traveled to Montana. I spent my first six months of life on a sheep ranch then my parents packed the truck and headed back to Alaska with me. We homesteaded near Tok Junction, in the interior, a gorgeous place with beautiful views of the Alaska Range. They built a log cabin there, and that's where I grew up. It was a long time before I realized it was anything out of the ordinary.

My parents are still adventurous. My mom's a gardener, who loves to be outside, and my dad is what I'd call an extreme fly-fishing guide in Alaska's Bristol Bay. My folks climbed a bit, and they took my brother and me top-roping a few times when we were young. Then, when I was fourteen, I went on a twenty-one-day Outward Bound course in Utah.

We hiked over the La Sal Mountains, down into Moab, then pretty much all the way to Cataract Canyon. And somewhere along the way, we spent a few days rock climbing. Just easy scrambling with our hiking boots and a rope, but I remember I did well. I was encouraged by the guides, and I was hooked! Part of the appeal was that the instructors were having so much fun. It seemed like a really fun way to play outside with good people.

But it was years later before I could dedicate much time to climbing. During high school, my family lived on Vashon Island, off the coast of Seattle, Washington. There's no climbing gym there. No rocks. It's an hour's commute by ferry to go to a climbing gym, and riding the ferry cost twenty bucks, so that wasn't a viable option for a high school student. At that time I was a passionate skier and snowboarder, so that's where my time and energy went.

When I started applying to colleges, I thought about schools where I could pursue my interest in climbing. I loved to ski, and I wanted to learn how to rock climb, so I focused on Colorado. I decided to go to Colorado College in Colorado Springs, because it had a cool class schedule. Students took one class at a time for three and a half weeks. Then you got five days off before starting the next class. So once a month you had this extra-long weekend, allowing you to travel and explore, which is what I wanted. Plus the school is located close to good climbing areas. You can boulder in the Garden of the Gods or climb at Shelf Road and the South Platte.

The program drew a lot of climbers and outdoor enthusiasts. So there was a built-in community of folks who were willing to teach me about climbing. That's where I met Madaleine, who became one of my primary climbing partners.

After I graduated with a biology degree and a minor in art, I spent a couple years doing biology fieldwork, but I soon realized that even during the coolest biology jobs, I was fixated on climbing. It seemed like I should give myself the opportunity to do one thing well [laughs], and I knew that if I really wanted to pursue biology I'd need to go back for more school, so I gave myself five years to go climbing and see where that led.

By the end of the five years, it was clear I was fulfilled by the climbing lifestyle. I'd discovered it was feasible to climb all the time and still make enough money through sponsorship and art. It's been pretty easy to keep doing what I love for another five years or for however long. So yes, I'm a late bloomer when it comes to climbing. I've got a lot of time to make up for. Lucky me!

I'm drawn to what I call adventure climbing, generally big-wall climbing. I like big walls, expeditions, and obscure kinds of things. That's what I excel in and pursue. But that being said, I'm trying to learn how to be a better sport climber, and I might even do some bouldering in Patagonia this coming season (2013). I love all types of climbing, but some forms come easier to me.

I love pure crack climbing. I learned to climb cracks in Indian Creek and I love perfect *splitters*. But it turns out there are a limited number of perfect splitters in the world! So then I started going to far-fetched lands to seek them out and discovered that the journey is just as much fun as climbing. I like hanging out with the crazy people I meet along the way and getting to see the world. So it's the intrigue of adventure travel and the beauty of remote landscapes that draw me to mountains and big walls.

ART

Growing up in the Alaskan bush, I spent a lot of time outside. But on those long winter nights, there's plenty of time to hang out. My mom's a great artist, and we would do art projects together. My parents valued anything I created, starting with my first drawings as a three-year-old. So I think those early experiences inspired me to be artistic and to try to capture the beauty of my environment. That remains important to me. *And,* you end up with this art object that you can share with other people. So it's a good deal all around [laughs].

ENJOYING THE SPORT

I'd say there are three things I love most about climbing. I love the physicality, the puzzle of using your body and your brain to move from point A to point B. I love being in beautiful places. And I really love the community of people, including the camaraderie and the trust that comes with the climbing lifestyle. I feel there's a special crew of folks out there who climb, and I have really special friends who I climb with in all these beautiful places.

That's why I go to Patagonia season after season. I *know* there are *other* places to go, but getting to see the sunrise on Cerro Torre is one of the most spectacular views imaginable. The same is true of the sunrise on El Capitan. Those things are really important to me.

I guess what I like least is that I get scared sometimes, and I don't like that. I don't like it when my fingers get really cold. That's definitely

Kate Rutherford dances up the Free Nose (12c) Black Canyon of the Gunnison.

a problem for me. And being hungry might be the hardest thing. Sometimes I'm not able to eat enough on a route. I can definitely get mean and stupid when I'm hungry.

FEAR AND RISK

Yeah, I know, I chose a style of climbing that requires a certain degree of suffering and not too many other women choose that. I don't know if that means they're smarter than me or not. Perhaps it's my childhood experience in Alaska, or the family values I learned as a child, but I'm pretty capable of enduring challenges in nature. Part of it's practice. You need to develop a sense of when a situation crosses a line from being merely uncomfortable to being dangerous.

And it can be lonely. It's not like sport climbing, where you have pretty much constant communication with your partner. Recently I began taking a third person along so I have a buddy at the belay to complain to [laughs].

Climbing El Cap is normally just fun in the California sun, so I've never felt anxious up there, but in Patagonia it can be cold and snowing and scary. I remember the first route I climbed there. We put up a new route on Aguja Guillaumet, which is a small peak near Fitz Roy, and we were two-thirds of the way up when it got dark and started to snow. I could see the headlamps of all my friends walking back to camp on the glacier below. I wanted to be with them. It was my first snowy, ice-climbing, alpine experience, and I was scared. I was sure I was going to get hypothermia. I was sure I was going to die. And my partner, Mikey Schaefer, was up there on lead, so what was I going to do? At that point I don't know if we could have even built a safe anchor

and rappelled off. So we just carried on, putting one foot in front of the other.

That's the way I deal with fear and anxiety. I break it down into simple steps. First you buy groceries. Then you pack your bag. Then you walk out the door and hike to base camp. You set your alarm. You wake up, get dressed, and start climbing. Simplifying it makes it possible for me. Otherwise I get overwhelmed.

So I prepare as best I can, and I head out with the knowledge that I will keep going until I'm forced to turn around. It's important to know that bailing is okay. My attitude is that I will work as hard as I can. I will go as far as I can, but if it starts storming or if my best isn't good enough, I'll turn around. There's always another day.

LOSS

I've lost friends to the mountains, and it's hard. It makes me wonder why we climb. Jonny Copp and Micah Dash were the first friends I lost, and their deaths created really a powerful, overwhelming sense of confusion for me about why I do what I do. But it was important, because it made me realize that Jonny and Micah were doing what they loved, and in the end, that's all any of us can hope for. It reminds us that life is fleeting and that loving our friends and family as much as possible is the most important thing. There's huge value in the people we love, so we need to be aware of that.

LESSONS

The biggest lesson I've learned from climbing is to have the courage and the commitment to put one foot in front of the other and keep going in the face of adversity. That really gets you a long

"Big Wall"
Kate jumars in
Colorado's Black
Canyon.

way in climbing and in life. It's important to try as hard as you can. Before I became a climber, that wasn't obvious to me. But success in climbing is directly related to how hard you try, so it's a lesson I've learned.

Plenty of people go through life without trying very hard—either physically or mentally—and they're okay with that. They're stable, they do the things they do, and that's fine. But I feel lucky to know how rewarding it can be to try superhard and discover how much you can accomplish when you do.

I still have so much to learn from climbing. It's endless! For one thing I still have to learn how to fall. I still have great anxiety around falling. I get scared, and when I get scared, I can then become *really* scared. I can push it pretty hard, and then all of a sudden, I want to cry, and I can't make that feeling go away. So there I am, ten feet above my last piece or whatever, crying. I would love to learn how to mitigate that [laughs].

But, as I said to a friend the other day, fear serves a purpose. She was saying, "Oh man, that was *sooo* scary. Why is it so easy for you?" And I said, "First, I practice dealing with this all the time, and second, it's a good biological response to be scared of this stuff. That's what keeps you in one piece."

STRENGTHS AND WEAKNESSES

My greatest strength is my ability to endure. I don't want to use the word *suffer*, because it's a bit weird to think I'm *good* at suffering. My perspective is that I'm willing to endure a bit for a great objective, and that goes a long way.

I don't have big muscles. My footwork is probably above average, but I'm no Brittany Griffith. But I do think that being able to dream big and to endure are areas in which I excel. I've been practicing that a long time. I grew up traveling through the winter twilight of Alaska in a dogsled! I'm comfortable with a wild way of being. It feels easy for me to be in these wild places on these dreamlike adventures. That's normal for me [laughs].

NOMAD

I've been on the road since I graduated from Colorado College in 2002, so it's been ten years. Part of that time I was living in my Toyota Tacoma. I also lived in a Chevy Astro with Mikey; then we upgraded to the fabulous Mercedes-Benz Sprinter. I think we spent nearly five years living in the Sprinter. Upgrading to the Sprinter made life on the road more comfortable. We were both getting frustrated with not having much personal space and not having any walls to put art on. The Sprinter has some good wall space. Mikey built it out, so it was a beautiful space to live in. That went a long way.

Living such a nomadic lifestyle is challenging, and at the same time it's really rewarding. But you make plenty of sacrifices. We didn't have a shower or a toilet. So you're constantly figuring out which friends you can stay with and where you can do laundry. And we definitely *did not* have cable TV [laughs]. So it's a romantic idea to live in this way, and it's a challenge to make it happen, but I think people are more intimidated by it than they should be. You get to see a lot!

CHROMOSOMES

I haven't really thought about the differences in the way men and women climb. It's always tough to generalize, because every climber is different in their objectives, their strategy, and their desires. But I do think the basic instinct to climb and have fun is universal. I think the gratification you receive and how inspired you are to climb is the same, whether you're a man or a woman.

That said I also believe women have more *rational* ways of going about things [laughs]. I think women have an instinct that discourages them from doing crazy things. So women have more to process and to come to terms with concerning the risks in climbing.

I was lucky because I didn't get any resistance from my parents about becoming a professional climber. In fact I think they're both jealous. I suppose it freaks my mom out a bit. She pretends she doesn't understand what all the pictures mean, like how high off the ground I actually am. But I'm fortunate my family accepts me as a climber. I think other women might not get that same support.

INSPIRATION

From a young age I was very inspired by Lynn Hill. I don't read climbing magazines or follow all the exciting happenings in climbing, but from the day I started, I somehow knew Lynn's name and all about her *rad* accomplishments. And I love it that she's a soul climber, that she climbs for the love of the sport.

And since I met Hayden Kennedy, I've been really inspired by him. His ability is astounding, and his joy, happiness, kindness, and just *pure stoke* are the coolest things I've ever seen! He's the most positive, excited climber I've ever met, and that's superrefreshing. It would be a great future

if everybody in climbing was as fun, nice, and honest as Hayden!

ACCOMPLISHMENTS

Free-climbing El Capitan via Free Rider (VI, 5.12+) with Madaleine was huge. I gave myself a lifetime achievement award for that one. Part of the importance for me was that I'd lived around the valley for a long time, and when I started climbing, free-climbing El Cap was something I never thought I'd be able to achieve. And then to do it with Madaleine was a treat.

My other huge personal accomplishment was putting up a first ascent on Fitz Roy, Washington Route 5.10, A2. It was a really big deal for me. Partially because I'd been trying for frickin' years to do it! I'd been close to the summit once before. Mikey, Dana Drummond, and I climbed the California route, and we got within what I know now to be ten minutes from the summit, but we had to retreat because it was stormy. That was a huge letdown. I'd been trying for five years to get that high. So that was a harsh deal for me that we were so close but didn't get to summit. Then Mikey and I went back and did the first ascent of the Washington route, and on our way to the top, we actually walked past the place where we'd bailed before, and I thought, "Oh my God, *really*? I had to do *all this* again just so I could walk another hundred feet!" So that was the realization of a huge goal for me to finally summit Fitz Roy, and climbing it via a new route was extra sweet.

PARTNERS

First and foremost when it comes to partners, it's important that you have fun with that person

Kate Rutherford and Madaleine Sorkin check the topo and sort gear by headlamp the night before a climb in Colorado's Black Canyon.

[laughs]. You also need to be willing to risk your life for your partner. If your partner's injured, then you need to do everything in your power to rescue him or her. So for me, when I go into the mountains with someone, I need to know I'm willing to do that and to trust that my partner will do it for me. On top of that your partner needs to have the same sorts of objectives and want to climb in the same style. It's amazing how hard it is to find those attributes in another climber.

So when you find a partner who is right for you, it's special. You have the camaraderie, the fun, the trust, and the mutual love of climbing to go and do great stuff. That's a unique bond that you won't necessarily experience in any other way.

RELATIONSHIPS

Climbing is my life. All my relationships are impacted by climbing. I put lots of energy into friends I've had for a long time, but if they're not climbers, it takes more effort, logistics, and planning to spend time with them. So yes, I make choices about friendships and relationships based on climbing. Maybe that's good and maybe it's bad. But you have to make choices somehow, so they might as well be based on climbing, right? Climbers share this crazy love; we all live in the same world, so to speak, so it's easier for us to relate to other climbers. It's *rad* that there are so many amazing personalities in the climbing world, so in the end it works out fine [laughs].

PHILOSOPHY

"Let the beauty we love be what we do." That quote by the Persian poet Rūmī has been my philosophy since I was a teenager. It's really grounding for me to have that sort of simple philosophy, one that relates to everything. Environmentally it's a way we can inspire ourselves and others to protect the places we love. And when I choose projects, I do so on the basis that one is more beautiful and aesthetic than another. And when it comes to people, really pay attention to those you love. It's worth doing that extremely well. In climbing and life I'm drawn to things I find beautiful.

How do you psych yourself up for a hard route?
I don't [laughs]. I try to pretend it's not a big deal. I try to eat well before the climb. I perform my lucky ritual, which is to blow in my climbing shoes before I put them on! The beauty of the project serves as my motivation. Once I've committed to trying the route, all I can do is try as hard as possible. As Mikey always says, "Just don't let go!"

What's your favorite place to climb?
Yosemite because it's big, powerful, and beautiful. The rock quality is good and there's a lifetime of climbing to do. Some of my favorite Yosemite routes are Tales of Power (12b trad, Cascade Creek), the Rostrum (aka the North Face, 11c trad, 5 pitches) and Astroman (11c trad, 10 pitches, Washington Column). I really loved free-climbing on Free Rider (VI, 12d trad, El Capitan), I think it's totally worth going up there and trying to free as much of it as you can. Even if you don't intend to free the whole thing, it's got such good climbing on it.

If you could offer one essential tip to other climbers, what would it be?
Try as hard as you can and have as much fun as you can. That's the way to be fulfilled.

One of the results of my lifestyle is having many photos and stories that I can use as a platform to inspire people and help preserve wild places. Climbing can be a bit self-serving, so I am inspired to share my love of nature with others and get them motivated to protect the environment.

THE FUTURE

I will always climb. That's my intention. And I'm excited to start creating a home, a home to come home to in the future. I'm ready to have a home base [laughs].

Kate Rutherford belaying Madaleine Sorkin during an ascent of the Free Nose in the Black Canyon.

MADALEINE SORKIN

erhaps the ultimate compliment in climbing is being called the *real deal.* "She's the real deal." When you hear that, you know a climber has proven herself repeatedly on challenging routes in her respective disciplines.

Madaleine Sorkin *is* the real deal. Again and again, on big-wall, multipitch routes around the world, Madaleine has proven herself to be as *real* as climbers get.

If climbing was a planet, then big-wall climbing would be a country all its own. Not even a country really, more like a remote, windswept and barren arctic archipelago. A place inhabited by individuals who thrive on deprivation, isolation, and sinew-snapping effort.

In the pages that follow Madaleine talks with courageous honesty about what it means to explore that with mindfulness and compassion. She also talks about being drawn to R-rated (that is run-out and risky) routes, about the volatile chemistry of climbing partnerships, about being a gay climber, and about being dedicated to the professional climbing lifestyle.

Being successful on big walls requires finding a partner who brings complementary skills and a haul bag full of *stoke,* and Madaleine has been lucky enough to find such a climbing partner in Kate Rutherford. In 2006 Madaleine and

Kate made the first female ascent of Moonlight Buttress (V, 5.12+) in Utah's Zion National Park. A climb which Madaleine says opened the duo's eyes to their own potential. In 2007 they made the first female ascent of the North West Face of Half Dome (VI, 5.12) in Yosemite and in 2010 they free-climbed El Capitan's Free Rider (VI,

Left, Madaleine Sorkin deciphers Qualgeist (12b) Black Canyon of the Gunnison. Above, Sorkin tops out on Tague Yer Time (12b) Black Canyon of the Gunnison.

5.12+), also in Yosemite. Then in 2013, on Sorkin's first trip to Chile's Torres del Paine National Park, they roped up again to climb Mate, Porro y Todo lo Demas on the North Pillar of Fitz Roy (900 meters, 11a) and the Red Pillar on Aguja Mermoz (450 meters, 12a).

With a variety of other partners, Madaleine also made such notable ticks as on-sighting Ariana (IV, 5.12-) and Heart and Arrows (IV, 5.12), both on the Diamond on Colorado's Longs Peak, and making the first free ascent of Women at Work (VI, 5.12 R) on Mount Proboscis in the Cirque of the Unclimbables in Canada. In one day she redpointed every pitch of the West Face of Yosemite's Leaning Tower (VI, 5.13- AO). In Eldorado Canyon State Park in Colorado (known for its bold and committing lines), Madaleine has climbed Surf's Up and Freeline, both 5.13 R.

In 2012 Madaleine had a breakout year. Teaming with Nik Berry, she freed El Corazon (VI, 13b) on El Capitan and traveled to the Karavashin Valley in Kyrgyzstan to bag the first free ascent of La Fiamma (VI, 5.12c R) on Pik Slesova and Sugar Daddy (VI, 5.11+) on Pik 1000 Years of Russian Christianity. In the United States she climbed the Hallucinogen Wall (VI, 13b R) in Colorado's Black Canyon of the Gunnison national park and the Phoenix (13a) in Yosemite. All in all, a year of accomplishments that would leave most climbers resting on their laurels, but for Madaleine it was just the beginning.

ROOTS

My name's Madaleine Sorkin. I was born in Miami, Florida, in 1982 and grew up in Bethesda, Maryland. My family's urban based; however, we spent significant time outdoors. My parents assigned a high value to nature, and I began to appreciate nature through them. Moreover, I was given space to be outside on my own and with friends.

I don't know if my development as a climber is the result of nature or nurture, but I do know I craved natural spaces from an early age, and as an athlete, I sought outdoor activities. I recall the excitement of my first overnight camping experience at a summer camp when I was nine. At that camp we spent a day rock climbing, and I liked it immediately. When I was fifteen, I went to an adventure camp in Colorado. Eventually I interned at the camp and became a guide. These experiences opened my eyes to the possibility of pursuing an outdoor lifestyle.

My first job at the camp was to work birthday parties at the climbing gym, and I immediately began identifying myself as a climber. I wanted to learn as much as possible. But climbing was relegated to the summers, because I played lacrosse until my junior year at Colorado College. At that time I tired of organized sports, and I shifted my focus to being a year-round climber.

Today I consider myself to be a competent all-round rock climber. I excel at bigger objectives, such as traditional, multipitch, big-wall climbing, because they inspire me the most. It doesn't have to be a *multiday* route. I desire long, singularly focused days, getting high off the ground. I *love* space. There's something about that element that I draw power from.

Madaleine Sorkin on the 5.11+ "Photo Finish" variation of the Free Nose.

STRENGTHS AND WEAKNESSES

My greatest strength is a stable mental state. Much more than physical prowess, mental stamina has gotten me up numerous climbs. Using climbing as a mindfulness practice has huge appeal for me. The focus demanded by climbing has increased my capacity to be less scattered in my life. I'm drawn to R-rated, that is, *run-out* (risky and difficult to protect) routes. Again, I suppose the appeal is the mental focus required. Perhaps this is because I feel pulled in multiple directions at other times in life. That said, I do not seek R routes every time I go climbing. But I do like challenging myself with dangerous consequences. On most rock climbs I can tell myself it's safe if I fall, but for R routes I'm forced to check with myself and find out if I'm up for the challenge. An important part of the run-out game is self-awareness. Climbers need to decide the appropriate level of risk and difficulty for them at any given time. That can be a complex decision.

I know climbers who tell of completing their hardest, most-dangerous climbs after they've broken up with a lover, lost their job, or experienced some other difficult change. I can definitely relate to times when life feels like it has no meaning. However, I've learned that those aren't the proper times for me to tackle stressful objectives. Attempting challenging climbs when I feel content is a healthier decision for me.

In 2006 I had a big accident that really brought this home. My rappel anchor failed. However, I would not have been in that situation, if I had not made some choices based on what I now call apathy. I realized afterward that I don't want to be in a dangerous place when the climbing doesn't mean anything to me.

CLOSE CALL

I was climbing in Nevada's Red Rocks with a new partner I didn't really like or trust. We'd just climbed a long, moderate route called the Resolution Route, and we were descending. My partner rappelled first. When I reached him, he was hanging from tattered slings on a vertical wall. When I saw the rappel anchors, I thought, "This looks like rubbish!" But it was late in the day, and I was tired. My partner was hanging from slings stuffed through two pitons. We should have cut the whole mess away and started over, but there wasn't an easy way to do it. So I decided to clip into the anchor as it was. I remember rationalizing, "I've rapped on crap like this before. It's getting late, and I just want to get down."

We pulled the rope, and my partner transferred his weight in order to rappel. When he did, both slings popped out of the pitons, and we both fell around fifty feet. I remember the wall passing in front of me and wondering if I was going to die. We landed on a long sloping ledge. I hit first, and my partner landed on top of me. I immediately knew my right leg was really screwed up. I was in shock, and I began to cry. My partner seemed to be fine, because he was jumping up and down, cursing excitedly about bad anchors in the desert. I was thinking, "This isn't happening." Then I began wondering if I could get myself out. Weighting my leg produced debilitating pain, and the hike out was three hours. Luckily another climbing party was nearby and they came to our aid. They lowered me down a low angle slab. Then we were in a sandy wash with boulders. Nine hours later we arrived at the trailhead. It was four in the morning. I went to the ER, and I was in a hallway with *all* the drunks of Las Vegas, and I got chewed out by a paramedic for not backing up my rappel. He didn't have a clue, but I was so fried, I just cried some more. I had a minor concussion, and I had popped the *bursa*, the sac of fluid beneath the patella, in my knee.

That accident flipped my attitude in a big way. I wanted to understand the mental state that led to it, so I'd be less controlled by emotional states in the future. Physically, I was unable to climb for six weeks.

To other climbers, it was no surprise that I continued to climb after that accident, but my family and nonclimber friends needed an explanation. I felt selfish that I still wanted to climb. I had to think deeply in order to articulate why I wanted to continue

MINDFULNESS

My process for dealing with fear and anxiety while climbing is similar to what I've learned from meditation. I notice my thoughts and emotions as they occur and try to accept them unconditionally. For example, a skillful response to anxiety is to allow it to simply exist, instead of letting my mind react. I do my best not to judge the emotion and instead be curious about what it is and what it needs.

I've learned through experience that I can't control everything that passes through my mind and body. Whether or not I want to be anxious, I've come to accept anxiety as a frequent visitor on challenging routes. When I become fixated on how anxiety is an obstacle to my success, I create more inner conflict (for instance, thinking, "Well I'm anxious, so maybe I shouldn't be here").

I'm talking here about when I'm on a big wall, confronting objective dangers like weather, rockfall, avalanches, or hypothermia. In those situations fear's an important and discerning tool. So a tension arises between the anxiety I *need* in order to be aware and make sound decisions and being overwhelmed by reactive out-of-control emotions.

Sometimes fear is just what's there. So first, I have to accept the fear. Then it's a question of whether I can stay present with the discomfort, allowing unpleasant emotions to exist without letting them overwhelm. In climbing I try to give the anxiety space to be, while actively cultivating higher states of mind, such as equanimity and loving kindness.

In the spring of 2012, when I was working on free-climbing El Corazon (VI 5.13R) on El Capitan with my friend, Nik Berry, I confronted a daunting array of negative thoughts and sensations. When we rappelled down to try the most difficult pitches three thousand feet above the ground, I was afraid, with knots in my stomach and shoulders. I reacted with even more negativity. Because I was fixated on freeing the route, I couldn't surrender to my emotional state as quickly as I wanted. I couldn't open to my experience as it unfolded.

El Corazon is a 35-pitch route with five 5.13 pitches, including a number of sections difficult to protect. After we rehearsed the crux pitches on rappel, it took Nik and me four days to free-climb the route from the ground up, and the effort wore me down mentally, emotionally, and, of course, physically. Since I was at my edge so frequently, I had to stay on top of my self-care if I had any hope of performing well.

In the fall of 2012, I participated in a week-long meditation retreat, and one thing I reflected on were the similarities and *differences* between climbing and meditation. In meditation you're typically in a safe place, where it's easier to welcome the feelings and thoughts that arise. Climbing, however, can take place in dangerous places, where welcoming visiting fears and anxieties might seem counterproductive to surviving the situation [laughs].

Since the retreat, I've been wondering whether learning to welcome all my emotions during meditation can better prepare me for the physically and emotionally challenging situations that arise in climbing. I believe that it can. Because when negative emotions arise, I can say, "Okay, I've been here before. I know I have the capacity to deal with this emotion."

There may be times when you're so broken down and so exhausted that you can't deal with your emotions very well. But because of your mindfulness practice, you might be able to simply allow those thoughts to arise and then let them pass away without getting caught up in the stories they're telling. It's much more life affirming for me to make decisions based on deeper self-awareness than on fleeting thoughts and feelings.

ENJOYING THE SPORT

What I love most about climbing is the connection I feel to the climb itself. It makes me feel like I'm part of the natural world. That's amazing. Then there's my connection to my partners, going through the ups and downs of the journey together, supporting each other, and having climbing as our muse. I also love the inspiration.

Wow! Just being goal driven about something I'm passionate about. That's a great gift! The thing I like least are the ups and downs I experience climbing, as well as the struggle I have integrating climbing with a more conventional lifestyle [laughs].

EVOLUTION

Climbing's helped me develop self-discipline. It's made me more serious. In fact, it's made me *obsessive* [laughs]. Big-wall climbing and expeditions require a lot of planning. That kind of organization is challenging. But when you're passionate about something, you want to learn the skills that will allow you to improve, and you learn quickly that if you're not scrupulous about preparation for a major climb, you're not likely to succeed.

PARTNERSHIPS

Just by virtue of being the minority gender in the sport, women have a different experience than men. While climbing, I've had to make conscious decisions based on my gender. From the start of my career, it was important to me to be treated as an equal. For me this means leading the same number of difficult pitches as my partner, if not more. Sure, I've had partners who were stronger, and it's *easy* in moments of doubt to give over the lead. It requires a lot of discipline to say, "No, this is a good challenge for me, so I'm going to lead this pitch, even though it might take me longer than you." Even if she's stronger, your partner should be willing to let you take your time. It's important for me to give a full-hearted effort. Those are my most satisfying climbs.

Madeleine Sorkin cruises the final pitch of Sheer Lunacy in Utah's Zion National Park half way through a one-day link up of Sheer Lunacy and Moonlight Buttress.

I like adventuring into the unknown, but when I do that, there's always the potential to go further than I desired and that can be traumatizing. In August 2012 I went on an expedition to the Aksu valley of Kyrgyzstan. My partner, Nik Berry, had less experience than me traveling internationally. While I was confident in our ability to climb together, I found myself lecturing Nik about traveling in remote areas.

Five days after our arrival, I became very ill with dysentery at the trailhead leading into the Aksu. From the capital of Bishkek, we'd traveled to the southwest part of the country, where we were dropped off. While we waited for the porters and donkeys that would escort us to base camp, I vomited continuously. No one spoke English, and we didn't have an adequate dictionary. Most importantly we didn't have adequate water. The nearby river was too filled with silt to filter, and the temperature was one hundred degrees. We knew little about the route to base camp except that the walk was supposed to take a day and a half.

The following morning we set out walking at five o'clock hoping to reach base camp that day. I was pathetic, shuffling along just trying to keep my depleted body moving. Every so often the porters, the donkeys, and Nik would wait. However, about five hours after we began, following a break, we started again and that was the last time I saw them. Without any discussion, I found myself totally alone and *very* ill in a foreign, inhospitable country, with no water treatment and no warm clothes.

That day was a surreal experience. On top of dysentery, I was experiencing the effects of dehydration and heat stroke. I had no idea where I

was or if I was even going the right way, and I was furious with myself, with Nik, and with the porters for creating such a reckless situation.

At seven o'clock that night I encountered some shepherd dwellings. A beautiful Kyrgyz family took me in, fed me mutton soup and naan (bread), and provided a place for me to sleep in a room with the children. I was moved to tears of gratitude for the hospitality, generosity, and concern extended to me by total strangers at such a difficult time.

Through sign language the family confirmed I was on the correct trail to base camp, and in late morning the next day, I continued up the Aksu Valley. My anger returned when I was stopped at a military checkpoint garrisoned by four young men with rifles and vodka (thankfully the encounter proved uneventful) and then again when I passed our porters returning from base camp. They informed me that Nik was there waiting.

When I finally arrived at base camp, Nik felt awful. After I slept, I tried to understand why he continued without me. His explanation was that he was afraid to leave our possessions, which included our passports and extra money, unattended with the porters. I tried to find some compassion for his position. However, I felt shattered, and I had little faith in our ability to work as a team or make mutual decisions. The bottom line was I doubted Nik's ability to take care of me in an emergency.

Already pushed beyond my limits, I struggled with all the thoughts and emotions that arose during the remainder of the trip.

Living through that experience challenged each of us greatly. I know I dealt with my

Madaleine Sorkin stays focused on the present moment on the Free Nose (12c), Black Canyon of the Gunnison.

emotions by reacting negatively to Nik (more often than I'd like to admit). But we developed more acceptance of and appreciation for our differences. The bottom line is we have different comfort margins when it comes to safety in remote areas, and that was the first time I was forced to be dependent on someone who's comfortable hanging it out there more than me. Eventually we rebuilt our partnership, and it probably became stronger than before.

After that trip, I learned how to be an advocate for my own needs, and Nik and I went on to do some really *cool* climbs. The biggest gift was freeing an existing aid line, La Fiamma (VI A3 5.9) in a ground-up on-sight style at 5.12c R. We each led pitches that challenged us appropriately, and we supported each other well, and that was satisfying.

During our return flight, Nik and I extended our stay in Turkey. We explored Istanbul, ate juicy figs, and sport climbed along the Mediterranean. That was excellent. We were able to decompress together, discuss our experience, and renew our friendship.

ACCOMPLISHMENTS

Any list of my accomplishments begins with Moonlight Buttress with Kate. We were the first female team to free-climb the route, and that experience expanded our idea of what was possible. It was a springboard to the future and remains a benchmark for how to try hard and inspire your partner to do the same. I've completed a number of female expeditions and first-female-team ascents. I often feel highly accountable to and supported by other women. Seeing another woman push herself can inspire me more than

observing a man do the same, simply because of the emotional and physical similarities I perceive. And often, it's just ridiculous, silly fun!

In 2009 I challenged myself with a goal to free-climb the *West Face* of Leaning Tower (VI, 5.13- AO, Yosemite National Park). I made six exploratory trips up the route to try various sections, each time with a different partner. During that process, I found my edge repeatedly, and there were days when the whole endeavor seemed useless. It was too hot. I got sunstroke. There were sections of climbing that at first I could barely climb at all. Mainly, it was really hard for me to have this singular goal and stick with it. A few days before my final attempt Jonny, Micah, and Wade Johnson all went missing in China. I met some friends on their way to China to help with the search. I ended up driving them around San Francisco, California, to acquire visas. Then we received the news that the body of one of our friends had been found. That news was devastating on a both a personal and community level.

I later learned all three men had died. I felt shattered by the news, by the utter meaninglessness of climbing, and by the realization that I was not at peace with the possibility of my own death. All in all, I was ready to pack up and drive back to Colorado. Then I spoke with friends in Boulder, and they said, "Hey, somebody needs to be going climbing right now. Why don't you go and do your project?"

So I felt strongly supported by my community, which helped me find meaning once more in what I was doing. The day I completed the West Face, Kate supported me, belaying and jugging behind me with snacks and water. That meant a lot. Thoughts and sensations related to dying were present the entire time. I cried inconsolably when I reached the top. The sun was fading in shades of purple and orange. It was a huge emotional release to connect with the sadness of our friends passing and to finally let go of this goal that had consumed me for so long.

In 2012 I broke through some perceived physical limitations with a new kind of energy, specifically when I climbed the Hallucinogen Wall in the Black Canyon (VI, 13b R) and El Corazon (VI, 13b R) on El Cap. They were a step up in technical difficulty from what I'd done before.

RELATIONSHIPS

I'm still trying to figure the whole relationship thing out [laughs]. I don't know what to say about it, except that it's a long and winding path. My family relationships are as strong as they've ever been. I'm fortunate to have a supportive, open-minded family. As far as a *significant other* goes, well, that's more conditional. My relationships work best when I've shifted my center to include the other person in decision making. My former girlfriend was also a climber, and she really understood the lifestyle as well as the passion and the amount of time climbing

---

How do you psych yourself up for a hard route?

Watching American Gladiator reruns [laughs]. Mainly I get psyched by thinking about how the objective will require me to draw from my existing toolbox yet present the opportunity for something new to learn and explore.

What's your favorite place to climb?

No matter what I say, I know that someday I'm going to be climbing in that place, and I'll say, "I friggin' hate this place," and my partner will say, "Oh yeah? You said in that book that this is your favorite area!" So okay, in Boulder, Eldorado Canyon is my favorite place to climb, and I love the Black Canyon of the Gunnison. If you've never been to the Black, then start with the Casual Route (II,

5.8 trad) or the Scenic Cruise (V, 10d, trad), and if you're a big-wall veteran seeking a mental test piece, climb the Free Nose (VI, 5.12 trad).

If you could offer one essential tip to other climbers, what would it be?

If you want to climb complex, multipitch objectives, start diversifying early in your career. Climb trad and sport, go cragging, climb multipitch, go to the gym, and go bouldering. Try it all! Keep opening yourself to new experiences. I see climbers becoming more specialized and more limited in the kinds of climbing they do. So be careful about looking at climbing solely from the number grade you pull down, because you will not become a great rock climber on that basis alone.

demands. But in the end we were unable to hold one another's different truths and find a way to move forward together.

It appears that those who embrace climbing as a lifestyle tend to find someone who's on the same page, basically someone who wants to spend all their time traveling from climb to climb. If that's not the case, the relationship requires even more empathy, understanding, and acceptance of the fact you'll be apart for long periods. To survive that requires two independent people. So yes, to be a full-time climber and have a relationship is challenging.

For me, being both a fiercely committed climber and gay doesn't give me infinite possibilities cultivating long-term relationships. So I live in Boulder rather than in a small town in Wyoming. It would be much harder for me to come home after months of climbing and not be able to tap into a gay community in the place where I live. These days I'm meeting more gay climbers, and I'm trying to cultivate that. For instance, I gave a slide show at an event called Homoclimbtastic. That was The people who attended the event were the most open, fun-loving climbing group I've ever experienced.

At first I thought, "Well, if I'm going to pursue climbing wholeheartedly, there isn't going to be room for a relationship." It's taken me a long time to open to more possibilities. I've learned that you always have to keep opening and then, sort of by magic, love develops.

PHILOSOPHY

My philosophy is to be intentional. The results of my actions are based on my intentions. Namely, if I choose to act from love, I will not have regrets. Climbing's taught me to follow my passions. I believe that one of the most important things you can do with your life is be true to yourself and share that with others. If you share from truth and integrity, that's truly a gift.

Index

About the Author

Recognized as one of the world's leading adventure photographers, Chris Noble is a writer and visual communicator, whose work celebrates the beauty of nature and inspires people to live healthier, more mindful, and more sustainable lives. He is a veteran of more than thirty expeditions, ranging from Denali to Everest to the jungles of Borneo, and his writing and photography have appeared in hundreds of publications, including *Life, National Geographic, Newsweek, Orion, Outside, Rolling Stone,* and *Sports Illustrated,* as well as in numerous books and anthologies. Noble also served as a contributing editor at *Powder* and *Outdoor Photographer* magazines. His commercial clients include Black Diamond, CamelBak, Nike, and the North Face. Noble has been a featured speaker at the National Geographic Society, the Banff Mountain Film Festival, the Mountaineers Club, and the Outdoor Photo Expo. According to *American Photo* magazine, "the secret of Noble's success is that there is no dividing line between adventure and his photography."

PROTECTING CLIMBING **ACCESS** SINCE 1991

ACCESS FUND

| JOIN US |
WWW.ACCESSFUND.ORG

Jonathan Siegrist, Third Millenium (14a), the Monastery, CO. Photo by: Keith Ladzinski